Jimmy Carter
and the Restoration
of Presidential Dignity

Jimmy Carter and the Restoration of Presidential Dignity

JASON FRIEDMAN

McFarland & Company, Inc., Publishers
Jefferson, North Carolina

This book has undergone peer review.

LIBRARY OF CONGRESS CATALOGUING-IN-PUBLICATION DATA

Names: Friedman, Jason, 1979– author.
Title: Jimmy Carter and the restoration of presidential dignity / Jason Friedman.
Description: Jefferson, North Carolina : McFarland & Company, Inc., Publishers, 2020 | Includes bibliographical references and index.
Identifiers: LCCN 2019053970 | ISBN 9781476674384 (paperback) ∞
ISBN 9781476638447 (ebook)
Subjects: LCSH: Carter, Jimmy, 1924- | Presidents—United States—Biography. | United States—Politics and government—1977-1981. | Political leadership—United States—History—20th century.
Classification: LCC E873 .F75 2020 | DDC 973.926092 [B]—dc23
LC record available at https://lccn.loc.gov/2019053970

BRITISH LIBRARY CATALOGUING DATA ARE AVAILABLE

ISBN (print) 978-1-4766-7438-4
ISBN (ebook) 978-1-4766-3844-7

© 2020 Jason Friedman. All rights reserved

No part of this book may be reproduced or transmitted in any form or by any means, electronic or mechanical, including photocopying or recording, or by any information storage and retrieval system, without permission in writing from the publisher.

Front cover: 1976 presidential campaign flyer (Library of Congress); United States capital photograph © 2020 Shutterstock

Printed in the United States of America

McFarland & Company, Inc., Publishers
 Box 611, Jefferson, North Carolina 28640
  www.mcfarlandpub.com

Acknowledgments

This book is the culmination of almost two decades of work. Along the way I have switched homes and careers. I have moved across town, across the country, and then back the other way. In between writing and revising what has become this manuscript, I have earned a master's and a doctorate. I have taught at four institutions of learning in four different states. I have taught rising eighth graders, graduate students, and every age in between. I am a scholar, a teacher, a husband, a parent, a friend, and I am sure there are other hats I wear, too. I want to thank everyone who has supported me along the way, everyone who has read a chapter draft or cheered me on, especially in the years when publishing was not an expectation in my job description. I am sure there may be names left off my list, but I assure you, the omission is unintentional.

First, I want to recognize the mentors I had during graduate school. These scholars helped to shape me into the historian and educator I am today. Thank you to Mark Kornbluh, Kirsten Fermaglich, Dean Rehberger, Gordon Stewart, the late David Bailey, Robbie Lieberman, Jonathan Bean, and Mary McGuire. I want to thank all my friends and colleagues who supported me in school. Thank you to my friends and colleagues from Faner Hall: Jay Knarr, Laura Slown, Trina Blasingame, Eric Jurgens, Daron Olsen, Deidre Hughes, Richard Baysinger, and Susan Baysinger. Likewise, thank you to my friends and colleagues from the now demolished Morrill Hall: Ted Mitchell, Ryan Pettengill, Erika Jackson, Carlos Aleman, Ben Sawyer, Joe Genetin-Pilawa, Dan Dalrymple, Jaime Dalrymple, Jennifer Gonzalez, Leslie Hadfield, Nik Ribiansky, Sowande Muskateem, Laura Cuppone, Gabe Henderson, and Lauren Anderson.

Acknowledgments

After finishing my degrees and after teaching at the university level, I moved to teaching high school. I think I have transitioned well, and in between the obligations of teaching at boarding schools, my manuscript developed. Thank you to those who have supported me along the way. More than colleagues, you are friends. Thank you to Dave Heldreth, Becca Heldreth, Yong Kim, Phillip Gablehouse, Chris English, Luke Austin, Brandon Hartley, Todd Eckenfelder, Matt Duncan, Curtis Condie, the late Geno Morgan, Josh McAlister, Todd Bucklin, Nick Church, Romona Reid, Jared MaGee, Claire Parker, Elizabeth Peterson, Kelly Harris, and Laurie Lambert.

Along the way I have received support and funding from various institutions. The history departments at Southern Illinois University and Michigan State University helped get me to the archives and trained me to make the most of the libraries on their campuses. I have lost count of how many visits I have made to the Gerald R. Ford Library and the Jimmy Carter Library. Every visit was an eye-opening experience.

Last but certainly not least, I want to thank my family. To my parents, Ted and Iris Friedman, thank you for supporting me at every stage of my life. Thank you to my kids, Andrew and Hayden Friedman, who are still too young to understand what my book is about or what it means that I am writing it. Don't worry, I will make them read it when they're older. To my family by marriage, you have welcomed me and supported me too. Thank you Tony and Dawn Reynen, Angie and Bill Becker, Lyn and Jason Little Nate Becker, and Zach Becker. Lastly, to my wife, Sandra Friedman. I have been writing iterations of this book for almost as long as I have known you. At each turn you have supported my writing and accepted the stress that comes along with it. I know presidential history is not your preferred reading genre, but I will point out that you did eponymously name our dog Carter.

Table of Contents

Acknowledgments	v
Preface	1
Introduction	2
1. The Carter Way: Creating a Tone of Openness and Responsiveness	13
2. The Path to Forgiveness: Draft Dodgers and the Debate Over Amnesty	31
3. Trimming the Trappings of Office: Presidential Yacht *Sequoia* and Jimmy Carter's Arsenal of Austerity	49
4. Water Project Cancellations: Public Works Appropriations and Parochial Interests	71
5. Jimmy Carter and the Reinstatement of Draft Registration	97
6. Jimmy Carter and Foreign Intelligence Surveillance	110
7. Jimmy Carter and the Legislative Veto: Fighting an Encroachment on Federal Comity	128
Conclusion	155
Postscript: Donald Trump and New Questions of Presidential Dignity	159
Chapter Notes	167
Bibliography	201
Index	209

Preface

Forty-four different men have served as U.S. president. Jimmy Carter is one of only a few who tried for a second term and failed. Due to his 1980 electoral defeat and for choices that he made during his time in office, politicians like Marco Rubio and historians like Clark R. Mollenhoff characterized Carter as a failed president. Though Carter's post-presidency service has been impeccable, the albatross of a negative perception of his presidency remains. This book joins a growing body of scholarship that disputes this historiographical view. For four years, Jimmy Carter improved the image of the White House and the reputation of the presidency. Based on archival research and examination of government documents, this book explores some of the important steps Carter took to restore comity in government and how Congress reacted to his efforts. In short, this book argues that the Carter presidency should not be viewed as a stain on the fabric of American history but rather as a ray of sunshine after a long storm.

Introduction

On a cold Washington, D.C., day in January 1977, Georgia Governor James Earl Carter, Jr., took the oath of office and became the thirty-ninth president of the United States. Carter began his inaugural speech by thanking his "predecessor for all he has done to heal our land." Such pleasantries are ubiquitous, a polite formality to reinforce the continuity of government and to suggest a moment of détente between the two rival political parties. However, the appreciation for now ex-President Gerald R. Ford seemed to go beyond the thunderous applause and standing ovation. Carter's words, "heal our land," spoke to the deep and divisive wounds Americans had suffered over the past decade. Carter genuinely respected the representative-turned-president from Grand Rapids, Michigan. Yet, inaugural speeches are manifestos. They are delivered not for the people on the dais next to the new president but for a much wider audience, for all of America and indeed the world. To Carter's nation writ large, memories of Watergate and the Vietnam War lingered. For them, America had just endured a staggering string of brazen presidential actions.[1]

Though to the electorate, these presidential tendencies seem a recent development; in fact, the lineage of expanding and aggrandized presidential power can be traced back long before secret wiretaps or the continuation of an unpopular war. Most scholars go back to Theodore Roosevelt, some go back to Abraham Lincoln, and others all the way to Thomas Jefferson. However, whether the imperial presidency began with the establishment of overseas protectorates, a naval blockade, or the Louisiana Purchase, there is consensus that the presidency reached crisis levels in the early 1970s.[2]

Traditionally the separation of powers in American government

Introduction

can be seen as a harmony between the branches or as a tug of war where no branch truly trusts the other because all want to have as much power as possible. James Madison suggested in *Federalist #51*—as have many others since—that the latter better reflected the intention of the founders and premise of the 1787 Constitution:

> To what expedient, then, shall we finally resort, for maintaining in practice the necessary partition of power among the several departments, as laid down in the Constitution? The only answer that can be given is, that as all these exterior provisions are found to be inadequate, the defect must be supplied, by so contriving the interior structure of the government as that its several constituent parts may, by their mutual relations, be the means of keeping each other in their proper places.

Madison further added, "If men were angels, no government would be necessary." Checks on power rein in the hubris of human nature. Regardless of the model, either cooperation or confrontation, over time an equilibrium developed whereby the branches' powers came to be defined. However, as the powers of one branch—the presidency—gradually began to expand in the twentieth century, that equilibrium destabilized.[3]

Within this framework, Richard Nixon merely represented the culmination of a long series of presidents extending the power and encroaching on congressional power. George Reedy, Lyndon Johnson White House staffer and press secretary, for example, argued that the founders' intention "was a solution which placed in office a monarch but limited the scope of the monarch's activities." This description is apropos in this discussion, as his view of the presidency seemed to come to pass. Reedy claimed presidential inaugurations had become an "apotheosis." Presidential power had become so expansive that ascension to the presidency was tantamount to a coronation.[4] In fact, by the Nixon presidency, many had begun to use a new term to describe the president's augmented powers: the "imperial presidency." The phrase comes from the eponymously titled 1973 book by historian Arthur M. Schlesinger, Jr. He argued that the gradual expansion of presidential power since the nation's inception left a plaque of monarchy on the White House. "Nixon's presidency was not an aberration but a culmination … [which] carried to reckless extremes a compulsion toward presidential power." However, in addition to proscribing the problem,

Introduction

Schlesinger alluded to the solution, calling for strong presidents within the Constitution framework; i.e., the president should be "neither a czar nor a puppet" and certainly "no larger than the law."[5]

Nixon's vice president and successor Ford did not exacerbate that trend, but his pardon slowed the recovery. By 1974, the Vietnam War and Watergate, extreme manifestations of aggrandized presidential power, were ubiquitous news stories and dominated conversations from the most remote and apolitical corners of the country to the halls of the U.S. Congress. Vietnam developed from a limited engagement to a quagmire as deceptive leadership and selective reporting betrayed the public's trust and faith in both the military and the government. Similarly, when Daniel Ellsberg leaked the Pentagon Papers in 1971, he exposed a long series of cover-ups and bad decisions dating back to the 1950s. Indeed, Lyndon Johnson and Richard Nixon were at fault, but they did not act alone. Dwight Eisenhower and John F. Kennedy deserved some of the blame.

Just as the Vietnam War wound down, news of the Watergate scandal ballooned. Americans stood agape as *Washington Post* reporters Bob Woodward and Carl Bernstein broke the story beginning in 1972. With the help of their secretive informant, Deep Throat (now known to be former Associate Director of the Federal Bureau of Investigation Mark Felt), they exposed the unthinkable as news unfurled about the botched cover-up of attempts to break in and subvert the opposition party's presidential campaign headquarters. In the words of Nixon's Chief of Staff—and chief henchman—Harry Robbins [H. R.] Haldeman, "No holds were barred unless something was explicitly illegal, and if a secure cover could be devised, even those limits were open." This attitude brought Haldeman to spy on political opponent Nelson Rockefeller and on the Democratic convention on behalf of the Nixon campaign in 1968, and to do more various dirty tricks after that.[6] When the Watergate burglars, the plumbers, were caught midway through their act of espionage against the Democratic National Committee headquarters in 1972, a chain reaction ensued that ultimately resulted in the first resignation of an American president from office. With a vote on the articles of impeachment imminent, Nixon announced on August 8, 1974, that he would step down as president, effective noon the next day.[7] Hence the official end to Nixon's pres-

Introduction

idency and the "nightmare" was 12 p.m., August 9, 1974, when Ford took the oath of office.[8]

Though many in Congress remained divided on where the nation should go next, they understood that something needed to change. These events and others made Americans and politicians aware of a disturbing trend: The power of the president, which had been in a state of steady expansion for some time, had reached crisis levels. Americans had lost faith in the White House and had come to distrust the leaders within. Gerald Ford would try to restore this faith, but even his squeaky-clean image would be irrevocably tarnished by his pardon of Richard Nixon. Though Ford framed the pardon in terms of "healing the nation" and helping the nation move past the dark days of Watergate, the American public fixated on absolution for a man who narrowly escaped impeachment. Most believed Nixon did not deserve amnesty. (Some Americans even accused Nixon and Ford of a *quid pro quo* deal where Ford ascended to the presidency in turn for pardoning Nixon. No evidence of this arrangement has ever been found.[9]) Ford learned that resolution and reconciliation could not be achieved on intent alone. Ford assumed the presidency midway through the midterm congressional election cycle and his pardon only added an exclamation point to the Watergate scandal. That November, Americans sent the "Watergate class" to Washington, a notably dovish and liberal (and mostly Democratic) set of freshmen senators and representatives who were elected in part on anti–Nixon coattails. Ford's best efforts fell short and the next presidential campaign cycle proved to be a referendum on not only Ford's job performance but on all the events that brought him to office.

Jimmy Carter ran a campaign that was in many ways more against Nixon than Ford. The 1976 presidential election gave the American public their first chance to vote in a major election since the United States' exit from the Vietnam War, the first election since the Watergate scandal culminated in President Nixon's resignation, and the first election since President Ford pardoned Nixon. In short, Americans had just experienced their first chance at electoral catharsis. Though President Ford made inroads toward reconciliation, the legacy of Watergate—and his pardon of Nixon—proved to be too big an albatross to shake. For many Americans, the Nixon and Ford presidencies

Introduction

seemed like an interregnum. Carter presented himself as a Washington outsider, a sales pitch designed to remind voters that he came to office *tabula rasa*, unscathed by the scars of scandals past. Carter continued Ford's efforts to restore American's trust and, as political scientist Douglas Kriner later asserted, "tame the imperial presidency."[10]

Carter understood this during his campaign, and when he took the oath of office he needed to convince the nation to trust their president once again. Midway through his inaugural address, Carter broached the issue of faith in government. "Let our recent mistakes bring a resurgent commitment to the basic principles of our Nation, for we know that if we despise our own government, we have no future." Carter understood the role inaugural addresses play in reassuring the American public. New presidents assure those who voted for them that they made the right choice and assuage the concerns of those who voted for someone else, all in hopes of bringing the nation together. New presidents seek to instill confidence in the American people. For Carter, this meant proving that he would be different than his predecessors. He needed to convey the image of a clean break. He would move the nation forward.

In reaction to the imperial presidential overreach made evident in the 1970s, Carter sought a government that respected the separation of powers, regardless of party lines. This included an acceptance that in past years the powers of the president had been stretched too far. Carter knew this required more than a change of leaders; it required a change in leadership style and in the choices leaders made.

As president, Carter sought a balance between king and doormat. Carter represented a dramatic shift in power. He did not represent the party of Watergate. His party had not expanded the Vietnam War into Cambodia or ordered the Christmas bombings. However, Carter could not rely on his party affiliation alone to convince the American people that he would be a different president. Carter had to restore the separation of power and repair the image of the White House—and its chief resident—with the American people. Separation of powers is more than the definition found in a civics textbook or in the *Federalist* papers. Constitutional balance is also about comity, a central theoretical framework of this book. Political scientist Eric M. Uslaner defines comity as "the adherence to a set of norms that includes courtesy and

Introduction

reciprocity, enhances collective action." Carter did not resort to dirty tricks. He stressed basic respect for individuals and the rule of law.[11] In essence, he tried to de-imperialize the American presidency; he tried to put Humpty Dumpty together again after his great fall.

Each chapter of this book addresses a challenge the president faced in an effort to rebalance the scales and restore an appropriate degree of power and respect to the office. This does not mean Carter's efforts were always successful. Along the way, Carter faced many setbacks and, at times, defeats. Carter's leadership style favored transparency and comity; however, it also suffered at times from naïveté and a failure to understand Washington politics adequately. Though not every chapter begins explicitly—or even implicitly—with the Vietnam War or Watergate, the conflict behind each chapter was inspired by larger issues that occurred in the years leading up to the late 1970s. To understand Carter's motives, the internal muses of him and his staff are crucial. Congressional debates and hearings are integral in understanding the motives and reactions of senators and members of the House. Federal comity is a two-way street of cooperation and a study based entirely on presidential sources would therefore be incomplete. To understand how Congress received these presidential efforts, it is imperative to explore their debates. This book examines some pivotal moments that helped define Carter's quest for comity.

Chapter 1 begins the story of President Carter's unique style and image. From transparency to austerity, it can all be seen in the promises and speeches Carter delivered on the campaign trail. This chapter addresses Carter's campaign promises to do things differently. Focusing on the year before Carter took the oath of office, this chapter examines Carter's ethics on the campaign trail and how that translated to his plan to shape the office he would assume in January 1977.

Chapter 2 addresses draft dodger and military resister reconciliation, the presidential policies of clemency and pardon.[12] Richard Nixon ended American ground troop participation in the Vietnam War but the chain of deception and deceit dates back far before he took office in 1969. Even still, pulling out American troops did not fully put the problems of Vietnam to rest. Ford's clemency program made inroads toward reconciliation but a pardon for draft dodgers did not come until Carter entered the White House. Though American ground

Introduction

troops had long since left Vietnam, the question remained of how to resolve the situations of these affected persons. To these young Americans, the impact and ramifications of the war continued long after the troops left the battlefield. Some served jail time while others fled into exile, forced to live abroad or lurk in America's shadows. As the nation remained divided over what ought to be these Americans' fate, two presidents tried to find common ground. They tried to heal a nation, to ease tensions between hawks and doves in the general population and in the halls of Congress, and to make amends for the aggrandized federal power that drove the Vietnam War.

Chapter 3 deals with Jimmy Carter's arsenal of austerity, including his restriction of limousine and helicopter use and the selling of the presidential yacht *Sequoia*. Owing to Jimmy Carter's populist style and outsider mentality, as president he tried at every turn to minimize the trappings of office. He believed the position itself had inherent prestige and anything beyond that was unnecessary. This rejection of excess coincided with his efforts to undo the imperial presidency. However, while Carter had clear success in reducing the fleet of White House helicopters and the use of limousines by executive staff, his move to sell the presidential yacht proved much more difficult and yielded much murkier results. The boat itself served political ends but fundamentally represented frivolous means. Carter did not see the political grease and capital the boat represented. Rather, Carter only saw a selfish perquisite for an official that should not be afforded such liberties. However, Carter's quest for austerity proved to be one of his first lessons in Washington politics as bureaucracy and red tape stymied some of his noble message. His efforts to de-imperialize the presidency were overshadowed by the means to his ends—how he sold the boat became more important than why he sold it. Thus, while Carter's austerity campaign had a mixed bag of results, the majority of the press coverage was on his follies more than his successes.

Chapter 4 addresses another early battle Carter waged to push for good government and fiscal frugality above politics: his efforts to review and to defund various questionable water projects. As with his sale of the *Sequoia*, his intentions were easier to say than to do. Carter hoped transparency and open communication would foster cooperation with Congress. Carter learned instead how much these projects

Introduction

meant to Congress. His proposals threatened the water supply of many senators and representatives. Even more problematic for Carter, his recommendations threatened their pork-barrel projects and all the political benefits and power that political pork represented.

Chapter 5 focuses on foreign policy, specifically Carter's reaction to the 1979 Soviet invasion of Afghanistan. Carter initially and quickly condemned the invasion, but the president did not commit troops into a conflict just to prove a point against communism. Carter struck a balance between aggressive consequences to Soviet bravado while not engaging the nation in another international conflict. Carter's solution included symbolic gestures. While the grain embargo and the boycott of the 1980 Olympics were important measures, this chapter discusses Carter's third action, the resumption of draft registration. Though Carter did not call for a return to a conscription-based military, Carter did resume collecting information about draft-eligible men. Carter would not go to war with the Soviet Union, but his symbolic gesture made it clear that America would be ready if war came. Afghanistan would not be the next Vietnam. Carter would not lead America into another quagmire.

Chapter 6 addresses an area in which Carter took specific legislative action to achieve a larger message of transparency. The brazen and sometimes questionable actions of past presidents were often done amidst a veil of secrecy. As president, Carter promised new degrees of transparency in actions and in conduct. Generally speaking, these sunshine laws—laws designed to shed light on actions—created strong debate about the limits of national security and the necessity of clandestine activity. One such debate manifested around the 1978 Foreign Intelligence Surveillance Act. Carter took a strong stand on when the government could use wiretaps and under what circumstances a warrant would be issued.

Chapter 7 continues the discussion of Carter's efforts to restore the balance of power in Washington. Throughout Carter's term in office, he fought against the legislative veto, one of the measures implemented by overzealous members of Congress worried about returning to the imperial presidency. Devised to be an added check on runaway executive power, fundamentally it gave Congress the ability to nullify executive decisions. In practice, the legislative veto represented

Introduction

aggrandized congressional power and more of an unbalancing than a rebalancing of federal power. Carter threw the weight of his presidency behind measures designed to expose the unconstitutionality of the power. In a time when politicians were trying to restore the trust and balance in government, the legislative veto represented a step in the wrong direction. In this chapter, as the ones before it, the internal presidential memoranda and external communications show the White House's reaction to these pressing issues. The debates and hearings of Congress similarly show the impact of the imperial presidency on the legislature.

Historian Charles O. Jones described Carter's style as indicative of the trustee model, "doing what's right, not what's political." Many in Congress felt the solution to an overreaching presidency was an overreaching Congress. Carter disagreed. He did not want the pendulum to swing too far in either direction. Carter often sought to avoid political saber rattling and arm-wrestling negotiations for power. Jones noted that Carter considered himself "above the system of bargaining" but also that his legislative strategy lacked effectiveness at times. His efforts to promote logic and good government over parochialism and politics failed to adequately catch on.

Carter had great intentions but sometimes his execution fell short. Historian Clark R. Mollenhoff characterized these shortcomings—and therefore Carter—as a failure. Garland A. Haas similarly described Carter's struggle to translate his leadership style into presidential success. I believe there is validation in his efforts, his attempts to restore comity and dignity to Washington. Edwin C. Hargrove framed the question as to whether Carter "made the most of his opportunities." Indeed, it is indisputable that, in some ways, Carter did in fact fail. He struggled to work with Congress and his inability to resolve the Iran hostage crisis before the 1980 presidential election damaged his likability rating. Overshadowing his reconciliation efforts, his incumbency advantage, and even his role in the Camp David Accords, these factors caused Carter to struggle and to lose the election.[13] The 1980 presidential election that brought the California governor and former actor to office could never have played out on the national and international issues the way it did had Carter not already sufficiently assuaged Americans' fears about political collapse. Carter acted to restore balance in gov-

Introduction

ernment but also to restore Americans' faith in government. In the modern Republican Party, President Ronald Reagan is lionized as the model to which every presidential candidate should aspire as they seek the nomination. Each president seeks to convince America they can restore American credibility abroad and prosperity at home in a Reaganesque manner. However, Reagan could never have been elected had the taint of Watergate and the Vietnam War not been addressed by Carter.

Though Carter's post-presidency humanitarian efforts have elevated his legacy, the four years he served as president represented an important transition in American history. Carter attempted the daunting task of taming the imperial presidency. Ultimately, as Americans watched a generation of their own sent off to fight a war in a far-off country, they sought solace in the belief that those doing the sending had a good reason for doing so and were responsible for the decisions they made. In essence, this book examines how Carter fully understood that Americans needed reassurance that they still lived in a republic—not a monarchy—where no one was above the law.

1

The Carter Way

Creating a Tone of Openness and Responsiveness

On the first Tuesday after the first Monday in November 1976, former Georgia Governor Jimmy Carter defeated incumbent President Gerald Ford. President-Elect Carter then had the better part of the next eleven weeks to transition into his new job. Every new president since Dwight Eisenhower scrambled to prepare in this short window of time. (The Twentieth Amendment shortened the transition window in 1933, though no new president was affected by this until the 1952 election.) In addition to the pragmatic questions facing the president elect, such as what school his daughter Amy would attend, more political questions loomed, such as whom Carter would nominate to the various appointed positions in his cabinet. However, one broader question that transcended any single political issue or any single nomination was how those elected and those appointed would conduct themselves in office. The question seems ubiquitous or obvious, but in the wake of Watergate it was no longer a *fait accompli*. This question of conduct is ideological, but it was not a new question to Carter and his transition team. He promised many different programs and initiatives during the campaign but above them all was a larger and broader promise. Bigger than any reconciliatory draft pardons or government reorganization, Carter promised honesty and transparency in governance. He sought to bring comity back to Washington.

Within days after the election, the man who would later be Carter's chief domestic policy advisor and executive director of the White House domestic policy staff, Stuart "Stu" Eizenstat, outlined immedi-

Jimmy Carter and the Restoration of Presidential Dignity

ate tone-related decisions that were needed built off past statements by Carter's transition team leader Jack Watson in a memorandum to Jimmy Carter. At issue was how those who were appointed would serve and how those poised to move into the West Wing would conduct themselves. Eizenstat suggested that to satisfy the various groups whose constituencies helped elect Carter, the new president would have to walk a fine line to satisfy all stakeholders.

> One important way to insure [sic] against a decline in public support which may result from unsatisfied demands is the initial setting—and a 4 year continuation of a White House tone which indicates you and your staff are truly committed to an open, a responsive, and a frugal and austere government.

Eizenstat believed the solution involved creating a "tone of openness and responsiveness." He compared the need for clarity in Carter's message to the efforts of California Governor Jerry Brown, who owed his popularity to his "no frills" tone. Carter's team recognized that Brown earned the second-most votes in the primaries and he represented a wing of the Democratic Party that had expressed stark reservations about Carter's nomination. Brown rejected "the multitude of limousines, the Mansion, and certain other frills of his office." Eizenstat continued,

> At the Presidential level a few steps can be taken immediately and followed-up periodically with similar ones—which can go a long way towards convincing the public of your commitment to an austere, non–Imperial Presidency and can maintain public support during what can be tough economic times. For example, you could (1) eliminate chauffeur service for many of the employees who now receive it (including certain though not necessarily all of the White House staff); (2) require tourist-class travel by government employees; (3) occasionally fly commercial yourself (as Nixon did during the Energy crisis); (4) sell the Presidential yachts [sic]; (5) eliminate much of the lavishness from White House dinners; (6) end the subsidization of low cost luncheons for the White House Staff; and (7) generally reduce much of the unnecessary pomp associated with the presidency.

I discuss many of these austerity measures in a later chapter, but the bigger issue is the perception of a Carter presidency. How Carter would frame his presidential narrative and how the new president could begin to deliver on the promises of the campaign mattered but transcending it all was the overarching call for transparency. Carter ensured that the American people did not forget the follies of the past two Republican administrations. Nor did he mince words when he

1. The Carter Way

campaigned against Gerald Ford, even as most voters recognized that he was also campaigning against Richard Nixon's legacy. Watergate scholar Stanley I. Kutler noted that Carter "slyly exploited the nation's memory of Nixon's pardon." Jimmy Carter knew to leverage the specter of Watergate as often as tactfully possible during the campaign. Eizenstat and others had specific policy and personnel recommendations, but the bigger picture superseded all other conversations.[1]

The issue of Carter's message pervaded his campaign and manifested itself in every issue Carter discussed. In the first presidential election since Nixon's resignation, the Democratic Party sought to exploit the Republican folly while providing a viable alternative. Crucial to this success—and pivotal to Carter's campaign—entailed providing more than an alternative; a better path was needed. Some voters are retrospective, casting their ballot as a referendum on the incumbent or the incumbent party. Carter needed to show what an honest and transparent leader could be. Carter never doubted Ford's resolve, but his pardon of Nixon tethered his legacy to Watergate; however, Carter recognized he needed to be more proactive. Carter needed to provide a positive example of leadership.[2]

The Kernel Event: Carter's Code of Ethics

Going into 1976, few Americans would have been able to pick Jimmy Carter out of a lineup and even fewer would have thought he would run (or was running) for president. To many voters, even after initial primary victories, they still found themselves asking, "Jimmy who?" Carter even surprised his own mother when he told her his intentions. When he initially told her that he would run for president, Lillian Carter replied, "President of what?"[3] Carter attributed his success to his unprecedented early presence in Iowa and New Hampshire. Carter sent his wife, Rosalynn Carter, to Iowa and she visited 115 towns before the caucus. The efforts paid off in those two states.[4] Though Carter garnered less than one third of the vote in each contest, he won a plurality of the votes. The momentum opened doors and gave Carter confidence, but it also brought scrutiny. He now found himself in the national limelight and his campaign recognized that their candidate

Jimmy Carter and the Restoration of Presidential Dignity

needed to better define his message moving forward.[5] Carter needed to frame himself in a way that would thrive under media scrutiny. On March 1, 1976, the day before the next two primary contests—Massachusetts and Vermont—Carter released a statement outlining his code of ethics.

Though Carter racked up some early victories, he still trailed in national polls. Other candidates were polling better nationally; Carter needed to work harder to make himself a household name. More than name recognition, he wanted his name to evoke images of a president who could restore comity and decency to the White House.[6] Carter framed himself as the answer to Washington politics and politicians perceived to be dishonest and imperial. "We ought not to lower our standards in government. Our government in Washington ought to be an inspiration to us all and not a source of shame." Carter pledged greater transparency in politics. He promised to be more open and more accountable. He welcomed public oversight and scrutiny in all but the most "narrowly defined national security issues." Though his proposals were phrased in broad strokes, Carter was painting a picture of Ford, Nixon, and Nixon's dirty tricks. Carter argued the special prosecutor should be a stronger position, an allusion to the 1973 Saturday Night Massacre. He suggested the Internal Revenue Service (IRS) should track who requests returns, evoking memories of Nixon's plumbers.

Carter's strategic invocation of the sins of Nixon proved to be a winning tactic. Stanley Kutler argued, "Jimmy Carter rode to victory in 1976 on promises of greater morality and efficiency in government." Kutler quoted Richard Nixon as saying, "We are responsible for Jimmy Carter," suggesting that Watergate and Nixon's follies in office set the stage for Carter's campaign and victory.[7] If 1974 ushered in a Watergate class of Democrats into the Congress, Carter would make a pitch for 1976 to be an election to usher a post–Watergate Democrat into the White House. Carter wanted to convince voters that he would stand apart from the follies of the Nixon-Ford interregnum.

> There is only one person in this nation who can speak with a clear voice, who can set a standard of morals and decency and openness, who can spell out comprehensive policies and coordinate the efforts of different departments of government, who can call on the American people for sacrifices and explain the

1. The Carter Way

purpose of that sacrifice and the consequences of it. *That person is the President.* [Carter's italics] The President ought to be personally responsible for everything that goes on in the Executive Branch of government, whether that be the appointment of major officials, the clear description of policy, the relationship of the Executive with Congress, the revelation of mistakes and mismanagement, if any, or violations of the law, should they occur, unfairness on any part of regulatory agencies and so forth.[8]

Carter made it clear. His ethical standard would be above reproach. Carter positioned himself as the anti–dirty tricks candidate without having to constantly mention Nixon. Carter lined up the facts for the electorate but left it to them to make the connections. This is something that would separate him from President Ford or Governor Ronald Reagan (who challenged the sitting president and nearly wrested the Republican nomination from him).

Reagan's challenge to the sitting president created a catch-22 for Carter's campaign. Carter needed to continue to hammer the dirty-tricks legacy and the sullied Republican Party, but in reality the campaign hoped the weaker candidate prevailed to the general election. Reflecting on Carter campaign's decision to "blast" Ford in the 1976 election, attacking his record and shortcomings, Carter campaign speechwriter Patrick Anderson pointed out that such a strategy of attacking Ford only strengthened Reagan's chances of getting the GOP nomination. Anderson noted, "In retrospect, we should have been doing everything in our power to make Ford, not Reagan, our opponent—we should have been strewing Jerry Ford's path with rose petals."[9] Although through the lenses of the post–1980 election hindsight, it may seem logical that Reagan was the stronger opponent; in 1976 the Carter camp wanted to minimize the incumbency advantage. In either case, Ford or Reagan, Carter sought to tether them to the legacy of Watergate, the debacle of the Nixon years of the Vietnam War, and a litany of other questionable behaviors of the Nixon-Ford interregnum.[10]

Around the same time as the Carter team published his statement of ethics, there was also a statement published about "secrecy." It declared that America's "gravest foreign policy blunders have resulted from decisions made in secret, decisions contrary to the basic inclinations of our people, decisions which would have been rejected had our people known of them." In this regard, Carter sought to distance himself from the major foreign policy debacles of the past decade, most notably the Vietnam War. Though the expansion of the war occurred during Lyndon Johnson's tenure in office, Carter banked on Nixon's expansion of the Vietnam War to Cambodia in 1970 and his Christmas bombings of 1972 to be fresher in the memories of the electorate.[11]

The General Election: Carter v. Nixon

By May 1, Carter had outlasted all of the other Democratic challengers. His numbers were strong; he was closing in on the requisite number of delegates for the nomination. On that day, his clear victory in Pennsylvania's primary only days before, Carter's last remaining opponent for the nomination, Senator Henry "Scoop" Jackson of Washington, dropped out. Thus, to the Carter campaign, the Pennsylvania victory was a turning point.[12] As the month of May rolled on, Carter began to pivot his standard campaign speech to the general election. Though a stump speech may vary slightly over the course of the campaign, the boilerplate speech becomes the standard for the politician's message. Who Carter would face off against in that contest was not yet clear; Ford had yet to stave off Reagan's challenge. This did not faze Carter—his message operated independently of whom he ran against.

On May 31, 1976, at a rally at Canyon Park in Rapid City, South Dakota, Carter delivered a typical stump speech, indicative of the larger message Carter sought to convey during the campaign. Carter lamented the follies of the Vietnam War, making sure to emphasize Nixon's war in Cambodia as well. Carter then shifted to railing against Watergate, from the crime itself to the cover-up; from Nixon's lies to his abuse of the FBI and the Special Prosecutor's position. Speaking of past folly, "sometimes we have been ashamed, and we have been embarrassed, and we have had to apologize for our own government." Carter wanted America to move forward. He pledged to make sure America could be proud of its leadership again.[13]

In line with pledging to clean up the reputation of the office of the American presidency and improve the image of the officeholder, Carter also pledged sunshine and austerity. To Carter, this meant a commitment to openness and transparency. Carter promised to be clear

1. *The Carter Way*

with his policies and methodologies. He sought to bring clarity to government where the perception of reality had been murky in past years. Carter also critiqued what he considered to be frivolous prerequisites of office. Similarly, Carter decried "wasteful spending" in the military and elsewhere in government. It is a short jump from this campaign promise to Carter's austerity measures in his first year in office. Helicopters, limousines, and the presidential yacht would be on the chopping block, but more to come on this in chapter three. Carter moved quickly to curtail limousine usage, to reduce the use of helicopters, and to sell the presidential yacht.[14]

Though Carter did not stand in Madison Square Garden at the Democratic National Convention to take his party's nomination until July, by June, Carter's nomination was a *fait accompli* and his campaign was in general-election mode. (In fact, in an even more optimistic move, by this point Carter had already chosen Atlanta attorney Jack Watson to begin preparing secretly for Carter's transition into office.) In anticipation of his party's nomination, on June 16, 1976, Jimmy Carter presented "A New Beginning," his statement to the Democratic National Committee and his recommendations for the party's platform. The first plank of Carter's recommendations called for "open, responsive, honest government, at home and abroad." Elaborating later in the document, Carter recommended more sunshine laws and a greater separation between the attorney general and politics and also between politics and money (i.e., lobbyists and campaign spending). Carter's second plank challenged Democrats to "restore a compassionate government in Washington, which cares about people and deals with their problems." This plank is laudable on its own, but in practice this is another opportunity for Carter and the Democratic Party to wave the bloody shirt of Watergate and the Vietnam War. Carter and his fellow Democrats tried at every opportunity to remind voters that the Republican Party is the party of Richard Nixon, with all the baggage that came with him.[15]

By August, Carter found himself circling back to where he had started. The primary season began with his code of ethics statement. A manifesto for his vision of government, Carter preached about how presidents should act and how his White House would be run. On August 11, 1976, Jimmy Carter addressed the American Bar Association

Jimmy Carter and the Restoration of Presidential Dignity

Governor Jimmy Carter and Senator Walter Mondale (D–MN) at the 1976 Democratic National Convention at Madison Square Garden in New York City (courtesy Library of Congress).

in Atlanta, and his code of ethics drove his narrative. Suggesting that morality and ethics are not a new idea, Carter started off his speech quoting the "ancient code of ethics": "We will not lie, cheat or steal, nor tolerate among us those who do." Carter intimated that this strict standard had dissipated during the previous eight years of Republicans controlling the White House. He argued that Watergate made Americans acutely aware of this deficit in leadership. Carter pledged greater accountability in leadership and greater scrutiny of those who serve in government. More than just an honest president, Carter wanted to eliminate the larger perception of corruption in the Washington establishment and federal bureaucracy. "If I become president, I will never turn my back on official misdeeds. I intend to take a new broom to Washington and do everything to sweep the house of government clean." In case anyone in the audience did not fully understand that his existential vision was a critique of the last eight years, Carter elaborated more bluntly later in the speech.

1. The Carter Way

> A prime responsibility of our next president will be to reestablish the confidence of the American people in the professions, in business and in the various departments that make up our government. In other words, to reestablish confidence in the American system.

Carter's pledge to reestablish confidence was a hallmark of his campaign and it would remain an underlying theme throughout his term in office. Carter read the polls. He understood the credibility gap. Gallup reported that the American public did not trust their leaders and did not expect their government to act in their best interest. Carter believed he could convince the American people to trust again. This began with how Carter would conduct himself in office. It reflected the policies he would pursue but more importantly how he would pursue them. Transparency and austerity would define his campaign and his presidency.[16]

As the election season wore on, the ethical contrast between candidate Carter and the Nixon-Ford interregnum became stronger. Speaking at a town hall forum in Los Angeles, Carter framed his campaign as the relief from the tumultuous events of the previous decade. Speechwriter Patrick Anderson dubbed this context Carter's allusion to the "national nightmare."[17] From the assassinations of the 1960s to the chaos of the wars in Southeast Asia, Carter positioned himself as a fresh alternative to a speckled past of national tragedy and failed Washington leadership.

> To want a change, to want a fresh start, to want government that is honest and competent again, is not a partisan issue. Democrats and Republicans, liberals and conservatives, all share those fundamental concerns.... In the last analysis, good government is not a matter of being liberal or conservative. Good government is the art of doing what is right, and that is far more difficult. To be liberal or conservative requires only ideology; to do what is right requires sensitivity and wisdom.

In 1976, two of Ford's biggest challengers came from outside the Washington establishment. Ronald Reagan, like Carter, would have been new to Washington, D.C. Carter believed that indicated that the American people wanted to see a change in leadership style and some new blood inside the beltway. This again reflects the fear of the incumbency advantage. Carter's assessment that the American people wanted new blood in Washington implied that the American people did not want the one candidate who did reflect the current establish-

Jimmy Carter and the Restoration of Presidential Dignity

ment: the sitting president, Gerald Ford. The Carter campaign was convinced that they would fare better against Governor Reagan than President Ford.

Carter argued that part of the problem stemmed from a government establishment that had lost touch with its constituency, the American public. Specifically, Carter chastised the perk-filled life of politicians: "It seems almost inevitable that if political leaders stay in power too long, and ride in limousines too long, and eat expensive meals in private clubs too long, they are going to become cut off from the lives and concerns of ordinary Americans. It is almost like a law of nature—as Lord Acton said, power tends to corrupt."[18] In contrast, Carter touted his austere lifestyle. Images of Carter's suits and carrying his own luggage bolstered his claims. Carter's rejection of the lifestyle many other politicians crave made his case easier to make. Spurning the ostentatious lifestyle made his criticism bite harder and made his austerity measures once in office more genuine. The efficacy of Carter's austerity campaign is discussed in Chapter 3.

As August rolled on, Carter continued to flout his code of ethics, framing himself as the alternative to the murky and at times nefarious Washington crowd. In a *Congressional Quarterly* interview, Carter made the case that he is best suited to work with Congress. (The implicit assumption is that the Democrats had and would maintain control of Congress.) When pressed in the interview, Carter asserted that being a Democrat was an advantage because Democrats were better at congressional relations.[19] Later that day, the Democratic nominee also spoke to crowd of Iowans at the Van Ryswyk farm near Des Moines, Iowa. The speech accentuated Carter's Southern and rural roots, especially his start in life as a farmer. He highlighted his similarities with the average Iowan and it was not until much later in his speech that the stump standards of the evils of Nixon's dirty tricks and the follies of the Nixon-Ford years came out. He could not go through his speech without pivoting toward an empathetic plea to the hurt and pain he believed Americans felt. Carter vowed that there would be no more Watergates, no more Vietnam Wars, and no more Cambodian invasions. Carter pressed for greater sunshine in politics and government, greater transparency and openness with the American people.[20]

1. The Carter Way

Transition

On November 2, 1976, Americans went to the polls. Though the margin of victory might not have been as high as Carter and his team had hoped, the champagne—or at least beer—flowed that night. Jimmy Carter had been campaigning for this office since early 1975 and now his investment in the campaign paid dividends with election success. However, by the time the election-night buzz dissipated, all efforts refocused on the transition. Carter advisors cautioned him against getting too cocky too early—not to presume he would win before the election happened. However, after Election Day, Carter's conversations about how he would run the White House were no longer "presumptuous."[21]

Though Jack Watson led the pre-transition team, by November it was clear Watson would not do it alone and, in the view of others, such as Hamilton Jordan, Watson should not do it alone. In fact, Watson and Jordan fought over how to divide the transition responsibilities. In the end, Jordan staffed the White House and Watson handled everywhere else. In practice, Jordan filled a more important role and his clout in the Carter administration grew. Even still, this formal division of labor left plenty of work to be spread around. (On Election Day alone, Carter received fifty transition papers on a wide range of issues.[22]) Watson hit the ground running, presenting the president-elect his transition memo for the Executive Office of the President the next day, November 3, 1976. Beyond the White House staff, Watson also had ideas about the Office of Management and Budget, the Council of Economic Advisors, and National Security Affairs. Watson's advice was not about which people should staff these positions but what types of people. Watson recommended loyal advisors but not sycophants. He recommended people who got the job done without worrying about which title their job contains. Watson made a specific point of warning Carter about "avoiding an imperial presidency." In capital letters, Watson urged Carter,

IN ORDER TO DO WELL, A PRESIDENT MUST REMAIN OPEN AND ACCESSIBLE. HE MUST ZEALOUSLY MAINTAIN CHANNELS THROUGH WHICH HE CAN RECEIVE DIVERSE INFORMATION AND JUDGEMENTS, AND THROUGH WHICH HE CAN BE CONSTANTLY CHALLENGED, DISPUTED AND FORCED TO RETHINK AND DO BETTER.

Jimmy Carter and the Restoration of Presidential Dignity

Watson wrote about the issue of personnel, but he was also talking about the larger issue of Carter's message. Though Watson and Jordan disagreed on many issues and often butted heads, on this issue they agreed. Carter came into office with what they believed was a mandate to organize and conduct himself in office better than his predecessors. Watson's advice captured the spirit of Carter's code of ethics: Americans were fed up with obsequious politicians who put themselves and their political gain first. Carter needed leaders who bought into the president-elect's *modus operandi*.[23]

Nine years later, Governor Mario Cuomo (D–NY) would famously quip that politicians campaign in poetry but govern in prose.[24] Had Cuomo said that to Carter or his transition team in 1976, I believe there would have been strong opposition. The Carter transition team intended to carry their message of the campaign through to the White House in its entirety. In an effort to foster accountability and preserve Carter's message to be honest and transparent, Stu Eizenstat and future Deputy Domestic Policy Advisor David Rubenstein compiled all the campaign promises they could find that Carter made during the campaign. They did not claim it was an exhaustive list, but it was comprehensive, covering "speeches, releases, letters, briefing transcripts, interviews, questionnaire responses, newspaper accounts, and certain other statements." Some were promises Carter made to "consider" items, others were promises to "support" actions, and still others were clear indications of intent to take certain action. Of specific importance was the section on general government, particularly reorganization, open and honest government, and election and campaign reform. Pledges were sometimes specific but often reduced to a promise where possible.[25] Many of these promises translated into policy measures, some of which are discussed later in this book. Concerns about austerity, for example, led Carter to sell the *Sequoia*. He advocated for transparency and reduced bloat and thus he later squared off with Congress over water projects. To paraphrase Cuomo, for Carter the poetry and prose would be one in the same.

Amidst the bevy of advice, Carter kept returning to his code of ethics and the leadership style the speech dictated. Working from his hometown of Plains, Georgia—rather than Atlanta or Washington, D.C.—the president-elect made sure his team understood his priori-

1. The Carter Way

ties. In a meeting with Carter, Special Council to the Carter-Mondale Transition Group John L. Moore, Jr., discussed how Carter could immediately demonstrate transparency and comity by fully disclosing his financial records, with the expectation that anyone who would work in his administration would do the same. Moore followed up with even stronger suggestions. Nominees and other potential hires would need to affirm that they would not accept any questionable contribution, compensation, *quid pro quo*, or compensation in kind. This included a promise that, if they left their government job, two years would transpire before they could take a job with a company that they had a professional relationship with during their tenure in government. Not quite a noncompete clause, but more a clause to prevent a conflict of interest.[26]

Various conversations and recommendations culminated in early December, with Carter's pollster Patrick H. Caddell circulating an "Internal Working Paper on Political Strategy." Caddell expressed a Cuomo-esque concern. Worried that Carter might flip-flop in office or walk back promises he could not keep, the pollster juxtaposed Carter's image as an outsider with strong moral authority with the commensurate connotation that he could be perceived as inexperienced. Carter was a risk, an unknown. Caddell noted as an example Carter's gaffe in his *Playboy* interview. Carter needed to balance providing fresh ideas with making sure he did not undermine his agenda with scandal or broken promises. Fundamentally, Caddell contended Carter won because the American public wanted "to 'feel good' about things." Julia R. Azari argued that Carter felt emboldened to follow through on his campaign promises. This "desire for change" reflected a base understanding that, in the wake of the Vietnam War and Watergate, Carter could turn the country around.[27]

Speaking to his suggested thematic goals for the Carter administration, Caddell conceded that Ford was correct "that bad times are being healed" or, as the outgoing president put it, America was recovering from "our long national nightmare." Caddell's first goal for Carter was the importance of healing the nation. By his account, Ford had started to move the nation beyond the baggage of the past but did not do enough: "Ford started the process to some extent. We have an opportunity to speed it along." Caddell's second goal for Carter was

Jimmy Carter and the Restoration of Presidential Dignity

restoring trust. "The public must have a sense that Carter wants to do the right thing. Basic faith in the institutions and our leader can be restored." These goals were not new nor were they different than recommendations Carter had received elsewhere. The American people wanted a change; they wanted a leader who would continue the healing while providing transparent leadership beyond reproach. Caddell did more than just rephrase what Carter already knew—he recommended a plan of action to deliver on his promises. He outlined a plan to prove to the American public his promises were not made in vain. Caddell recommended making sure Carter's early victories be small, succinct, and clear. Carter could build momentum and a track record of doing what he set out to do. Basically, Caddell encouraged Carter to rewrite the script on how a president acts and implements policy in order to convince the public that Carter is a different type of leader than his predecessors. This involved new rhetoric but also a "new style." Caddell suggested the new style be "one of austerity," of cutting back on "imperial" frills and perks. Caddell recommended symbolic actions to accomplish the "life style" image achieved by Governors Jerry Brown and Michael Dukakis. (Brown in California and Dukakis in Massachusetts had run on platforms of reform and rock-solid guarantees.)

Caddell balanced generic new-style messages with policy-specific recommendations. Caddell juxtaposed big plans about criminal justice and the environment with more symbolic plans about style and image. For example, in his suggested time line, in the first week between a foreign policy tone-setter and a budget announcement, he recommended that Carter make a "symbolic gesture in terms of personal style." Caddell suggested Carter make an "ostentatious" appearance with a guest like Bob Dylan, Martin Luther King, Sr., or perhaps a conservative. Caddell's recommendations for the first month included symbolic actions such as cutting down limousine use and pardoning draft dodgers. Fundamentally, Caddell stressed that Carter needed a good start: "Carter needs to gain personal credibility and restore the trust of the people."[28] Caddell's script played out in early 1977, as Carter strategically tackled austerity and comity in initiatives big and small. Whether overhauling the water projects process or discouraging the playing of "Hail to the Chief," Carter carried his code of ethics to the White House.

Though Carter historians Burton I. Kaufman and Scott Kaufman

1. The Carter Way

argue Caddell's report failed to adequately account for congressional interests, they concede the paper did help chart the "legislative and political course" Carter embarked upon as president. While it is true that Carter struggled to work with Congress, Caddell's memo helped Carter focus on his message. Carter considered Caddell's paper such a good read that he sent a copy to the vice president-elect to read. Carter suggested Vice President Walter Mondale find him when he was done so the two could discuss the memo. Part of Carter's new approach to the presidency would be a greater, more inclusive role for the vice president. He welcomed the soon-to-be-former senator from Minnesota into his inner circle. Consistent with Caddell's memo, Carter wanted Mondale to be more active in government and be another role model Americans could respect. Just as Carter was poised to move into 1600 Pennsylvania Avenue, Mondale would be moving into Number One Observatory Circle.[29]

In a memo subsequent to and building on Caddell's paper, Mondale responded directly and formerly to Carter. Mondale's memo spoke about a new role for the president beyond the traditional (and in some cases constitutionally mandated) big three of chief executive officer, commander in chief, and party leader. Those first three he deemed self-explanatory, but he added a fourth job, "chief elected officer." Mondale elaborated, "the Chief Elected Officer under our federal system in relations with the Congress and with state and local government and interest groups." This is clearly a point of emphasis. Mondale and Carter stressed this relationship on the campaign and now it was time to demonstrate how Carter planned to lead in this regard. To satisfy all four roles, Mondale suggested the following themes:

1. Carter as a President who will unify the country, healing past divisions, so that we can get on with meeting the problems of the future, rather than those of the past.
2. Carter as an outsider who intends to shake things up in Washington, through government reorganization, conflict of interest rules and other reforms.
3. Carter as a leader who is close to the people, who cares about their problems and is determined to give them a government that is courteous, compassionate and helpful.

Jimmy Carter and the Restoration of Presidential Dignity

4. Carter as a President who knows how to manage the Federal bureaucracy, to make it work efficiently and without waste.

5. Carter as a President who can restore trust, by his openness and candor and by his commitment to preventing abuses of the past.

6. Carter as a leader who is energetic and effective in working to solve national problems, such as the recession, inflation, energy, and international problems such as arms control.

Mondale understood Carter's vision and his code of ethics, both on an ideological and a policy level. He evoked the standard set by Franklin Delano Roosevelt, whose first hundred days in office set the tone for his presidency in 1933. Mondale challenged Carter to do the same, making recommendations about budgets and other momentum-building initiatives. Beyond what issues a Carter White House would tackle when, Mondale laid out a strategy to translate Carter's campaign promises into presidential practice.[30]

On January 22, 1977, two days after Carter became president of the United States and moved into the White House, he viewed his first movie in the White House theater room. In an ironic twist, Carter and his wife watched *All the President's Men.* Carter admired the underlying story of crack reporters Bob Woodward and Carl Bernstein sleuthing out the Watergate scandal; however, the story also brought a wave of emotions to the new president. The new president felt discomfort knowing he occupied the same residence and held the same job as Richard Nixon, who "had brought such disgrace on the White House and the presidency itself." Carter took solace in his faith that he could do better, that he would never "let the same thing happen" while he was president.[31]

American politics in the 1970s floated into previously uncharted waters. The decade saw a vice president and then a president resign from office. In both cases, Gerald Ford filled the vacancy. By 1976, Gerald Ford found himself running as an incumbent president who had never been previously vetted in a national election. Jimmy Carter knew this, and he knew that the American people had not yet forgotten about the circumstances that brought Ford to power. Carter reveled in every opportunity possible to remind voters about the tumultuous events of the past few years.

1. The Carter Way

President Jimmy Carter entered office with confidence. In this photo a couple weeks into his term, he stands behind his desk in the Oval Office, sporting a big smile (courtesy Library of Congress).

Carter's use of those scandals to debase his opponent and the opposition party had the added effect of reminding Americans that in previous years the White House had been shrouded in secrecy (often with criminal outcomes). Carter campaigned that past presidents betrayed the public trust. Whether or not Carter privately agreed that Ford needed to pardon Nixon, publicly Carter happily capitalized on the public animus toward Ford for letting Nixon off the hook.

Amidst all the controversy and scandal Carter ran against in the campaign, he knew he needed to promise a better alternative, and then deliver on that vision from day one. Carter argued that a Democratic victory would return confidence to the White House. It would return transparency and dignity to an office that had recently lacked both. At no point in the campaign or the transition did Carter back off his commitment to an "open" presidency or to his commitment to transparency. He strove to use language "people down in Plains" would

Jimmy Carter and the Restoration of Presidential Dignity

understand. He pledged press conferences, fireside chats, town hall meetings, and a new relationship with Congress.[32] Carter entered office with a lofty plan, replete with visions of a better way of conducting government. He would soon learn how well it stacked up against the Washington establishment.

2

The Path to Forgiveness

*Draft Dodgers and the Debate
Over Amnesty*[1]

The issue of amnesty for draft dodgers circulated around Washington, D.C., long before the Vietnam War ended. In the early 1970s, doves in Congress floated proposals while American ground troops continued to serve in Vietnam and elsewhere in Southeast Asia. However, regardless of the progress of the Vietnam War or the provocative debate by members of the House and Senate, President Richard Nixon maintained that reconciliation could never become a formal consideration. In a January 2, 1972, interview, Dan Rather asked if there was a scenario in which he could see amnesty being granted. Nixon curtly replied, "No." Nixon believed that nothing needed to be done for those who rejected the call of military service. Despite the persistence of draft dodger amnesty advocates, a truly viable solution would not come until Jimmy Carter.[2]

Though American ground troops formally left Vietnam in March 1973, the war itself continued on for two more years until the fall of Saigon in May 1975. In this respect, it could be said the war lasted longer than Richard Nixon, who resigned amidst the threat of impeachment in August 1974. This juxtaposition only adds to the irony of Gerald Ford's pardon of Nixon on September 8, 1974. A month after taking office—and two weeks before announcing his clemency program—Ford offered a "full, free, and absolute pardon" to the Watergate president for any or all offenses he may have done. Not until September 16, 1974, did Gerald Ford announce his Presidential Clemency Program. Adding more sting to this juxtaposition, clemency, by definition,

Jimmy Carter and the Restoration of Presidential Dignity

is not a pardon. Neither full, nor free, nor absolute, Ford's actions were bold but incomplete. Ford's program allowed resisters to expunge their spotty service record and earn reentry into American society by performing sufficient alternate service. Ford framed the program as an alternate path for young men to fulfill their debt to society. Though a bold step toward reconciliation, Ford's solution faced opposition from conservatives and underwhelming enthusiasm from liberals. Approximately two and half years later, on January 21, 1977, Carter fulfilled a campaign promise to do more for those who dodged and to heal the nation. Building off of his own personal and moral beliefs and the statistical reality that, despite Ford's efforts, many young men chose not to participate in his clemency program, the day after he took office Carter offered a full and unconditional pardon to all draft dodgers. Directed toward violators of the Selective Service Act, it applied broadly to those who chose jail over service and to those who fled into exile in Canada or elsewhere. For other resisters—such as deserters—Carter

Draft card protests, such as this man's act at the Selective Service System on March 19, 1970, typified the frustration and tensions Americans felt with the draft (courtesy Library of Congress).

2. The Path to Forgiveness

enacted a Special Discharge Review Program, guaranteeing a case-by-case review of their situation to ensure that all veterans had the discharge status they deserved.[3]

In many ways, the reconciliation solutions of America's thirty-eighth and thirty-ninth presidents had similarities. Both solutions tried to resolve one of the lingering legacies of the Vietnam War, while walking a middle road between hawks and doves. Both presidents were decorated Navy veterans—Ford earned two Bronze Stars and Carter served as a nuclear technician in the early days of the America's nuclear submarine program—but despite their own military past they understood reconciliation represented issues broader than respect for military service. No solution could have appeased the entire country; however, these men tried to satisfy as many Americans as they could. Ford tried to move the nation beyond the divisive issue of draft resistance, but his efforts fell short. Carter recognized that more could be done for those who dodged but, more generally, he saw reconciliation as an extension of his larger push to restore the image of the presidency. Carter's pardon exonerated the young men in jail or in exile, but it also recompensed for the sins of past leaders who perpetrated the war.

In every declared war and in the Civil War, presidents have enacted broad sweeping amnesties and pardons to reconcile the situations of those who chose not to serve in the military.[4] Article II, Section 2 of the Constitution reserves the power to pardon (and grant reprieves) to the president and the president alone. Since the founders wrote those words two centuries ago, the definition of pardons and reprieves has expanded to include variants of the power, including clemency and amnesty. "Clemency" suggests leniency but not automatic absolution. Like partial debt forgiveness, clemency makes restitution easier, but some restitution remains necessary. Gerald Ford considered clemency to be less than a pardon or amnesty. Some amnesty advocates, especially many members of Congress, used those two terms interchangeably, arguing they connoted the same action, but not Jimmy Carter. Drawing on his strong Christian background, the president recognized there was an important distinction. To Carter, "amnesty" meant absolution for a transgression or transgressions, often (though not exclusively) with the implication that transgressors were morally in the right. "Pardon" carried the same legal weight, however there would be no moral implications attached. Usually, amnesties are given broadly while pardons refer to narrower measures. Carter followed this classification when he called his solution a pardon. He used semantics to temper his proposals but also to reinforce that pardoning is the president's purview. Presidential pardons promote comity rather than abuses of power.[5]

Congressional Reconciliation Debates

Long before any presidential reconciliation action, members of Congress debated amnesty and proposed their own solutions. Undaunted that the Constitution's pardon clause denied them the power to act, various determined senators and representatives tried to force a debate on an issue ignored by the Nixon administration. They rested their proposals on an obscure Supreme Court case that, when taken out of context, appears to sidestep the otherwise clear language of Article II, Section 2 pardon clause. In the 1896 case of *Brown v. Walker*, the Supreme Court held that while the power to grant pardons and reprieves has been vested in the president, "this power has never been held to take from Congress the power to pass acts of general amnesty." Legislative attorney John D. Sargent of the American Law Division of the Congressional Research Service filed a report in 1972 with Congress in which, based on the precedent in the *Brown* decision, he argued, "Congress does have the authority to enact amnesty legislation." However, even Sargent admitted congressional action had only been in select cases and, even then, under limited conditions which generally included a mandate that superseded the Constitution's pardon clause.[6]

Whether those in Congress thought they could affect amnesty unilaterally or not, their crusade reflected a sin of the Nixon administration but also an abuse of comity. Whether the members pitched conditional amnesty or unconditional amnesty, they framed it as action needed when the president would not act. They critiqued President Nixon for not doing more for these draft dodgers, but in the process, they glossed over their own abuse of power. The spurious precedent

2. The Path to Forgiveness

set by the *Brown* decision amounted to congressional overreach into executive power more than the natural extrapolation of *stare decisis*.

Conditional amnesty meant that the draft dodgers had to earn their amnesty. Representative Don Edwards (D–CA) advocated an amnesty review board and alternative service. He promoted a conditional solution because he believed those who fled were not all "cowards," but they were not all "heroes" either. Representative Frank Horton (R–NY) concurred with Edwards' sentiments, deeming alternative service and a case-by-case examination the only way to determine if amnesty was warranted. He considered blanket amnesty inappropriate in light of all the men who served dutifully.[7] Conditional (case-by-case) amnesty supporters would ultimately rally around Ford's clemency program.

In contrast, unconditional amnesty meant that the draft dodger would be offered reconciliation without any requirement of restitution. Two notably liberal New York representatives spearheaded the case for unconditional amnesty in the House. Representative Edward I. Koch (D–NY) began his push for reconciliation in 1972, even before the war was over. Similarly, Representative Bella Abzug (D–NY) advocated amnesty to "exonerate and reconcile with draft dodgers and deserters," in an effort to reconcile American society as a whole. Like Koch, Abzug proposed amnesty bills. In 1974, Abzug proposed a bill that provided "full and complete" amnesty, expunging the records for all draft resisters. Amnesty reflected the dovish agenda that Koch and Abzug hung their hats on.[8] Senator Philip A. Hart (D–MI), the "conscience of the Senate," best paralleled Koch and Abzug's efforts, championing the cause of amnesty until his death in 1976:

> What better time than now for the president or the Congress, or both to extend to those huddled masses of American exiles living in Canada and elsewhere the right to breathe free in their native land.... Better to blanket in a few liars than to commit to exile forever the thousands of others who believed, erroneously or not, that what they were doing was morally right.

Amnesty, to Hart, was not an admission that someone was right or wrong but a tool of reconciliation to put the past behind. Hart admitted there might be people who would benefit that should not but contended that it was better to forgive a few too many than deny forgiveness.[9]

Jimmy Carter and the Restoration of Presidential Dignity

Despite the persuasive prowess of these three savvy politicians, there were many members of Congress who opposed amnesty. Their sentiments paralleled the opinion of many Americans who believed nothing ought to be done for draft resisters. They opposed reconciliation because they believed there was no negotiation needed; the *status quo* represented the best solution to the problem. Sometimes these sentiments graduated to accusations of "cowardice," or even stronger language such as "self-retired veterans" or "slackers anonymous." These derisions were common amongst anti-amnesty supporters, though senators and congressmen usually followed up with more detailed arguments.[10] Some opposed amnesty because they disagreed, such as Representative Edward J. Derwinski (R–IL), who believed these young men should come home and "face the music," while others like Representative Philip Crane (R–IL) likened the actions of draft resisters to the civil disobedience promoted by Dr. Martin Luther King, Jr. Crane argued civil disobedience connotes a willingness to be punished for one's beliefs. Draft resisters should return to America and face prosecution under the law.[11]

More complex arguments against amnesty generally rested on two contentions. The first argument regarded the negative precedents amnesty would set. Former Republican presidential nominee, outspoken hawk, and conservative icon Senator Barry Goldwater (R–AZ) argued that to show leniency to any individual or group of individuals would set a devastating precedent for the ability to raise an army in the future. No draft would be able to be called without the assumption that noncompliance is okay. Furthermore, the notion of serving would seem less than dignified.[12] Goldwater failed to consider that amnesties have been issued after past wars and did not affect the ability to conscript future armies. Others, like former Chair of the National Republican Congressional Committee and House Armed Services Committee member Representative Bob Wilson (R–CA) or Veterans' Affairs Committee member Representative Sam Hall (D–TX) suggested amnesty refuted rule of law. It sent the message that lawbreaking would be excused; that amnesty begat anarchy. Even when President Carter later pardoned draft dodgers per his constitutional powers, they still seemed convinced the action was anarchistic.[13]

The second main argument regarded the respect for those who

2. The Path to Forgiveness

served dutifully. Former Dixiecrat presidential candidate and conservative Republican pillar Senator Strom Thurmond (R–SC) stated the argument most forcefully. Amnesty should not be "doled" out undeservingly, it should be "dosed" out responsibly. Thurmond argued that peacetime service should not be offered as a path to amnesty or as a means to polish "spotty" wartime records. Draft resisters should not be allowed to don the same uniform and reap the same benefits as someone who served dutifully. The spirits of the brave men who fought should haunt those who support the "cynical double standard" that is amnesty. Thurmond summed up this argument by noting, "[i]f this country's moral fiber is to regain its consciousness, then we must teach our citizens that they have rights and they have responsibilities, and that the two go together like ham and eggs." This argument might seem a bit ironic coming from a politician with a pronounced record against civil rights legislation. On the other hand, Thurmond's own argument concedes that there is atrophy in the country's moral fiber. Though Carter and Thurmond would be on opposite sides of the amnesty question, they both recognized a need to move the nation forward.[14]

In an ironic twist, before he became president, Congressman and House Minority Leader Gerald Ford (R–MI) presented a similar argument against amnesty. On March 24, 1973, he discussed his position in his weekly radio address, contrasting the suffering and heroism of Air Force Major (and former prisoner of war) Joe Shanahan with "those men who call themselves Americans but live in Canada or Sweden or 'underground U.S.A.' because they refused to answer the call of their country." Ford stated clearly to his constituents that unlike some of his fellow legislators who demanded "total forgiveness" and "total amnesty" based on historical precedent, he disagreed with their propositions. He added that the facts actually show that, historically, draft evaders pay for their actions. Congressman Ford told his radio listeners that he supported the position of President Nixon and opposed any endorsement of these men's actions.[15] Two years later, as president, Ford would reverse his stance. Still against "total" solutions and congressional action, as president he embraced executive clemency as a necessity for progress.

Ford's Clemency Program

On September 16, 1974, Ford issued Executive Order 11803 and Proclamation 4313, establishing his clemency program. When ascending to the presidency, Ford promised to "throw the weight of [his] presidency into the scales of justice on the side of leniency and mercy." Later, Ford reflected, "There was no magic wand that I could wave to restore people's trust, but there *were* some specific steps I could take to nudge the process along." Clemency presented a reserved solution. During "Question-and-Answer" session in the months after the program's announcement, the president characterized clemency as "earned amnesty for draft evaders." The phrase "earned amnesty" sounds good, but in practice the two are incompatible. If amnesty is offered, no restitution should be required. True amnesty is a *mea culpa*, conceding the moral high ground to the recipient. Earning reentry suggests it is a reward or a deal, rather than an entitlement. In fact, this is how Ford described his program elsewhere. He clarified that it was

President Gerald Ford announces his clemency program for draft evaders on September 16, 1974 (courtesy Library of Congress).

2. The Path to Forgiveness

not a "free ride" but a chance for people to earn a second opportunity at mainstream society.[16]

Ford's clemency program was a case-by-case conditional amnesty. The clemency program had different divisions to assist different types of potential clemency cases. The first category was those draft law offenders who had yet to be convicted or punished. Ford offered these individuals an option to fulfill their civic duty by means of twenty-four months of alternate service. Alternate service referred generally to duties similar to those assigned to conscientious objectors. The second category of potential clemency cases involved those persons already convicted of draft law offenses. The clemency program offered a review of their case to determine if their status needed to be amended. To review these cases, Ford established the Clemency Review Board.[17]

An ally from across the aisle, Senator Edward "Ted" Kennedy (D–MA) defended Ford's plan, commending the president for trying to reconcile the nation. Kennedy assured Ford that the majority of Americans would appreciate the clemency program, emphasizing that "reconciliation is the precondition for the nation to move forward again." Kennedy believed reconciliation helped individuals but also helped the nation. The senator from Massachusetts reasoned that for most cases the call for healing outweighed the call for justice. "Many Americans would accept the hardship and suffering—even though self-imposed—which many of these young men already have suffered in defense of their deep moral convictions as sufficient." Kennedy supported "earned reentry,"—e.g., clemency in return for some modicum of alternate service similar to Ford's program—though he hoped Ford would eventually warm to the idea of a more comprehensive amnesty plan. For the moment, Kennedy pledged support and "whatever additional assistance" Ford wanted. This spirit of bipartisanship struggled under the weight of Ford's other act of leniency: his pardon of Richard Nixon. Ford's pardon eviscerated his political capital and angered many members of Congress, including Kennedy. It would not be until Jimmy Carter became president that doves would be fully satisfied.[18]

In light of the diverse congressional feedback and in the spirit of transparency and federal comity, the day Ford announced his clemency program, he invited congressional leaders from both parties to meet with him and his staff. "Hard-line conservative" Representative F.

Jimmy Carter and the Restoration of Presidential Dignity

Edward Hébert (D–LA) worried that by being too lenient, Ford would set a bad precedent for future crises. Senator Strom Thurmond (R–SC) concurred: "I want to help you unify the country, but I am concerned. Eddie Hébert expressed my views. There is no worse crime than this. This is setting a dangerous precedent. You can exercise your pardon authority, but we should let the courts go through the legal processes." Conversely, House Majority Leader and vocal Vietnam War critic Senator Mike Mansfield (D–MT) congratulated Ford on his action, noting he is "continuing a tradition that was started by President Washington." Ford responded to Mansfield and Hébert,

> Thanks Mike; but Eddie, I hope this meeting illustrates that we can have frank discussions in these meetings without affecting personal relationships. I think the restrictions we have imposed will keep them from having clean hands. The [Joint Chiefs of Staff] think it would not undermine military discipline, but others in the Pentagon differ with that.

More than just having such a meeting with congressional leadership—which in itself represented a gesture lost at times by past presidents—Ford invited and respected (though he did not necessarily follow) the input and suggestions from members of Congress. "Frank discussions" and "personal relationships" were two things that had been lost during the Johnson and Nixon administrations. Ford burned many bridges and strained bipartisanship with his pardon of Nixon. This meeting tried to ease some of those tensions.[19] Ultimately, Ford's efforts at transparency and comity would be undone by the limitations of his clemency program and his full pardon of Richard Nixon. Both of these issues became campaign talking points for Carter in 1976.

As the impact of Ford's announcement set in, the reactions reflected the gamut of the American political spectrum. Critiquing Ford's clemency program, Senator Barry Goldwater (R–AZ) commented: "I deplore very deeply and greatly the fact that our president, my president, whom I want to back as much as I can, has taken this step that is like throwing mud in the face of millions of men who have served their country."[20] Conversely, some members called for greater leniency. When Ford enacted his clemency program, Representative Bella Abzug (D–NY) declared on the floor of Congress that she was happy to hear he had taken the "first step" and "rejected revenge, favored leniency, and ordered a review of the cases of individual draft resisters." How-

2. The Path to Forgiveness

ever, she believed that more than a "second chance to work their way home" ought to be done for those who protested an immoral war. Ford needed to take the next step of universal and unconditional amnesty, especially in light of his pardon of Nixon. She considered it ironic that Ford pardoned Nixon but only offered consideration for draft resisters. As the clemency program ran its course, Abzug chastised Ford for giving America a "half-a-loaf" solution to silence supporters for amnesty and noted that his "earned reentry" program was failing its goal of reconciliation and reintegration. Abzug attributed this failure to the fact that clemency was not amnesty, it was "strained mercy." She advocated complete expungement, effectively rendering the records of draft resisters *tabula rasa*. In her view, extension would not be enough; true success required the wiping clean of records, which could only be successfully achieved by a universal and unconditional amnesty. For this reason, Abzug approved of Carter's pardon of draft dodgers two years later, but she wished he had also pardoned resisters.[21]

Ford's clemency program ended on September 16, 1975. Approximately 6 percent of the 350,000 eligible men actually applied and of those roughly 21,500 applications, only about 8,000 received clemency. Most draft dodgers who did not avail themselves of the clemency program understood their choice. They would not return if they had to justify themselves with alternate service. Despite the dismal numbers and success-rate statistics, Ford tried to claim victory. In the words of White House Special Counsel Richard Tropp, "the clemency/amnesty issue is now a dead letter and a part of history. This particular wound of the Vietnam War is, to the extent that it ever humanly can be, healed." In a brief statement, Ford announced that the program had been a success for all who sought it out. He added that he believed "these young Americans should have the opportunity to contribute a share in the rebuilding of peace amongst ourselves."[22] Ford ignored the droves of draft dodgers insulted by his half-a-loaf solution. He also ignored his critics who were still steaming over his pardon of Nixon. Some balked because they wanted Nixon's head on a pike, while others balked because they felt that draft dodgers deserved the same deal.

Ford did not resolve the amnesty debate but the debate did shift its focus. Anti-amnesty proponents modified their position and merged with the conditional amnesty advocates. Together they accepted Ford's actions but wanted no more amnesties to be offered. The sentiments of pro-amnesty advocates also shifted their framework in light of Ford's actions. They now argued that Ford's action was an appropriate beginning, but more amnesty measures were needed. Pro-amnesty advocates believed that conditional amnesty provided insufficient reconciliation for draft resisters. They wanted more. They wanted amnesty. They did not know it, but what they wanted was Jimmy Carter.[23]

Carter's Proclamation of Pardon

In 1976, Carter made reconciliation a campaign issue. As part of his commitment to restoring the relationship between the White House and the nation, Carter also used the tactic to remind voters that Ford's solution did not work adequately. An additional wrinkle to the platform plank was the promise of a pardon evoked Ford's pardon of Nixon. In the *United Press International* on August 24, 1976, Carter laid out the connection:

> I don't think that the person that pardoned Mr. Nixon—I think it was President Ford—specified that Nixon was guilty or not guilty. I'm not going to say whether those young people were guilty or not guilty. I'm just going to say "what you did, whether right or wrong, you are forgiven for."

Ford repeatedly maintained that, while he wished more individuals had taken part in the program, he had no intention of offering additional leniency.[24] This rhetoric created a clear distinction between the candidates, especially after Carter's August 24, 1976, American Legion speech. Speaking before a hostile audience, Carter pledged, "I do not favor a blanket amnesty, but for those who violated Selective Service laws, I intend to grant a blanket pardon." Carter later added,

> If I am President, I will issue a pardon for all those who are outside our country or in this country, who did not serve in the Armed Forces. I am going to issue a pardon—not an amnesty. I think those kids who have lived in Sweden and Canada or who have avoided arrest have been punished enough.

Carter's technical distinction reflected his belief that amnesty carries a connotation of moral absolution. A pardon cleans the offender's slate, but Carter believed amnesty cleaned the slate and implied the offender was justified in doing what they did. Beyond any allusion to

2. The Path to Forgiveness

Carter's devout Christian faith and the role of pardoning transgressions, the distinction allowed the presidential candidate to woo the pro-amnesty vote while trying to respect those who chose to serve dutifully.[25]

While both men offered visions for healing the nation, their solutions had clear differences. Neither man condoned draft dodgers, but both wanted to reunite them with mainstream American society. On September 23, 1976, Ford and Carter faced off in a presidential debate in Philadelphia and, as expected, the issue of amnesty arose. The moderator asked Ford about his stance on amnesty. Ford maintained that he was against an "across-the-board pardon of draft evaders or military deserters." In response, Carter clarified what he defined as amnesty and pardon: "Amnesty means what you did was right. Pardon means that what you did, whether it's right or wrong, you are forgiven for it. And I do advocate a pardon for draft evaders." Carter wanted to "heal [the] country after the Vietnam War." Making good on his campaign promise and demonstrating his commitment to heal the nation, Car-

President Gerald Ford and Governor Jimmy Carter during their first presidential debate in Philadelphia, Pennsylvania (White House Photography courtesy Gerald R. Ford Library).

ter's pardon closely resembled the promise made in that Philadelphia auditorium.[26] Carter ultimately won the 1976 election. Though Ford later proclaimed that he thought he lost because of how he handled the New York City financial bailout, other factors such as amnesty, the larger legacy of the Vietnam War, and Watergate likely played more decisive roles.[27]

Carter promised quick action to reconcile the issue of draft dodgers, and on January 21, 1977, his first full day in office, the new president made it his first executive order and proclamation. A symbolic gesture to reunite families, the act also emphasized Carter's commitment to convey a more positive image of government. As his transition team had recommended, Carter's reconciliation was a way to gain momentum and assure the public that he would do what he promised. Carter issued a "full, complete and unconditional pardon" to all draft dodgers but "specifically excluded" deserters. Carter instructed Attorney General Griffin Bell to dismiss all relevant pending indictments, to cease all relevant pending investigations, and to refrain from opening any relevant new ones. All persons previously precluded from reentry into the United States were now able to do so. Any individual who participated in Ford's clemency program was eligible for Carter's pardon, eligible to have his status upgraded. Senator Ted Kennedy (D–MA) said Carter had taken a "major, impressive and compassionate step toward healing the wounds of Vietnam." Continuing Ford's effort to heal the nation, Carter acted swiftly on this campaign promise.[28]

In conjunction with Carter's pardon for draft dodgers—those who never entered the military—he implemented his Special Discharge Review Program to provide a forum to veterans. Some felt they were assessed with the wrong discharged status. Beyond the micro-level political argument for reconciling those who served along with those who did not, Carter's review program had other political values. It provided the possibility for leniency while respecting those who served dutifully and did not need the review. Though the program proved especially helpful to undesirable and clemency discharges (for which an upgrade in status is significant), all discharges were eligible for review. By framing his program broadly, Carter promoted a program to ensure all veterans—including those who served dutifully—were eligible for review and could be afforded the discharged status that they

2. The Path to Forgiveness

earned. Also, Carter's program implied that there might be larger systemic problems in the executive branch of government, in this case the Department of Defense and the Department of Veterans' Affairs. By promoting a program that called for external review of discharge policy, Carter demonstrated a commitment to righting past wrongs and doing so in a transparent manner. Carter recognized a potential problem with executive bureaucracy and moved to fix it. Carter accepted that the federal bureaucracy—in this case the Department of Veterans' Affairs—might have exacerbated the resister and discharge problems. Carter also reformed the Veterans Administration—especially in terms of the medical care given to veterans. Carter appointed distinguished Vietnam War veteran (and future senator) Max Cleland to be the Administrator of Veterans' Affairs. Cleland sustained severe grenade injuries during the war, resulting in the amputation of his right arm and both legs. Cleland carried Carter's message of reform to the Veterans Administration. The war ended on some sour notes, but Carter wanted to put the war behind America while respecting those who served dutifully.[29]

Unable to veto or stop Carter from implementing his pardon, anti-amnesty advocates in Congress responded (in the final action on amnesty) based on the powers that were within their purview. Much like the congressional proposals to usurp the executive power of pardon, some members of Congress used creative methods to circumvent the president when he used his pardon power. Congressional hawks recognized that they could still sabotage funding for Carter's program; however, since pardoning required no funding, members focused instead on those veterans who sought to have their discharge status reevaluated. They set their sights on Carter's Special Discharge Review Program.

Representative John T. Myers (R–IN) went even further. He added an amendment to the 1978 Fiscal Year Budget. Myers sought to circumvent the pardon clause by treating the exiles as aliens before treating them as pardonable Americans. Myers sought to prevent Carter's pardon from applying to exiles who had renounced their American citizenship. Senator Mark Hatfield (R–OR) cut through the subterfuge of Myers' amendment, noting it "would effectively gut President Carter's pardon program for Vietnam-era draft resisters." While Hatfield's concerns focused on draft dodgers—a group whose pardon had already been carried out—his sentiments also applied to wrongly discharged veterans still in need of a discharge review. Myers' maneuver garnered support from the anti-amnesty camp, desperate to land one final punch. For example, Senators Ernest "Fritz" Hollings (D–SC) and Bob Dole (R–KS) based their support for the Myers Amendment on the respect for those who served dutifully and especially for those who died in combat.[30]

On June 24, 1977, Leon Ulman, Acting Assistant Attorney General from the Offices of Legal Counsel, wrote Deputy Counsel to the President Margaret McKenna about Myers' amendment. Ulman cited numerous Supreme Court decisions reiterating that the power to pardon "cannot be modified, abridged, or diminished by the Congress." Ulman conceded that Congress had plenary power over immigration, but quickly added that this power was not the basis for congressional action in this matter. Myers designed the amendment to nullify Carter's pardon and its effect. McKenna later described the amendment as having has "some serious constitutional problems." Hatfield concurred, "Denying him the funds in effect is denying him the power to exercise his constitutional authority."[31] While the balance of power between the president and Congress often fluctuates, Myers' amendment represented precisely the problem of politics threatening comity. In an effort to circumvent Carter's constitutional prerogative, Myer tried to aggrandize Constitutional authority for partisan gain.

After weighing options which ranged from passive acceptance of the bill to an outright veto, Carter followed the compromise solution advised by White House Counsel to the President, Robert J. Lipshutz and Chief Domestic Policy Advisor Stu Eizenstat, whereby the bill would be signed into law but with a stern signing statement. On August 3, 1977, Carter signed the bill into law, but with his signature he expressed his

> ... strong disagreement with [the Myers Amendment].... [The Myers Amendment] purports to prohibit the use of funds appropriated under this act to carry out the Executive order.... I am advised by the Department of Justice that this aspect of [the Myers Amendment] is unconstitutional. It amounts to interference with the pardon power which is invested in the President by the Constitution.

Frustrated by congressional attempts to derail his reconciliations efforts, Carter regretted that he had to sign the budget bill even though

2. The Path to Forgiveness

it threatened his discharge review program. He feared that if he vetoed the bill on principle, the public reaction would be about government shutdown and would blame him rather than see the scheming of congressional amnesty opponents. Carter worried the public would not see a comity violation but a president who put politics above the best interests of the nation.[32]

Beyond the practical value of Carter's pardon, there was the bigger symbolic value of this shift in policy. More than just a shift in White House Vietnam War policy, it furthered Carter's agenda for his time in the White House. Ten years after the Gulf of Tonkin Resolution begat increased draft calls, the attitude of the executive office changed with respect to the draft. Ford's clemency program gave draft dodgers a path to forgiveness, but the alternate service seemed insulting to those who believed they did nothing to apologize for. They never supported the war and resented the idea of returning to serve the war machine in any capacity. Ultimately, Carter's pardon provided reconciliation for draft dodgers. Carter never endorsed draft dodging, but he did not tack on conditions to draft dodger's reentry into American society. The pardon provided closure for those individuals for whom conscience trumped patriotism. It signaled to the American public there would be no questionable Cambodian invasions or presidential pardons during Carter's tenure in office. Carter wore his faith on his sleeve. He would preach forgiveness over punishment. He would restore the image of the White House and the president as fighting the good fights and trying to move the nation forward.

American ground troops withdrew from Vietnam in 1973. This made for a tidy end in the rhetoric of Richard Nixon and in the minds of other like-minded politicians. However, just like Hubert Van Es' infamous photograph of the fall of Saigon, reconciliation made clear that the 1973 Paris Peace Accords did not totally resolve all the lingering issues surrounding the Vietnam War. Months before North Vietnam finished its sweep through South Vietnam and its capture of Saigon, Gerald Ford tried to sweep away the issue of draft dodgers. Ironically, hawks felt he did too much and doves felt he did too little. Others thought it unfair that draft dodgers needed to earn reentry into American society while Richard Nixon received a full pardon. Some Americans earned their clemency discharges but for many others they did not believe they should need to earn their way back. They waited for a better deal. They waited for Carter's pardon.

The year 1977 brought a détente to America. Draft dodgers could rejoin mainstream American society. Though the Cold War continued, there was no hot war demanding the service of young Americans. In fact, until 1980, there was not even a draft registration. Carter's first act as president of the United States removed the sword of Damocles hanging over draft dodgers and their families. Carter resolved an issue that had been eating at Congress—and absorbing their time—for almost a decade. Carter's pardon demonstrated how the Constitution should work and how the actions of an honest president can help the nation move forward.

3

Trimming the Trappings of Office

Presidential Yacht Sequoia *and Jimmy Carter's Arsenal of Austerity*

By the time Richard Nixon left office, his style of leadership left an air of arrogance and hubris associated with the White House. Though Arthur M. Schlesinger, Jr., did not coin the phrase "imperial presidency" until 1973, by the mid–1970s instances of aggrandized power and eccentric regal proclivities proliferated. They extended beyond Nixon's handling of the Vietnam War or his relationship with Congress, though those did upset the balance of comity and strain the constitutional balance of power. Nixon also pushed more subtle and symbolic gestures. In the early 1970s, Nixon changed the dress of the White House guards, then still called the Executive Protection Service. Their old garb proved too plain for Richard Nixon's tastes. Secret Service historian Philip H. Melanson remarked, "The new outfits looked like they might have been borrowed from the Vatican or from a Sixteenth-Century French palace."[1] Inspired by European royal guards, the uniforms included gold-trimmed tunics and peaked hats. The change served no purpose beyond the visual image, as Nixon tried to maximize the regality of his office.

Nixon also invited controversy over some capital improvements made to his personal residences. While every president in the modern age had some modifications made to their home in the name of national security after taking office, allegedly some of the amenities added to Nixon's estates came into question and prompted a congressional investigation. The House Subcommittee on the Treasury, Postal

Jimmy Carter and the Restoration of Presidential Dignity

Service, and General Government Appropriations of the Committee on Appropriations held hearings, investigating the "improvements" spending on Nixon's properties in San Clemente, California, and Key Biscayne, Florida. At the hearings, officials from the Secret Service made it clear that the alterations to Nixon's properties were all within the letter of the law and all the alleged frivolities (such as ice makers and air conditioners) were actually for the legitimate use of security staff. Though the Secret Service testimony exonerated the president, the impact on the president's image stuck. The caricature of the imperial presidency extends beyond warfare and spying. The imperial presidency also implies a unique yet extravagant presidential lifestyle and sense of luxury.[2]

Gerald Ford worked to restore the credibility of the presidency, but his pardon of Nixon eviscerated much of his clout and political capital. Thus, Carter represented the first president with a clean slate and an unencumbered chance to restore Americans' faith in their chief executive. Part of his larger campaign platform of austerity and

President Jimmy Carter and First Lady Rosalynn Carter walk on Inauguration Day, January 20, 1977 (courtesy Library of Congress).

3. Trimming the Trappings of Office

honesty, the former peanut farmer vowed to improve the image of the presidency and eliminate some of the trappings of the office. Reflecting on his vision, Carter later noted:

> Although we altered little in the White House itself, I wanted to make some basic changes in how a President lived and governed. In addition to the gesture of walking down Pennsylvania Avenue, I tried in many other ways to convince the people that barriers between them and top officials in Washington were being broken down. A simpler lifestyle, more frugality, less ostentation, more accessibility to the press and public—all these suited the way I had always lived.

This commitment to austerity and determination to stand by his promises translated to a series of actions designed to subdue the luxury of office. Restricting limousine usage and selling the presidential yacht were two of the more prominent and publicized measures undertaken by Carter, but they are two of many. Overall, Carter sought restitution for the "trappings" and "perquisites" by trying to refine the public face of the presidency.[3]

To this end, Jimmy Carter's austerity reflected his common-man style and acted as a harbinger of his attitude toward presidential power. Alluding to his predecessors and the appearance that they relied on fiat rather than respect, Carter made deliberate moves to be different. Some gestures were symbolic as much as they were political, such as "serving only beer and wine at the White House and dispensing with the playing of 'Hail to the Chief.'"

> Watergate had been a largely unspoken though ever-present campaign issue, and the bitter divisions and personal tragedies of those recent events could not quickly be forgotten. So, in spite of Ford's healing service, the ghosts of Watergate still haunted the White House. We wanted to exorcize them and welcome friendlier spirits. However, in reducing the imperial Presidency, I overreacted at first. We began to receive many complaints that I had gone too far in cutting back the pomp and ceremony, so after a few months I authorized the band to play "Hail to the Chief" on special occasions. I found it to be impressive and enjoyed it.[4]

Though Carter's initiatives begat mixed reactions and results, his efforts proved to be just as important as his successes. After many manifestations of the imperial presidency, Carter fashioned himself as a man trying to do the opposite. In Julia R. Azari's words, "Carter focused on changing the image of the office." Gaddis Smith noted, "Jimmy Carter believed that Watergate and Vietnam indicated that there was a lack of

Jimmy Carter and the Restoration of Presidential Dignity

spiritual health and that now somehow there would be a rebirth, which he would lead." Similarly, Laurence I. Radway noted, "turning down the heat and doing away with imperial frills" made "Joe Sixpack satisfied and pleased with Carter."[5] This dovetailed with his larger campaign to be the simple, straightforward, anti–Washington common man from Plains, Georgia, who came to Washington to counteract the imperial *status quo* and clean up American government.

Carter was not the first president to try to abandon "Hail to the Chief." Ford often replaced "Hail to the Chief" with the University of Michigan fight song, (Hail to) "The Victors." Ford's alumni pride almost caused an international incident. On a 1975 visit to China, the Peking band played "Victory for MSU" (Falcone Fight), the fight song of Michigan State University—the University of Michigan's rival. Reports say, however, that Press Secretary Ron Nessen chose not to stress the issue. It is not clear whether China deliberately tried to snub Ford or truly committed an error. Needless to say, had China played "Across the Field" (Ohio State University's fight song), there might have been a war.[6] Still, Ford's gesture seemed to come across more as the affinity of a former Wolverine football player than that of an austere president. Indeed, Ford was not above asking the Secret Service to wake him up while he was traveling abroad just to find out the score in a Michigan–Ohio State game. (Michigan lost.)[7]

While Ford did spurn some trappings of office, Carter advanced a more coherent austerity strategy. Still, some trappings would prove hard to avoid. James Fallows pointed out that this is especially true when foreign affairs were concerned. "There were also familiar allurements of foreign affairs: the trips on fabulous Air Force One, the flourishes, twenty-one-gun salutes, and cheering multitudes along the motorcade routes." In this Carter is not alone. Speaking of John F. Kennedy, Louis Koenig noted, "If the president himself lags in donning monarchic trappings, others will put them on him." Despite Kennedy's austerity efforts, the press dubbed his White House a modern Camelot.[8]

When Carter first took office, his austerity campaign ranked high amongst his priorities. During the transition, Frank Moore warned that Carter had an eight-week window to establish his austerity campaign.[9] When preparing for his first interview as president, Press Secretary

3. Trimming the Trappings of Office

Jody Powell instructed Carter to name-drop one or two "hard items," such as the limousines issue or draft amnesty. Powell encouraged the president to steer the conversation toward his "determination to live up to campaign promises and not get enmeshed in the trappings of the office."[10] Carter reiterated this message numerous times in the early days of his presidency. Speaking on his efforts to make the government more efficient, Carter said,

> And I can hope that I can exemplify this attitude in such a way that it might inspire you to do the same thing. I've tried to eliminate some of the artificial trappings and respect that's openly paid to me. I feel that the Office of Presidency is substantial enough and has an adequate amount of respect already.[11]

From the moment Carter entered office, he emphasized his common-man image. In the age of limousines and Secret Service details, no newly minted president before or since has opted to walk down Pennsylvania Avenue to his new home as opposed to riding in a limousine motorcade. "I felt a simple walk would be a tangible indication of some reduction in the imperial status of the President and his family."[12] Carter also meant for the walk to emphasize his simpler lifestyle and austere attitude, a break from the pomp of his predecessors. Walking down Pennsylvania Avenue suggested that there would be no regal guard at Carter's White House and that this president would never hide from the American public.

Motion to Dispose

Following his campaign promises to subdue the trappings of the presidency, Jimmy Carter began considering "retirement" options for the presidential yacht *Sequoia* before the Electoral College finished counting the votes. The idea was inspired partially by a television report in late 1976 by Roger Mudd calling for a "crack down on White House perquisites." Allegedly, Hugh Carter, special assistant to the president, known to his colleagues as "Cousin Cheap" (Hugh and Jimmy were cousins), had a handwritten letter on his desk from the president, citing the Mudd report and calling for him to investigate the selling of the *Sequoia*. Despite the president's deliberate call for the boat's sale, skepticism remained as to whether Carter would

Jimmy Carter and the Restoration of Presidential Dignity

make good on his promises. *Washington Post* reporter Joseph Kraft questioned whether Carter's symbolism and promises were genuine or merely manipulations to garner votes. On one hand, Kraft pointed to the signs visible from the campaign. Carter wore denim, carried his own bag, and attacked the Washington establishment. "Stressing these themes cost Carter absolutely nothing and while they may not be bogus, they certainly do not pass the test of authenticity. Moreover, the same stress on cut-rate, if not costless, symbols of openness had continued in office." Kraft then noted Carter's moves in office, including the Inauguration Day walk down Pennsylvania Avenue, the rollbacks of limousine use, and lowering the thermostat in the White House. However, Kraft feared Carter was hiding secrets and manipulating Washington politics. He critiqued the president for not pushing his austerity campaign into the private sector. Kraft doubted Carter's sincerity, predicting that his campaign was a ruse and after the first big crisis it would be business as usual.[13] Carter proved Kraft wrong. Intent to dispel the regal image of the office and unaware of the political value of White House perquisites, Carter moved quickly to sell what he saw as an unnecessary luxury. Swiftly moving to follow through on his campaign promises, by March Jimmy Carter had already decided the *Sequoia*'s fate. Carter requested detailed information regarding his options for the boat's "disposition."

The practice of presidential yachts dates back to Rutherford B. Hayes, though the use of riverboats for similar ends can be traced back to Abraham Lincoln. (During the Civil War, Lincoln often rented out the *River Queen*, a privately owned steamer.) Hayes acquired the USS *Dispatch* in 1880, making him the first president to have an official yacht. Between Hayes and Carter, ten boats served off and on at the pleasure of the sitting commander in chief. Administered by the Naval Administrative unit, "to provide yachting and other support services to the President for both official and social functions," the boats were a special segment of the fleet. The last in that line of boats was the presidential yacht *Sequoia*. Built in 1924, the *Sequoia* served off and on as the naval refuge for various presidents since 1933. It contained a master stateroom with a king-size bed and topped out at an eleven-knot flank (maximum) speed. A modest boat as yachts go—even presidential yachts—it still commanded respect and provided a distinguished escape.[14]

3. Trimming the Trappings of Office

When Hugh Carter described Carter's options and the pros and cons of each, he also described the possible political fallout, reminding his cousin that presidential yachts dated back to 1865 and should Carter dispose of the *Sequoia* it might impede future presidents from replacing the yacht. (Hugh) Carter preemptively scuttled any option that did not fit with the president's larger political message. For example, he nixed the possibility that the boat be given to the Department of Defense for use by senior Pentagon officials. Such an option, though a fortuitous deal for those senior Pentagon officials, would be antithetical to Jimmy Carter's austerity motives. Carter believed government workers should focus on the cheap and efficient job of government. Carter did not just think the president should not have an official yacht, he believed that yachts—like fancy dressed guards and other superfluous accoutrements—did not belong in government. Reassigning the boat elsewhere in the government would defeat Carter's attempt to reduce extraneous perquisites and shrink frivolous expenditures. Carter did not oppose an imperial presidency only to enable an imperial congress or an imperial bureaucracy. Carter wanted to return government to the business of governing, free from the arrogance of power and the trappings that imply the same.

As a corollary to the pros and cons of selling the boat, Hugh Carter outlined four possibilities for executing the sale if the president so chose. Option one was deactivation and disposal, with the intent that the craft be sold off if the Department of Defense or the General Services Administration could not find a suitable non-pleasure use for it. This option would have netted a savings of $800,000. The second option called for the transfer of the boat to the Navy Historical Museum. This plan would have saved approximately $600,000, though $100,000 would need to be earmarked for upkeep as such funds did not exist in the museum's budget. The third option bypassed the reassignment search of option one and went straight to the public sale, for a total savings of $800,000. The last option deactivated the boat as a presidential yacht but allowed it to remain in the Navy inventory for use as the Defense Department saw fit. This option would save less than $50,000. Hugh Carter added as an afterthought that the prospect of transfer to the Smithsonian Institution had been considered but the scientific and historical organization did not have the requisite space.[15]

Jimmy Carter and the Restoration of Presidential Dignity

Ultimately, Hugh Carter concluded, the "*Sequoia* itself does not serve a function that is necessary for the well-being and security of the nation." He reduced the dilemma to the dyad of austerity versus tradition. Focusing on the details and the larger political agenda, both Carters underestimated some of the political ramifications and implications of the boat's sale. The president and his assistant missed the political capital the yacht created. Bringing members of Congress on the presidential yacht was one of the unwritten ways to grease the skids inside the beltway, a consideration neither Carter gave adequate weight. To President Carter, the symbolism of the gesture of selling the yacht took priority and any adverse political implications were collateral damage in his fight for austerity at the White House.

Solidified by Hugh Carter's recommendations, on March 30, 1977, the president instructed Secretary of Defense Harold Brown to "[p]lease deactivate the *Sequoia* and have it disposed of through public sale. Despite its distinguished career, I feel that [the] Presidential yacht *Sequoia* is no longer needed." Carter subtly made the sale public the next day in the *Weekly Compilation of Presidential Documents*. Buried in the weekly newsletter, "The White House announced that the President has requested that the Secretary of Defense dispose of the Presidential yacht *Sequoia*, by offering it for public sale." Reduced to a brief statement, Carter's austerity campaign began to take tangible shape. With a frugality of words, Carter introduced his simpler lifestyle and common-man presidential attitude.[16]

Washington Post writer Judith Martin covered the *Sequoia*'s sale, reporting that Carter considered the expense of maintaining a presidential yacht "unjustified and unnecessary." Martin considered Carter unique in his resolve as compared to past presidents. She noted that, ironically, despite all the rhetoric by past presidents against excessive luxury and wasted spending, they all enjoyed their yachts.

> So with all that selling and saving, how come each of those luxury-hating Presidents, and every President in between, has passed hours cruising on the Potomac River or beyond in his very own Presidential yacht? In fact, the U.S. Navy has operated Presidential yachts—often two of them per President—during every administration since Rutherford B. Hayes.

Martin buttressed her argument with the financial incentives. She coyly noted that while the numbers "rock back and forth," overall the

3. Trimming the Trappings of Office

sale would save the American taxpayer money, especially considering that operation costs included the salaries of Navy and Coast Guard personnel assigned to the yacht.[17]

As word of Jimmy Carter's decision spread, new prospective buyers and mediators offered their suggestions for disposal. Inside Washington, the Associated Press reported that a House panel considered purchasing the yacht. Representative Phillip Burton (D–CA), Chairman of the House Interior Subcommittee on National Parks, put the *Sequoia* purchase plan in a larger, wide-ranging, national parks bill. The bill would place the boat under the jurisdiction of the National Park Service, where it would be open to the public for a small fee to cover its upkeep. Regarding bidders, Judith Martin quipped that for all the prospective bidders, the one person clearly not interested in the boat was Jimmy Carter, "who ordered it sold as an economy measure."[18]

However, amidst an otherwise benign bidding process (not counting the presence of *Hustler* publisher Larry Flynt, Jr., or daredevil Evel Knievel, both of whom bid on the boat), Jimmy Carter nearly lost a valuable ally in Congress over a prospective bidder.[19] On April 26, 1977, a frustrated Representative John W. Jenrette, Jr. (D–SC) wrote White House Congressional Liaison Frank Moore. The letter referred to a personal friend of Jenrette's interested in bidding on the *Sequoia* who was discouraged that tours were restricted. The logic given for this policy was to prevent nonserious bidders from cadging free tours of the boat. Jenrette assured Moore that he could vouch to the Department of Defense that the client was a serious bidder prepared to offer over $1 million for the boat.[20]

Page two of the letter reveals Jenrette's underlying and more pressing concern. The incident had made him look weak. When Jenrette told his constituent that a tour would not be possible, the client then contacted Senator Strom Thurmond (R–SC) and a tour was arranged. Besmirched, Jenrette reminded Moore that he had been an early supporter of Jimmy Carter and his administration and he requested an investigation of the double-talk and the snub. For a president who campaigned on and pledged to restore communication in government and trust in its leaders, these accusations were particularly threatening. This was especially true given that Jenrette and Thurmond's party affiliations made partisan favors an unlikely alternate explanation. Jenrette was one of the "pioneers" amongst Southern Democrats, who became more moderate as a reaction to changing politics, demographics, and civil rights. He stood in stark contrast to the conservative icon of Thurmond.[21] Carter's goal would be achieved but at the cost of some ruffled feathers. Carter placed policy above politics even if it burned bridges. Jenrette felt snubbed, but Carter's transparency and austerity did not stop at party lines; however, even Carter admitted his attempt to rise above politics blew up in his face. In an effort to appear as a president who would not get sucked into backdoor politics, Carter missed a chance for cooperation.

Having seen the letter, Carter's Special Assistant for Administration Herb Upton believed firmly that Jenrette clearly "talked with the wrong people and got the wrong info"; however, he concluded that the issue needed further investigation and directed that a reply letter be sent. After discussion, White House Military Office Director W.L. "Bill" Gully sent the official reply to the congressman. Gulley apologized for the confusion, contending that some paperwork mishaps had caused the response delay and the tour mix-up. The director assured Jenrette that the White House neither intended to mislead or embarrass him nor prevent his constituent from touring the boat.[22] In a situation where perception mattered more than facts, it was politically better to eat some crow at the White House and apologize for the inconvenience than to give the story legs. Deflecting any blame to Jenrette would risk creating an imbroglio that would distract from Carter's message of selling a presidential luxury in the name of simplicity and economy.[23]

Sequoia Follies—Growing Pains in the Common-Man Campaign

Pushing headstrong into symbolic gestures with major political implications, Carter learned the hard way that the inside politics he campaigned against were impossible to avoid. The Jenrette fiasco was not be the only gaffe on his path to undo the imperial stigma of his office. The main impediment to a smooth sale involved political infighting amongst the Washington bureaucracy. On May 24, 1977,

3. Trimming the Trappings of Office

Secretary of Defense Harold Brown sent the president a handwritten note informing him that the sale of the *Sequoia* had been carried out. Thomas Aquinas Malloy of Leisurecraft, Inc., submitted the winning bid. However, the bid remained in abeyance pending "an emergency meeting of representatives from the Department of the Interior, Defense and Justice to determine whether the sale is legal." Reporting for *The Washington Post*, Judith Martin quoted Under Secretary of the Interior James A. Joseph's correspondence with the secretary of the navy, who made the "strong recommendation that [he] proceed no further with the sale until determining whether the yacht qualifies as an historic monument. It's clear that the Sequoia is likely to meet the criteria for the National Register."[24] Though Thomas Malloy secured the winning bid, it turned out that Carter had not placated all of the necessary government agencies.

Robert M. Utley, Deputy Executive Director of the Advisor Council on Historic Preservation, sent a letter dated April 21, 1977, to Francis B. Roche, Director, Real Property and Natural Resources, Office of the Assistant Secretary of Defense, regarding the lack of consultation regarding the sale of the *Sequoia*. Utley contended that the boat's "historical value" qualified it for the National Register of Historic Places. He figured that, legally, the *Sequoia* was subject to the council for evaluation and the Department of the Navy could not sell the boat unless the council so permitted.

On May 20, 1977, James A. Joseph, secretary for the Department of the Interior's Office of the Solicitor, sent a letter to Secretary of the Navy W. Graham Claytor, Jr., regarding the National Historic Preservation Act of 1966 and how he saw it applying to the *Sequoia*. He suggested the boat be submitted for "determination of eligibility for the National Register." Continuing her coverage of the sale and the larger "due process" scandal, Judith Martin noted, "[I]f the yacht is sold to Malloy on Monday without its historic significance being sought, the Navy Department could be open to a lawsuit from the Department of Justice or anyone else charging that due process was not followed in the sale." Continuing Utley's crusade, Joseph reminded the top sailor that the *Sequoia* had a long and distinguished history and that the Advisory Council of Historic Preservation had jurisdiction to determine its fate.

Jimmy Carter and the Restoration of Presidential Dignity

Martin reduced the scuffle to the Navy's duty to sell the boat as per the president's request versus the Department of the Interior's prerogative to designate the boat as a historic monument. She concluded the latter agency would not prevent the sale to Malloy (whose intention was to use the boat as a "historical tourist attraction") but did resent the lack of consultation. In a moment of candor, Advisory Council member Leon Scherther expressed the real concern: "I know what happens to these yachts. They end up as gambling casinos in the Bahamas, or floating whorehouses. This could be a very interesting floating museum, but the maritime preservationists can't afford to compete with the multi-millionaires." Nixon had tried to preclude past presidential yachts from being sold for "gambling casinos" or other "notorious use." However, the boats did not sell until that stipulation was removed. Scherther's fears were heightened by the presence of Jack Gallagher, vice president of Larry Flynt Publications (the company behind *Hustler* magazine), as a bidder. However, Flynt himself said, "[P]eople think of us as being in a seedy room, taking dirty pictures. But we're just as concerned about our corporate image as any other corporation." Flynt claimed he intended to donate the vessel to the Ohio Historical Society.[25]

In reaction to these concerns, Deputy Counsel to the President Margaret McKenna cited the statute governing the sale of real property. The rules distinguish between items of historical significance from those merely of historical interest. She contended that the *Sequoia* fell into the latter category and, hence, the president's prerogative prevailed, and the sale should proceed unimpeded. Any further questions could be resolved by the secretary of the interior. Deputy Administrator of the Panama Canal Joseph Cornelison countered that the original statute applied only to property already included on the National Register of Historic Places. However, the executive order expanded the statute, allowing agencies to bring to the attention of the secretary of the interior any property within their jurisdiction that they deemed qualified for inclusion in the National Register. If the property is determined to belong on the National Register or is in question of belonging, then the agency is required to request judgment from the secretary of the interior, whose judgment in the matter is final. Only if the secretary approves the property for inclusion in the register is there

3. Trimming the Trappings of Office

any further action to be taken by the agency. If the property does not qualify, however, then the agency need not make any further responsibility to referral to the secretary of the interior. The twofold test for inclusion in the National Register is based first whether it is "associated with events that have made significant contributions to the broad patterns of our history [or] associated with the lives of persons significant in our past." The caveat is that properties achieving significance in the past fifty years are ineligible for consideration for the National Register unless they are of "exceptional importance." Cornelison concluded that though the boat met the first two categories, its significance materialized only in recent times and this fell under the caveat.[26]

On May 23, 1977, White House Counsel to the President Robert J. Lipshutz reduced the council's complaint to a political slight, adding that all the bad press over due process had shadowed the larger importance of the sale, such as the symbolism and the money saved. Lipshutz and McKenna sent a memorandum to Press Secretary Jody Powell listing the official time of sale and confirming that the Historical Preservation Advisory Council, after consulting with the Department of the Interior and the Department of the Navy, suggested conditions of sale, to which the purchaser agreed.[27] Thus the Council had been consulted, placated, and satisfied while the Navy successfully covered itself legally. Though the Council seemed placated, in a future memorandum to his fellow council members, Robert R. Garvey, Jr., Executive Director of the Advisory Council on Historic Preservation, elaborated on what he considered a snub by the White House. John G. Kester stated that Garvey's memorandum was "not entirely accurate, and does not appear very supportive of the President." The bottom line of the memorandum reiterated that the Council was not consulted before the boat was retired and sold. Garvey felt its requests to be consulted should have been heeded sooner.

The sale was finalized and the boat sold. A major White House perquisite was no more, but the president struggled to get the credit. The process story clouded Carter's austerity message. Press coverage gravitated to the story of how the boat came to be sold and the administration's follies in doing so, more than the underlying message of why Carter chose to sell the boat in the first place. Judith Martin and the other White House reporters framed their coverage as an evaluation of Carter's Beltway savvy at the expense of his image as an austere and conciliatory president. Carter divorced the boat from the presidency but failed to use the sale as an opportunity to reassure the public. Rather than a new transparency in Washington, the American people read about politics as usual. Bureaucracy and pride muddled Carter's efforts to de-imperialize the presidency by removing a trapping of office.

Sequoia's *Legacy*

The true test of Carter's impact on the legacy of presidential yachts was not fully realized until a future president tried to bring back the perk. No sooner than Carter left office in 1981 did his successor Ronald Reagan face the decision to follow Carter's lead or reacquire a presidential yacht. As Reagan pursued his initial budget, Carter's legacy frustrated his successor's economic policy plans. This was made clear on June 17, 1981, when Representative Henry González (D–TX) took to the House floor to critique President Reagan. He chastised the new president's hypocrisy of "asking all Americans, and especially the poor, to make sacrifices" while he himself was "looking for a yacht." González juxtaposed the president's economic stability plan that the congressman felt sought "to take away the very bootstraps by which [the President] exhorts the poor to raise themselves" with the president's renewed interest in a yacht after it had been recently docked on the Potomac River. The congressman criticized the president for even considering reacquisition of the *Sequoia*—or any boat—on the grounds of its cost. He pointed out that even if Reagan took back the *Sequoia*, the upkeep would still be expensive. González ended by sarcastically berating Reagan, noting that while he did not "begrudge" presidential perks, he wondered if perhaps the president could give some of the resultant jobs surrounding the use of a presidential yacht to those who had lost their jobs because of the rest of Reagan's decisions.[28]

González' speech came just as the White House reached a similar conclusion, indefinitely postponing efforts to restore the presidential perquisite of a presidential yacht. The buzz in the White House and in Congress stemmed from the announcement of the *Sequoia*'s new

3. Trimming the Trappings of Office

owner, the Presidential Yacht Trust. The tax-exempt organization reacquired the boat and planned to restore it to its former glory and offer it (at no cost to the taxpayers) to the president for his use, if he so desired. Trust member Richard W. Arendsee noted, "The American people want a symbol of elegance in their country. We're the richest country in the world. This boat is not a gift to Reagan, it's a gift to the history of our country. We've only got 200 years of history—so why dump 50 of them?" In short, the trust's *a priori* motivation sought to undo the fundamental basis and ultimate purpose of Carter's initial action. Arendsee essentially sought to restore one of the trappings of presidential office. Before the decision, White House Military Office Director Edward Hickey had been investigating potential boats amongst the "ships in mothballs" at the Customs Bureau previously seized in drug-smuggling raids. White House Press Secretary Larry Speakes noted there was displeasure amongst some people at the White House over President Reagan's inclination to recommission a presidential yacht.[29]

However, as the Reagan years ended and the next decade brought the Clinton years, it became clear that Carter's noble effort to minimize superfluous luxury had brought unintended consequences.[30] On April 17, 1998, *Washington Post* reporter Ken Ringle criticized the boat's initial sale as "one of the least enlightened moments of the Jimmy Carter presidency." Ringle's argument juxtaposed Carter's motivation—"purportedly for economic reasons"—with the history of presidents since Carter vacationing to places like Kennebunkport, Martha's Vineyard, and St. Thomas. Ringle concluded that they still ended up on the water but flew there via Air Force One, which costs $26,000 an hour to operate. Even still, for all that Carter sold off or got rid of, even he kept the crown jewel of presidential getaways, Camp David. Carter frequently used the Marine base formerly known as Shangri-La as an escape for himself and as a place to entertain dignitaries and other notable guests. This is different from times when the president of the United States uses retreats for work. Camp David falls in both categories and Carter clearly saw this. Any doubt in his mind surely vanished after the eponymously named accords were signed there in 1979 between Israeli Prime Minister Menachem Begin and Egyptian President Anwar Sadat.

Ironically, Carter's boat sale, designed to cut costs and reduce what he saw as ostentatious luxury, proved to have the opposite effect twenty years later. Carter tried to save the taxpayers money and remove the trappings of office. Ringle contended that without a presidential yacht, presidents since Carter have turned to other outlets for their pleasure. These alternatives have proven to be equally lavish in nature but often come at a much greater cost to the taxpayers.[31] Ringle's argument is based on a false premise. Neither Carter nor Ringle could prove a president would have opted for a boat cruise in lieu of a destination vacation. His criticism of Camp David also fails under the utility the location provides. Neither the Camp David Accords nor the "Crisis of Confidence" speech would have happened had Carter not had Camp David. Presidents before and after Carter used that space as a different work setting as well as a place to relax. Carter proved Camp David was more than bungalows and a golf course.

Limousines

Beyond measures that tamed what Carter saw as frivolous perquisites of his office, the president also moved to trim the fat off his staff's perks. During the transition period, Stu Eizenstat recommended to the president-elect that chauffeur use be eliminated except for a motor pool to transport staff members to Capitol Hill during the day. "I think the President-elect's elimination of this perquisite would stand as a significant symbol of his commitment to a lean staff and a cost-conscious operation."[32] Eizenstat sought to present Carter with a wide array of options—anything that could trim the budget and the appearance of frivolity.

Carter embraced Eizenstat's recommendations. Once in office, Carter moved quickly on initiatives to make the government more "competent and compassionate." These changes would begin at the White House. Amongst the initiatives he cited were the elimination of "some expensive and unnecessary luxuries, such as door-to-door limousine service for many top officials, including all members of the White House staff." In a "Report to the American People," Carter added,

3. Trimming the Trappings of Office

> Government officials can't be sensitive to your problems if we are living like royalty here in Washington. While I am deeply grateful for the good wishes that lie behind them, I would like to ask that people not send gifts to me or to my family or to anyone else who serves in my administration.

Intent not to get caught up in the pomp and formality of the office, and in an effort to have his common-man image be reflected in his staff, on his second day as president Jimmy Carter began to investigate coordination of chauffeured car use at the White House. Carter later reflected,

> I wanted to eliminate some of the perquisites of Washington officials, beginning with my own immediate political family. Despite some subtle but persistent objections, I issued the appropriate orders. There were a lot of news stories when senior White House staff members began to arrive for work in their own automobiles, without chauffeurs—the great publicity confirmed to me that the change was long overdue. One of the White House drivers said that, before we arrived, he had ferried the pets of staff members to veterinarians as part of his driving duties! This man, a retired Army sergeant, had been offended by the extravagance of staff "perks." He felt much closer and at ease with my White House staff—the kind of change I wanted.

Carter initially tried to place the same restrictions on his own limousine usage. However, while the president always travels on land via armored car, getting those cars to those locations was (and remains) a ballet of ground and air transportation. Carter failed to realize the major logistical project transporting the president of the United States entailed. Carter's intention was to preempt coordination concerns and maximize efficiency while minimizing cost. However, over time he came to realize that some of the "special arrangements" were necessity more than frivolity.[33]

Complimenting Carter's internal inquiries, on January 31, 1977, Senator William Proxmire (D–WI) sent a letter to Hamilton Jordan identifying himself as Chairman of the Subcommittee on Priorities and Economy in Government of the Joint Economic Committee and expressing his long-standing interest in the distribution and use of official cars by government officials. His letter served to remind the White House that the law, Title 31, Section 638a, stipulated that officials' cars could only be used for government business and are expressly forbidden from taking people to and from their homes. As such, he sent a list of inquiries regarding the use of official cars in the White House: who had them and how much they cost.[34]

Jimmy Carter and the Restoration of Presidential Dignity

On February 10, 1977, Hugh Carter responded to Proxmire's letter and questions pertaining to who amongst the White House staff had assigned cars and, in some cases, drivers. When drivers were used, they earned $10,500 a year. There was no overtime pay since they were military drivers. The last question regarded the operating costs for vehicles. Hugh Carter said that each car was leased for $600 per year, including incidental maintenance (such as oil and antifreeze). The motor pool paid for gas, which in 1976 (under Ford) ran to $45,600. Hugh Carter expected that number to be lower in 1977.[35]

That same day, Secret Service Director H.S. Knight followed up on Carter's inquiry with a history of the program. Knight noted that armored car service began in the wake of President Kennedy's assassination and the review of Secret Service procedures made by the Warren Commission. Knight laid out the entire fleet of armored cars and their assignments, including the prospects for 1977 regarding acquisition and retirement of armored vehicles and use by visiting foreign dignitaries in 1976. Knight concluded by noting, "The problem of organized terrorism and the use of explosives and automatic weapons in terrorist acts continues unabated. The use of armored cars by the Secret Service is, therefore, considered a necessity."[36] Carter heeded the director's assessment of necessity, but he still saw fat. In response, Jimmy Carter instructed Treasury Secretary Mike Blumenthal to "minimize purchase of armored limousines, buying only those for which we are firmly & irrevocably committed."[37] Thus Carter tried to minimize expenditures and luxury while recognizing that security and the dignity of office ought not to be compromised.

To help compensate for the smaller fleet and to maximize the utility of the remaining limousines, Carter relished opportunities to invite guests into his limousine. Not only would this maximize time in a president's busy schedule and give appointments some valuable face time with minimal interruptions, but it also allowed Carter to, in effect, carpool. This saved money and was environmentally friendly. For example, Jimmy Carter traveled to the October 21, 1977, Jefferson-Jackson Day Dinner with Jim Maloney of the Polk County Courthouse in Des Moines, Iowa. Both men planned to attend the event anyway and traveling together saved money while giving the two politicians time to meet.[38] Surely Jim Maloney would also attest it is a humbling expe-

3. Trimming the Trappings of Office

rience to travel in the United States presidential state car. More than the average Lincoln Continental, if the vehicle did not awe the guest passenger, their company would.

Helicopters

Following a theme of economic and environmental conservation in the transportation of the president and his staff, Carter also moved to eliminate five of the thirteen helicopters in the White House fleet, cutting back helicopter usage 38 percent for an annual savings of $2 million. The remaining aircrafts were the larger helicopters in the fleet. Helicopter operations cost over $4.3 million, though the reductions would be offset in part by reassigning some equipment and crew elsewhere. Nonetheless, presidential usage of the aircrafts required more strenuous maintenance regimens, which would mean a net savings when the helicopters were reassigned.

The warrant for the shift was twofold. First, the president has little use for the smaller helicopters. Also, should the president need a smaller helicopter, there were ones available from the Department of Defense. The only catch was that they were not configured for the president (having webbed seating, for example, instead of customized seats). The number of pilots assigned to the White House, two, would not change. "The reduction in the helicopter fleet follows similar actions by the President in reducing the number of vehicles, exclusive of Secret Service cars, from 56 to 31, and the sale of the yacht *Sequoia* for $286,000, at a savings to the taxpayer of $800,000 yearly in operating, maintenance and personnel costs."[39] Overall the president's motivation was saving taxpayer money by cutbacks in frivolous and unnecessary amenities.

The headlines of austerity aside, Carter soon realized that some luxury stemmed from necessity. While the average person does not have a fleet of helicopters at their disposal, Carter learned that helicopter usage remained a practical necessity of office.

> I soon learned that there were other times when presidential privileges were a necessity; some special arrangements simply proved more practical than my old way of doing things. I understood this clearly on my first trip home to Plains

Jimmy Carter and the Restoration of Presidential Dignity

three weeks after the inauguration. I had instructed the Secret Service that, to save money, we would go to Plains by motorcade instead of by helicopter. But I discovered that because of the tremendous amount of effort that had to go into traffic control for road intersections, it was much less expensive to go by helicopter. A good portion of the Georgia State Patrol had been marshaled to block every country crossroad for more than sixty miles! It was obvious that I was not simply one of the people anymore.[40]

Carter accepted that pragmatically—and, in the big picture, economically—helicopters made more sense than a lengthy motorcade on a cordoned-off highway. At a minimum, he realized that some government expenditures can appear frivolous to some but are actually necessary and requisite when compared with the alternative. Though Carter's helicopter program—like his other simpler lifestyle initiatives—did not manifest as clear successes, his efforts reaped their own reward. Carter set out to do something for the right reasons and he followed through as promised. He made a campaign promise and then turned intent into transparent action. Though the president felt he had won a personal victory by reducing the fleet size, such actions did not create groundswells of public praise.

Unlike his predecessor Richard Nixon, who had the White House guard don regal uniforms, Jimmy Carter tried at every turn to minimize the trappings and reverse the monarchical ambience of the White House. Where past presidents had talked a lot but done little, Carter followed through on a platform of austerity and simplicity. While in office, Carter scorned some of the perquisites and eliminated others that were uniquely and exclusively available to the president because of his prestigious position.

Though limousines, helicopters, and yachts are not monumental initiatives in the traditional sense that new presidents often pursue in their first hundred days, Carter's choice of battles operated at a symbolic level as well as at a pragmatic one. Following Nixon, who placed the White House guards in regal uniforms, and Ford, who pardoned Nixon, Carter's image as the common-man president was as much about eliminating government perquisites as it was about appearing to be a president of transparent motives and one who is beyond reproach.

Tallying up the political victories and losses may not bear a solely positive outcome for Carter's austerity campaign; however, the sym-

3. Trimming the Trappings of Office

bolism and the initial gesture remains a bold move to counter the previously prevailing negative image of the president. True to the common-man style and in line with his frustration with luxury he deemed ostentatious as displayed by his predecessors, Carter enacted compact solutions to change the narrative and the optics. Indeed, in light of the tarnished presidential image, Carter's battles counted more than his victories. Public faith and trust would take time to reestablish. Change would not happen overnight, but Carter did not stop trying.

In December 1977, Senator Gary Hart (D–CO) proclaimed that Carter "had demythologized the imperial Presidency." However, Hart worried that Carter had also "sacrificed some of the psychological weight and power that the Presidency had accumulated since Roosevelt's time." Public Broadcasting Service reporter Robert MacNeil, speaking about Hart's characterization, asked Carter if by "making [his] the Presidency of the common man and ridding [himself] of some of the imperial trappings [he] may have thrown away some of the clout?" Carter responded,

> Many people think so. The pomp and ceremony of the office does not appeal to me, and I don't believe it's a necessary part of the Presidency in a democratic nation like our own. I'm no better than anyone else. And the people that I admire most who have lived in this house have taken the same attitude. Jefferson, Jackson, Lincoln, Truman have minimized the pomp and ceremony and the pride, personal pride, that accrues sometimes to Presidents. I don't think we need to put on the trappings of a monarchy in a nation like our own. I feel uncomfortable with it. But I doubt if I feel quite as uncomfortable as the average citizen.

Long-term unintended consequences aside, Jimmy Carter's initial motivation and agenda should not be lost.[41] Campaigning against Washington, against Watergate and imperial presidencies, Carter's symbolic actions were an important corrective for a nation that had endure a tarnished presidency.

Jimmy Carter demonstrated his honesty and accountability by following through on campaign promises. In general, Carter's actions sought to restore the faith of the American people in the legitimacy and purpose of the Presidency. In a decade that saw secret wars in Cambodia and Laos (as part of the larger war in Vietnam), as well as the first sitting president to resign from office, Jimmy Carter proved to be a president that Americans could trust once again. His gestures were po-

Jimmy Carter and the Restoration of Presidential Dignity

litical but also symbolic. Carter's austerity measures and anti-trappings initiatives sent the message that the president was no longer trying to be king or turn the White House into a palace, but instead was focused on being the leader of the nation and the head of one of the three co-equal branches of American government.

4

Water Project Cancellations
*Public Works Appropriations
and Parochial Interests*

In the middle of a Senate floor debate about the Public Works Appropriations for 1978, Senator J. Bennett Johnston (D–LA) took to the floor to refute his colleague, Senator Thomas McIntyre (D–NH)—and by extension President Jimmy Carter—as well as to defend the Atchafalaya channelization project in Louisiana. In this moment, Senator Johnston broke party ranks. He stood in opposition to his fellow Democrat from New Hampshire and the leader of his party, the president. For Johnston and many others in Congress, the issue of water projects cut across party lines. In this case, geography determined the battle lines. Senators (and members of Congress) from states without water were battling against those from states where water abundantly flowed. However, even that distinction is naïve. The real distinction laid between those in Congress whose states benefited from these pork-barrel water projects versus those who did not.

When Johnston took the floor on June 30, 1977, his argument focused on the merits of the Atchafalaya water project. He explained how the project benefited the surrounding region economically; making his case for continued funding. However, Johnston admitted something that few other senators and members of Congress had the frankness to say outright. Though an absolute reality and business as usual in politics, the correlation between those in Congress fighting to save funding specifically for their pet projects comes across as narrow and self-serving. However, rather than deny the connection or claim it was merely a coincidence that the senator from Louisiana rose to defend a project in Louisiana, Johnston owned it: "Do I have a parochial interest in this? You bet I do."

What Johnston did not mention is that the project really only benefited two oil-rig-construction companies based in the Gulf of Mexico. *New York Times* reporter John B. Oakes criticized Johnston and others in Congress for abusing pork-barrel appropriations. For the Atchafalaya, Oakes reported the cost to the American taxpayer at $20 million. It would also destroy irreplaceable wetlands and disrupt important shrimp and shell fisheries. Oakes' argument did not fall on deaf ears. In addition to the national and international readership of *The New York Times*, two brave representatives pointed to Oakes' article (but only as they still assured their colleagues that their projects were the good ones that should be funded). Representatives Jim Tucker (D–AR) and Romano L. Mazzoli (D–KY) printed Oakes' article into the *Congressional Record* for the members to see, but in the same breath they defended the Cache Valley water project and the Richard Russell Dam, each in their own home state.[1]

The environmental impact the Atchafalaya caused—and the impact of many other projects—formed Carter's argument for defunding almost two dozen projects. Carter knew he would be ruffling some feathers at the other end of Pennsylvania Avenue, but he entered the fray convinced that logic and good government would prevail. While the White House made a persuasive case on environmental and fiscal grounds, the president did not adequately account for the vested interest of legislators such as Johnston. Carter threatened one of the main avenues for constituent services—Carter threatened congressional pork. Carter campaigned on general promises of respect and cooperation with Congress, as well as specific promises to review water projects and eliminate bloat from the federal budget. In fact, Carter found himself in a dogfight against Senator Johnston and others like him in the Senate and House not willing to let logic and fiscal prudency jeopardize their ability to bring federal dollars back to their home districts. Pork projects are a prime medium for constituent service that helps reelection campaigns, allowing them to continue their tenure in office.[2]

4. Water Project Cancellations

Nineteen Projects

One month into Carter's term in office, the new president moved on efforts to reel in spending he deemed frivolous. He called for cutting an array of projects from the federal budget. On February 14, 1977, Carter received a letter signed by dozens of senators and members of Congress expressing their support of Carter's efforts to review environmentally and economically questionable projects. The idea of trimming spending and saving tax dollars appealed to these legislators from both sides of the aisle.[3]

Four days after receiving the declaration of congressional support, the White House framed Carter's response. Carter and his staff in the West Wing wanted to be clear from the outset. The president's intention would be consultation and communication with Congress. Confrontation might be inevitable with a controversial proposal, but Carter tried to soften the backlash with interbranch diplomacy. The letter, drafted by Stu Eizenstat, ended, "I look forward to working closely with Congress to develop a coherent water resource policy." The deliberate phrasing constituted more than just an olive branch from the new chief executive. Carter, Eizenstat, and the entire West Wing took steps to frame the letter as cordially as possible. Carter wanted to follow through clearly on his campaign promises. Cooperation would be nice, too, but Carter could not guarantee Congress would come to the table with their sleeves rolled up. The president promised comity and transparency in Washington. Carter's response took the form of a formal letter to Congress, inviting channels of dialogue along Pennsylvania Avenue.[4]

One week later, Carter officially announced his intentions. Per his campaign promise, he committed to reduce government spending. Acting under the authority of the Impoundment Control Act and with the consultations of Major General Ernest Graves, director of Civil Works for the Army Corps of Engineers, Carter outlined nineteen projects that he considered "unsupportable on economic, environmental, and/or safety grounds." The Senate published Carter's letter the next day and referred the issue to the Committee on Environment and Public Works. This would be the first time the nineteen projects slated for defunding would be formally read into the *Congressional Record*.

Jimmy Carter and the Restoration of Presidential Dignity

Though Carter thought his actions flowed from congressional support for budget reform, he had not explicitly floated the idea of water project cancellation past his legislative counterparts, especially his fellow Democrats. Carter employed a trustee approach to the problem: He hoped that doing what he felt was right would transcend parochial interests. Historian Charles O. Jones noted that Carter resented these water projects as the "worst examples" of pork-barrel legislation.[5] It is not clear how big Carter expected the battle ahead of him would be, but the letter proved to be just the opening salvo.

Carter knew what it would take to implement his proposal. Both for practice and optics, Carter stressed his desire to work "closely with Congress" to review the projects in question; favoring that only ones that are "economically and environmentally" sound receive funding approval. To paraphrase Jean Baptiste Colbert, Carter wanted to pluck as much bloated government spending from the budget as possible with the smallest possible amount of hissing from senators and members of Congress.[6] During the campaign, Carter promised to make better use of taxpayer money and to the trim the budget where possible. Carter drew a direct line to his action on water projects. For those projects, Carter recommended no FY 1978 funds be earmarked. Carter directed Secretary of the Interior Cecil Andrus and Secretary of the Army Clifford Alexander, Jr., to work with the Office of Management and Budget and the Council on Environmental Quality to evaluate the viability of the projects and whether funding should be reinstated. Carter estimated the potential savings at $5.1 billion.[7] His letter made his intentions clear. He highlighted what he believed to be superfluous spending and he intended to work with Congress to trim the federal budget and remove ineffective bureaucracy.

With Carter's position formally announced, commentary and concern percolated throughout Congress and the nation. Both were handled delicately, whether it was a call from KUED radio based in Salt Lake City or the Republican leadership. The Utah radio station—like many other media calls—concerned a local project. For KUED, it was the cancellation of the Central Utah Project at Bonneville. They wanted the White House to comment for a news piece they would be airing.[8] In many ways, the concerns of Congress were local concerns, too. Carter expected that he would have friends and foes in Congress. Some

4. Water Project Cancellations

would laud his efforts but others, regardless of party, would buck at the threat to a project in their district. Each project represented pork-barrel legislation, an opportunity for senators and representatives to bring home the bacon. Legislators live or die on their ability to bring money to their district and Carter had just threatened their revenue stream. Historians Burton I. Kaufman and Scott Kaufman wrote,

> Unfortunately for Carter, pork-barrel politics had been sacrosanct on Capitol Hll for many decades. Lawmakers also viewed the hit list as further evidence of the president's political indifference to Congress. Even Carter acknowledged that his new administration had sometimes "inadvertently" given Congress cause for complaint by not conferring with the congressional leadership.[9]

Carter tried to grease the skids. He tried to curry the favor of Congress. Some congressional feathers would be ruffled, but Carter would act as respectfully as possible. A calculated decision, Carter banked on the greater good to prevail over regional interests. His position would prove naïve but to what degree had yet to be determined.

Within days, the floors of Congress were filled with legislators making variations of the same NIMBY argument. NIMBY (Not in My Backyard) refers here to the passionate defense as to why the funding for a water project located in their home district (or in the case of senators, their home state) should continue. For example, Senator George McGovern (D–SD) rose on January 31, 1977, to talk about water policy. His concern focused on the threat of drought that plagued his state. He advocated for the Oahe Irrigation project. Comparably, in the House on February 22, Representative Bernice Sisk (D–CA) spoke about Carter's "attempt to stop construction of vitally needed water projects in the west." Sisk decried Carter's plan as "deplorable." Sisk had helped approve two of the nineteen projects—the Auburn Dam (in California) and Central Arizona Project. Sisk argued that those two projects were integral to the water needs of the region. Sisk concluded by arguing the damn closings were politically motivated: "What does concern me somewhat in this current development is that the bulk of the projects targeted for cutbacks are in States which did not support the current administration. I would hope that we can begin healing the wounds, not deepen them." I have not found any substantiation to this claim. While Sisk's home state of California did pledge their electoral votes to President Gerald Ford in the 1976 election, half the states containing water projects slated for defunding pledged their 1976 electoral votes to Carter. Two days later, after Sisk's comment, freshman Representative Bob Stump (D–AZ) accused Carter of welshing on his promise of transparency. Stump accused Carter of proceeding without adequately consulting the state elected officials, including the Arizona governor. He suggested that this snub contradicts Carter's pledge to "conduct the affairs of state openly." Stump opposed Carter's proposal to cancel the water project in his district, the Central Arizona project. He argued the cancellation would have a detrimental economic impact on the region. In so many words, Stump criticized the president for attempting to cancel his pork project.[10]

Nobody in Congress made their regionally and pork-based argument more persuasively than Senator George McGovern (D–SD). On March 1, he took the floor to speak about the Oahe Irrigation Unit. McGovern worried that Carter's Water Project Review Panel might act too hastily and not give the attention needed in evaluating the viability of water projects. In practice, McGovern's real concern centered on Carter's intention to scrap the Oahe project in McGovern's home state of South Dakota. McGovern, in large part due to his personal objection to the panel's recommendation about the Oahe project, argued that Carter did not have the ultimate authority to reject any water projects. At best, the president could advise. He encouraged the Congress as a body to recognize that "the opinions that will ultimately be advanced by [Carter's Water Projects Review Panel] must, under our system, be advisory. The final responsibility for the evaluation and funding of these projects rests with the Congress." Senator Barry Goldwater (R–AZ) later made a similar argument (in this case in the context of the Central Arizona project in his home state), accusing Carter of being either "totally uninformed on the nature of the project or that he has no regard for the truth." Goldwater, like McGovern and others, felt Carter was wrong about water projects in general but the argument quickly narrowed to a NIMBY concern about their local project.[11]

On March 7, Representative Teno Roncalio (D–WY) took to the floor to express his "confidence" in President Carter. He characterized Carter's first hundred days as an "auspicious beginning" as important as Franklin Delano Roosevelt's. Roncalio disagreed that Carter's water projects cancellation would cause a "confrontation" with Congress. He

4. Water Project Cancellations

saw the reviews as useful. Roncalio included a recent *Denver Post* article by Leonard Larsen. Larsen's article argued that while some water projects were pork, the Colorado projects were not. Those projects were vital. Cutting pork is noble but care must be taken to distinguish between pork and vital projects. Ultimately, Larsen launched a scathing attack against the president. "The Carter administration action on water projects appears to have been not only dumb but bordering on dishonest."[12] Roncalio, echoing Larsen, went on at length to argue that pork was bad, but his pet project was not pork. This variant of having his cake while eating it too was not the unmitigated support for which the White House had hoped.

Carter's staff found itself writing many senators, members of Congress, and governors who were worried about their projects. For example, Stu Eizenstat drafted a letter for Carter responding to Senators Edward Muskie (D–ME) and William Hathaway (D–ME) at the request of Frank Moore. The response addressed their concerns of Carter's decision to delete FY 1978 funding for Dickey-Lincoln School Lakes Project in Maine. Muskie and Hathaway cited recommendations of the Council on Environmental Quality, the Office of Management and Budget, and the Army Corps of Engineers. They argued the water project would produce energy—reducing New England's dependence of foreign oil. This was a good argument to make to Carter, though the administration's response pointed to other alternatives that would accomplish the same goal while not damaging natural resources in the process. Separately, Muskie went so far as to request personal notification before any decision was made.[13]

Muskie bluntly declared his grit and made clear he would play hardball to make sure his position was heard. Senate liaison Dan Tate sent a memo to White House Congressional Liaison Frank Moore about a conversation he had with Senator Russell B. Long (D–LA). The message was simple: Carter needed to play ball with Congress. If the president pushed forward to defund projects in key members' districts, then the president would find himself in for an uphill battle. Long threatened to put key legislation "in the deep freeze" until Carter's projects review finished. The delay would severely waylay the president's agenda. In Tate's words, "the President might not get what he wants unless certain members of Congress get what they want."

Long's pork project on the Atchafalaya River was on the list of nineteen to be chopped. Tate also relayed that Senator Edmund Muskie (D–ME) would hold up other legislation (he mentioned specifically the Third Concurrent Budget Resolution) until the fate of the Dickey-Lincoln water project (in Maine) was resolved. To make sure Moore did not miss the message Tate conveyed, he ended his memo by stating, "The threat was hardly veiled."[14]

Not everyone in Congress reacted negatively. Sometimes, the reaction displayed confidence in Carter's decision. Senator William Proxmire (D–WI) rose to support Carter's water projects plan. "I support President Carter's decision to follow through on his campaign promise to eliminate unnecessary water resource projects." Proxmire read into the record a position paper Carter had shared during the campaign. The president, trained as an engineer, was in a unique position to assess recommendations of the Army Corps of Engineers.

> The President's decision to eliminate funding for 19 particularly bad projects from his fiscal year 1978 budget is the right way to begin fulfilling his promises to redirect the Nation's water resource policies. This Presidential opposition to the dear old pork barrel is the hardest kind of promise to keep.[15]

Not unsurprising, the support came from a Democrat from a water-rich state. He had no pork-barrel water project of his own to defend. Beyond party bias, a stronger determinant of allegiance on this issue was regional bias. Indeed, senators and representatives defended their local pork-barrel projects but support for Carter often came from the water-rich Eastern states, while those in the South and West were more critical of his efforts. Senator Proxmire hailed from a state with adequate water resources and had no water project under threat of defunding.

In a memo to the secretary of defense, the secretary of the interior, the director of the Office of Management and Budget, and the secretary of the army, Stu Eizenstat noted that the White House "had already run into a political hornet's nest" and their group would "stir up more action on the Hill."[16] Carter needed support in Congress, especially from his own party. When a prominent member, such as Muskie, threatened political hay if the president did not capitulate, Carter's charm offensive was clearly falling short of expectations. Carter truly had disrupted the hornet's nest and he was getting stung.

4. Water Project Cancellations

In addition to correspondence from Congress, the president received comparable communications from state governments too. For example, North Dakota Lieutenant Governor Wayne Sanstead invited the president to visit his state and address the senate over which he presided. The upper chamber of the North Dakota legislature had recently passed Senate Resolution 10, which specifically invited President Carter to come and speak. Carter declined the invitation but spoke in his letter specifically to the Garrison Diversion water project located in North Dakota. Carter stressed that all projects receive a rigorous review. Carter could not visit each project himself, but he wrote to assure the lieutenant governor—and the state senate over which he presided—that the process would be fair and balanced, and it would only target projects worthy of review.[17]

The White House also received a flood of correspondence from concerned citizens, especially residents in the vicinity of various projects. For example, B. Kevin Molloy of McMinnville, Tennessee, wrote Media Liaison Jim Purks to commend the president on his decision to cease production on the various water projects. Molloy added that another project worthy of consideration was the Duck River Dam in middle Tennessee. Molloy proceeded to give his assessment as to why the Duck River Dam was worthy of Carter's scrutiny. Purks thanked the citizen for his civic effort and reminded him that even if Carter did not add that dam to the portfolio for consideration for fiscal year 1978, that did not mean it might not be considered in fiscal year 1979. Similarly, Gerald L. Pond of Clear Point, Alabama, a newspaper reporter and disabled Vietnam War veteran, wrote about the Tennessee–Tombigbee Waterway project. Pond wanted to know what the president's final decision would be. When Media Liaison Jim Purks wrote back a week later, Carter had yet to make his final decision.[18]

I wrote to Kevin Molloy personally in 2017 to follow up on his correspondence with President Carter forty years earlier. Molloy, with the benefit of the perspective of time, appreciated the job Carter did as president.

> I would first like to begin by saying that I do not feel that President Carter receives the credit he deserves for being a very intelligent and caring President. His approach to the presidency was one of honesty, integrity, intelligence and caring about the people of the Unites States and the world as a whole. He also

cared deeply about the environment, peace and restoring trust in America and its government.

He believed Carter had good intentions for his water projects, but it took longer to implement than he desired. Carter forced the culture shift away from large dam projects, but it was not be clear until after he left office. Molloy admired Carter's communication and transparency as president. Molloy felt Carter followed through on his campaign promise, but he became embroiled in a fight with Congress in the process.

> [C]onsistent with his campaign promises, his review of water projects was just one step he took to reevaluate government and restore cooperation with Congress. However, Congress did not agree with his approach and this became an early battle with Congress and may have ultimately impacted his ability to work with Congress. However, by taking a strong stand on projects that he felt were inappropriate for environmental, fiscal, safety or other practical purposes, he showed his integrity and intelligent approach to the Presidency. He took great strides to improve government for the people and maintain an honest, smart and transparent presidency.

In 2017, as in 1977, Molloy respected Carter even as he provided feedback. It takes initiative and a sense of civic duty to write a president.[19]

Establishing a Dialogue

In an effort to continue Carter's commitment to respect for Congress, the president held a meeting at the White House on Thursday, March 10, 1977. Twenty-eight senators and twenty-eight members of Congress—fifty-six legislators in all—came to the Executive Office Building across the street from the White House to discuss the nineteen water projects affecting their districts. Carter sent Frank Moore and Stu Eizenstat to meet with this large group to assuage the concerns of the affected members of Congress and earn their support for his program. "The members of my Cabinet and I will work closely with you to see that our water resources goals are achieved through sound expenditures of public funds which benefit the most people at the least environmental and safety risk."[20] To the White House, the meeting with Congress had been a success. The groundwork had been laid and the issue at hand discussed. Members of Congress met the principles

4. Water Project Cancellations

for the administration including Secretaries Andrus, Alexander, and Council on Environmental Quality Chairman Charles Warren. Each described their roles in the process. Studies would be made of all water projects Carter designated for defunding. "I will insist that this review be open and on the merits. The recommendations I will make on April 15 will be based on sound information and on public hearings. I intend to take fully into account employment, power, and economic considerations."[21] The administration beat home the point that no unilateral action would be taken. For example, Office of Management and Budget Director Bert Lance made a point of emphasis that the projects scheduled for cancellation would only be approved through investigation and with the opportunity for input and feedback from members of Congress.[22]

Four days later, after giving Congress the weekend to process the White House meeting, Legislative Assistant Ann Dye shared the results of their research on how Congress is likely to vote on the water projects. She theorized that without the support of Western members (minus Representative Phillip Burton [D–CA], who was on board), there were only 141 votes for Carter's plan. Burton, the head of the Democratic caucus who had just a few months earlier lost a narrow vote for House Majority Leader to Jim Wright (D–TX), and House Minority Leader John Rhodes (R–AZ) (who favored the Arizona project) were key votes to have on board. Any hope of Rhodes' support quickly faded three days later when Rhodes had harsh criticisms of Carter's plan inserted into the *Congressional Record*. This would not be a simple legislative victory.[23]

Dye's analysis sketched out various scenarios including the potential for veto override. If Congress sent Carter a bill he could not sign—if Congress refused to defund key water projects—could the president veto the bill with impunity? Not only would a veto override make the bill law, but it would weaken the president politically. The more detailed analysis looked at the House's reaction to previous public works bills and the volume of correspondence so far on the water project initiative.

> This study produces 168 Members. It takes 146 votes to sustain a veto. With regard to the Members listed, the following caveats should be noted: (1) state delegations tend to hang together on water project votes, particularly Califor-

81

nia, Texas and other western states: (2) western state Members are particularly "water-conscience" at this time; (3) how Members voted in 1976 <u>does not</u> determine how they will vote in 1977.

Twice during Ford's administration, the House overrode a veto on public works bills and on a third occasion the Congress passed a water projects bill by a wide margin. Political analyst Norman Ornstein described a weak president as Gulliver, dominated by congressional Lilliputians.[24] Dye saw the bigger picture. Carter wanted to win but it was more than just this program on the line. He could not afford to end up like Gulliver.

In light of Dye's findings, Environmental and Natural Resources Specialist for the Domestic Policy Staff Kathy Fletcher wrote to Stu Eizenstat the next day with strategies for framing the cancellation of water projects. Fletcher suggested that while pitching the fiscal conservatism would be beneficial, it would be prudent to also include emphasis on other issues to offset concerns. For example, Fletcher suggested coupling it with efforts to support family farmers, jobs creation, and conservation of water and soil.[25] The next day, Carter formally wrote to Congress, reaffirming his commitment to involve the members of Congress, especially those who had reservations about the larger initiative or specific projects on the cut list.

Carter acknowledged the members' concerns with his decision to review water projects. He made every effort to convey sincerity and to be genuinely receptive to their plights. Carter reiterated the broader theme of cooperation and transparency; the return of comity and respect to Washington politics.

> It is essential to involve the Congress in developing a coherent water resource policy, which we have not had in the past. Towards this end I will arrange a meeting with Congressional leaders from all relevant committees to meet personally with me in order to establish a dialogue and close cooperation on this issue.

Carter proceeded to present his stock logic behind his program: the idea that many of these water projects have proceeded unchecked and unaudited for years. In an effort to assuage the concerns of Congress, Carter pointed out that the nineteen projects were out of a total of 325 projects surveyed and the reasons for cancellation were often difficult to overlook. For example, one project "would be built in an

4. Water Project Cancellations

earthquake zone, potentially jeopardizing the lives of thousands of people." Another project "appeared to be in violation of an international treaty, and Canada has repeatedly asked the United States to suspend construction." Still, Carter did not want to proceed without consultation with Congress. Carter closed by reiterating his desire to work with the legislative branch of government. "In cooperation with Congress I want to insure that our future water resource policies meet the real needs of this nation. I look forward to working with you in that enterprise." Carter understood that members would have concerns with projects that affected their districts. He assured members that he did not reach his list of nineteen projects lightly but based on qualitative and quantitative evidence pointing to the targeted projects.[26]

By the end of that week, more information would be given to the press but it would be buried in the Friday news dump. Eizenstat told Carter he agreed with Lance's memo on Water Project Deferrals, but the press would not get the information until Friday at 3 p.m. (News that the White House wanted to minimize was often sent out Friday afternoon. The Saturday paper was the least read paper all week and the column space would be divided among however many stories the White House threw at them.[27]) The memo regarded action being taken on specific water projects and the delayed release allowed Congressional Liaison Frank Moore and his staff to reach out to the affected congressmen and senators. At issue was use of the Impoundment Control Act of 1974 to embargo funds earmarked for some water projects. Pending more thorough reviews, the administration sought to stall some questionable projects. Either because they did not accept the direct appeal from Moore and his staff or because they read the Saturday newspaper, many members of Congress did not see the merits of Carter's action. A story as big as this would not be lost in the trash. Whether it was Representative Dennis DeConcini (D–AZ) or Senator Barry Goldwater (R–AZ) defending the CAP (Central Arizona project) or Senators George McGovern (D–SD) and James Abourezk (D–SD) taking the floor for the Oahe Irrigation project, regional interests transcended party affiliations.[28]

As the debate over the projects moved forward, transparency and communication remained key features of White House strategy. Kathy

Jimmy Carter and the Restoration of Presidential Dignity

Fletcher and Domestic Policy staff member Kitty Schirmer suggested to Stu Eizenstat that Carter hold more hearings on more water projects. The more hearings held, specifically a decision to discuss more than just the ones most likely to be cut, would give Carter more leeway when he decided to cut some of the water projects. It made his final decision easier to defend. In practical numbers, thirty-five projects were originally brought under scrutiny, but Carter only wanted to have hearings for twenty-five. Schirmer and Fletcher suggested that all thirty-five should be afforded hearings. More hearings would make the president appear more transparent and make his decisions cut more methodical as a fraction of the projects brought to a hearing. In general, Carter needed to be receptive to all constituencies and all positions regarding each project.[29]

Despite Carter's efforts to open broad lines of communication, there were groups who felt their voices were not adequately consulted. Most often, these were defenders of various projects eager to explain to the president why their local project is not the bad pork like the others are. For example, Senator Carl D. Perkins (D–KY) spoke out about Carter's decisions about dams in his home state of Kentucky. Though the Paintsville Dam had been on Carter's initial list of dam projects to reevaluate, it was removed from the strike list. Two other Kentucky water projects (the Yatesville Dam and the Dayton Floodwall) were not. Perkins praised Carter for coming to what he believed to be the right decision about the Paintsville Dam. Perkins empathized with Carter's struggle to familiarize himself with so many water projects in such a short time. Perkin's praised the president for reaching a conclusion about the Paintsville Dam consistent with his own views and those of his Kentucky constituents. The implication was that Carter ought to reach a similar conclusion about the other two Kentucky projects under question.

On the flip side, while water project proponents lobbied for their pet projects to escape the chopping block, water project opponents cried politics over pragmatism when these exchanges between politicians and the president seemed too fortuitous. The *Lexington Herald* reporter Don Walker noted that Paintsville Dam opponents believed Carter acquiesced to political pressure rather than sound science and practical decision-making.[30]

4. Water Project Cancellations

Especially when consulting major political players, the White House took careful measures to frame the narrative, assert their position, and promote comity. Prior to a big meeting with the vice president and key senators, Frank Moore strategized on the best way to frame Carter's positions on water resource management. A consistent policy would frame the administration's decisions, allay confusion, and preempt some parochial positioning. Moore coordinated with the Army Corps of Engineers as well as the Bureau of Reclamation and other agencies. Moore sought to reconcile any potential conflicts between agency policy and the president's prerogative. The goal was a consistent and clear message to present to the senators based on what was best for the nation.[31]

On April 5, 1977, Moore and Mondale met with Senators Robert C. Byrd (D–WV), Hubert H. Humphrey (D–MN), Alan Cranston (D–CA), and Russell B. Long (D–LA). Humphrey, deputy president pro tempore of the Senate, was the only senator who had not been at the big meeting with administration principals a month earlier. In his report back to Carter, Moore said, "We received the water projects story, and Dr. Byrd says the patient is in intensive care, has no discernable pulse, and prospects of survival are nil unless it receives an immediate Presidential transfusion." Moore and Mondale took Byrd's "prescription" to heart and moved quickly to call senators to check their status on the issue. Moore admitted to the president his analogy might sound "silly" but he considered it apropos to convey Byrd's thoughts accurately. These senators spoke for their colleagues. Parochial interests were a constituent service. Pork-barrel projects were prime reelection fodder. Carter anticipated resistance to his cancellation proposals. The next step was an official statement reminding the Congress and their constituencies that national priorities trump regional interests.[32]

An Official Statement

On April 6, 1977, Craig Raupe from Frank Moore's office shared a statement that had been discussed with White House staff—including President Carter—at lunch the day before. In Raupe's words, the statement gave the White House "an out-to-water situation without losing face for anyone." The statement reiterated that Congress is the "primary forum" for national debate and therefore it was logical and constitutionally prudent for the president to look to Congress to have these debates. "The President can, and should, recommend, advise, cajole, appeal to the people and, on occasion, veto, but it is the Congress that ultimately decides." Carter remained committed to policies that served the best interests of the American people, but Carter accepted that these policies ultimately required legislation. This, in turn, meant, "Congress has the last word." Carter elaborated,

> In my view, it is the responsibility of the Chief Executive to review all ongoing Federal programs to determine where changes should be made, either in broad policy or specific application. That is what I am doing now with respect to certain water projects. When my reviews are completed, I will have recommendations to make to the Congress. Congress will then decide whether to adopt my recommendations.

Carter's defined his long-term goal as shifting the way business in Washington was conducted. Carter wanted to foster comity and collaboration between branches of government while maintaining presidential power. Historians Burton I. Kaufman and Scott Kaufman described Carter's relations with Congress on this issue as "at loggerheads."

> Although Carter modified his hit list by dropping some items and adding others, and although he promised to meet with lawmakers "to establish a dialogue and close cooperation in this issue," he was determined to excise the remaining projects. "Prepare dam project statement listing those which will be eliminated or cutback," he instructed Eizenstat. "In every case, itemize objections in strongest terms." Congress responded by soundly defeating (252 to 143) an administration-sponsored admendment to cut $100 million of funding for water projects from the budget.[33]

Carter had adjusted his "hit list" of which projects were targeted but it was to no avail. In a decade that blurred those lines and fostered mistrust of the White House and the motivations of the presidents therein, Carter sought to make his intentions and his methodology abundantly clear. Carter campaigned on a promise to work better with Congress, but to a degree he took cooperation for granted. He underestimated the reelection imperative and the role of pork-barrel water projects. Carter's proposals threatened that political ecosystem, disrupting business as usual. Carter's failure to garner support did more than just sustain a system of questionable water projects. Carter's po-

4. Water Project Cancellations

litical gamble squandered leverage and momentum. The first hundred days of a presidency are so important, and Carter had bungled this opportunity.[34]

By mid–April, Carter moved to finalize his position. Few in Congress had their positions swayed but Carter maintained his position that the process of consultation ensures comity and respect for the deliberative process. "I intend to cooperate with the Congress in accomplishing reform in the water resources area, and I hope that the Congress will cooperate with me in eliminating wasteful and destructive spending on water projects." The Liaison Office had contacted almost every senator and member of Congress. Out of 535 legislators, 529 had been contacted.[35] The White House knew threatening pork-barrel projects complicated congressional relations. He desperately needed détente.

By the close of business on April 16, all the research and investigations had been taken into account. The White House announced their decisions and their plans moving forward. The assistant to the president for domestic affairs and policy sent the memo to the secretary of the interior for his final approval. Andrus called it "an excellent draft." With the blessing of Andrus, as well as the Office of Management and Budget and Secretary of Transportation Brock Adams, Secretary of the Army Clifford Alexander, and others, Eizenstat sent the memo to the president for his final approval. The memo, when published, framed the projects' cancellations in terms of money saved but also in terms of benefits in kind.[36]

With Carter's approval, the White House released its official statement on water projects two days later. Carter laid out his revised recommendations for cancelling and truncating various water projects. From environmental concerns to budget savings, Carter presented his major policy initiative.[37] The announcement reiterated Carter's commitment to working with Congress to determine which projects ought to be cut. Carter wanted to ensure the public benefited from these projects and not just special interests. Carter also sought to improve the mechanisms for ensuring dam safety in America, to recoup the costs of dam projects from those who benefited, and to improve water conservation efforts and create public works projects in conjunction with approved water projects. Some projects were to be cut, others were to be modified (meaning the budget slashed, but not cut), and others were going to be funded as requested. In total, Carter reviewed thirty-two water projects.[38]

Carter's message was met with mixed results. Supporters championed his candor while critics questioned his logic. For example, first-term Colorado Governor Democrat Richard Lamm wrote President Carter following the statement on energy and water projects. The governor read about Carter's efforts to shift funding away from "expensive water projects," firing back that the dams provided substantial alleviation of drought conditions. Lamm worried about the "quality of advice" the president received about the West. Lamm spoke about Colorado but also about Wyoming, Utah, and California. His concerns about the best interests for water in Colorado amounted to a pitch for a different approach for the entire Western third of the country. The White House response offered little comfort beyond the company line: "The President hopes to improve all our water resource programs by making certain they are effective and efficient."[39] Carter grew thick skin to absorb the ire of the nation, but he was not deterred from his plans.

In anticipation of meetings with key House leaders, including Majority Leader Jim Wright (D–TX), Chairman of the Committee on Public Works and Transportation Harold T. "Bizz" Johnson (D–CA), and members of districts with affected projects, the West Wing drafted a letter to the larger Appropriations Committee, of which Public Works and Transportation is a subcommittee. The White House chided the committee members for not including more of Carter's recommendations about water projects in their public works bill. Carter reiterated that his recommendations would save the American taxpayers $4 billion, $200 million of which would be realized for FY 1978. In a condescending tone, as if a parent were admonishing his or her children, Carter berated the legislators for not helping to balance the budget. The letter stated that the bill would cost more and bloat the budget. Some of the projects approved by Congress were deemed poor spending choices by the administration. Specifically, the bill would restore funding for six projects scrapped by the administration as part of a compromise between Congress and the White House. The letter derided Congress' motivation to continue to study some of the projects (funding them in the interim) when the administration had already de-

4. Water Project Cancellations

termined the projects were bad ideas. At the meeting, Carter stressed his desire for the deletion of the eighteen water projects while both sides sought to avoid a veto.[40]

The next day, Mondale, Eizenstat, and Moore reported formally to Carter about the reaction of Congress. The Public Works Subcommittee reported to the full Appropriations Committee that all but one of the water projects were funded in their entirety. The subcommittee report recognized the environmental and safety concerns, but it did not sway their final recommendations. The trio predicted that the full Appropriations Committee would vote for "virtually full funding for the projects." As reported, the subcommittee plan did provide any budget savings. Early trial balloons to quash the funding for the water projects were defeated in the House of Representatives. Carter and his team needed to press harder if they wanted their changes in the FY 1978 budget. Mondale, Eizenstat, and Moore reported that the Senate would not take any action until the House had reached its final decision. Ultimately, his advisors recommendation waived the president off of fighting over 1977 funds to focus on the following year's budget. The trio recommended the president criticize the committee's decision but stop short of threatening to veto any resultant budget bill. Based on past votes on similar water project and budget issues, Mondale, Eizenstat, and Moore feared Carter's veto might be overturned. Secretary Andrus took a more optimistic view. When asked if he would recommend Carter use his veto power, he responded, "I can't for certain until I see the finished product, but if Congress does not give consideration to our recommendations, I will recommend a veto. I would suspect that if the bill is vetoed, that veto would be sustained."[41] Carter could, of course, lobby against a veto override. Carter's advisors recommended he stress the budget savings above all else, targeting the blue dog Democrats and fiscal conservatives. In the meanwhile, chess moves such as hinting a veto is likely might have swayed some senators and representatives from voting the measure up in the first place. The subsequent letter to members of the House Appropriations Committee was succinct.

> I am deeply disappointed by the failure of the Subcommittee on Public Works to include my recommendations on eliminating unnecessary water projects in the bill they have reported out on May 3 to the fill Committee on Appropriations.

Jimmy Carter and the Restoration of Presidential Dignity

My recommendations, announced April 18, were the result of a thorough and detailed review. They would save the American taxpayer nearly $4 billion, including nearly $200 million in FY 1978.

If wasteful spending is to be curtailed and the Budget balanced by FY 1981, the Congress will have to assist me in eliminating needless and counterproductive projects and program. I look forward to working with you to achieve these goals.[42]

One such blue dog Democrat, Gunn McKay (D–UT), had been in the Cabinet room meeting. One week after meeting in the White House so that West Wing staff could woo his support, McKay took to the House floor to sound off about Carter's plan. Specifically, McKay defended the project in his backyard, the Bonneville Unit of the Central Utah Project. McKay argued that Carter's designation of projects such as the Bonneville Unit were premature. McKay disputed Carter's characterization of the projects as "bad." Point by point, McKay refuted six criteria that McKay attributed to Carter's decision calculus. He refuted the president's math. He argued the project would not cost more money and it would in fact bring money into the local economy. McKay argued that there would be no negative effect of downstream salinity and that the local Utes supported the project. McKay was not the only one to take to the floor to defend a project dear to his or her home district. With the bill reported out, many more came out of the woodwork. The language varies, but the argument remained the same: "The project in my district is important. This project should be funded." In other words, NIMBY.[43]

The Vote

On June 2, 1977, Representative Tom Bevill (D–AL) introduced HR 7553, the Public Works for Water and Power Development and Energy Research Appropriation bill. A bill "making appropriations for public works for water and power development and energy research for the fiscal year ending September 30, 1978, and for other purposes."[44] With an imminent floor fight, Eizenstat and Moore prepared an amendment to be introduced that would embody the president's recommendations. Their goal—at minimum—sought to convey that a

4. Water Project Cancellations

veto would be sustained. The administration wanted to make it clear that if Carter had to veto, he would, but that his veto would not have the votes to be overturned. Carter needed to shore up his support. Earlier in the year, only 143 members had voted to cut the budget for water projects.

Kathy Fletcher sent a memo to Stu Eizenstat the same day reporting on her work with Jim Free to prep for the upcoming floor flight. It was Fletcher and Free's idea that the president personally reach out to the 143 members who voted for budget cuts (and 63 members who had proposed the cuts earlier). Carter needed to confirm their support and seek out the support of more. Frank Moore warned that sending the letters that Eizenstat (Fletcher and Free) proposed would cause "an uproar with Bizz Johnson, Jim Wright, etc." However, Moore conceded that they needed "a baseline vote for sustaining a possible veto."[45]

In the other chamber of Congress, the Senate Appropriations Subcommittee had deleted nine water projects and curtailed a tenth in response to Carter's recommendations and the administrations strong showing on the House floor on June 13. The question remained whether Carter would commend Senator John C. Stennis (D–MS) as the architect behind this for this compromise or rebuke him and push for all of Carter's programs. Carter's advisors concurred that his best option was to "hang tough" and not endorse Stennis and his efforts before the big meeting with members of Congress. Too much early concession would weaken his position at the meeting and diminish his chances for desired results. Carter needed to retain all the support he could for the votes ahead.[46]

One week later, news of the debate on the floor of Congress began to flow in. House Liaison and White House Lobbyist Rick Merrill wrote to Frank Moore with his reflections and observations on the water projects vote in Congress. He first commented that there was no "Carter coalition" in the House but in fact the members voted based on geography—based on the stake their region had in various water projects. Members from New England and the mid–Atlantic supported the administration while opposition swelled from members in the South and West. While some liberal Democrats "bucked" the regional pull and supported the administration, mostly geography trumped party affiliation. Merrill suggested that in order to reform a coalition, Carter needed at least sixty Republicans and enough money to grease the wheels.[47]

Three days later, the Senate took up the discussion of Public Works Appropriations 1978. Most critiques from the Senate floor devolved quickly to NIMBY concerns for the projects in their home districts. For example, Senator Floyd Haskell (D–CO) declared, "from the day the President's water project hit list was issued some viewed the situation as a classic test of wills between the newly elected President and the Congress." Haskell framed the fight in the terms he believed local farmers across America would see the fight. To him, Congress stood defending promises made to farmers over the years to provide them adequate infrastructure to sustain themselves. Some projects have been restored but others—like the one in Haskell's state of Colorado—were still under scrutiny. Similarly, the Tennessee–Tombigbee (Tenn–Tom to those who know it) was originally on the "hit list" but it was swiftly reinstated. The Tenn–Tom was environmentally sound despite being one of the criteria Carter used to choose projects to be slated for defunding. A second factor was safety and Haskell pointed out that if the Auburn Dam was scrapped, there could be serious concerns for the Californians living downstream. The third factor was the benefit-cost ratio. Put another way, "What do we get and what does it cost us?" In this case, Haskell points to the Tallahala project, which was threatened and then reinstated.[48] Haskell's crescendo praised new standards but felt they should not apply to existing projects. To prove his point, he presented an analogy using ice cream cones.

> What is at work here, I am afraid, is the same kind of selfishness which ruled the little boy sent to the store to buy two identical ice cream cones: The one he dropped was his sister's. Well, in this case, Colorado and the West are the sister and we are upset. We do not object to the application of new standards to water projects so long as those standards are not made retroactive.
>
> I would be delighted to work with the administration in drafting new standards against which to judge water projects. Such standards are long overdue. But in the name of fairness and commonsense let us apply those standards to all future projects, not those which have been promised for years and which are, in many cases, substantially underway.
>
> That approach is basic, Mr. President. The present approach puts the position of reneging on a promise—not a promise casually made, but one stated and restated for years.

4. Water Project Cancellations

Haskell later took to the floor to propose an amendment to reinstate the projects cut by Carter. The amendment failed, but this tied to his idea that Carter's proposal was an *ex post facto* proposal.[49]

Soon thereafter, Senator Thomas McIntyre (D–NH) offered a similar half-a-loaf support. He commended Carter for his efforts, proposing an amendment to fund some projects but not others. He argued that the president can only recommend; ultimately Congress must decide.

> The President recognized the difficult choices that must be made to restrain inflation and to place our budgetary process back in balance and I believe we in Congress have an even greater responsibility. The President can only recommend; we appropriate. The President has recommended after careful study that several water projects, however worthy, still do not meet the ultimate test of the budgetary give and take. He has found that some of the proposed water projects are wasteful or unsafe or economically unjustified or environmentally unsound. His conclusion is that we simply cannot continue to pursue this type of budgetary expenditure. The final and ultimate determination, however, must be made by Congress.
> Is the President wrong? Are these projects worthy? These are the questions. I believe the President's findings are correct. I believe we must make the hard choice and I know as surely as everyone in this body that we cannot construct these water projects and at the same time meet all our other pressing priorities. We in Congress have the ultimate responsibility. I only hope that we can find the courage and wisdom to make the right choice.

McIntyre described the trade-off as one of the tough choices members of Congress are both empowered and charged with making. Every project has pros and cons.[50] Senator Milton Young (R–ND) rose directly afterward to oppose McIntyre's amendment because it would cancel the project in his home state that had been previously approved. A similar critique came from Senator J. Bennett Johnston (D–LA). He accused McIntyre of not knowing the facts about the projects, as he did not serve on the Public Works Subcommittee or the Appropriations Committee. Johnston, conceding his vested interest in the project, then laid out the case for continued funding. "Do I have a parochial interest in this? You bet I do." He spoke about all the jobs his local water project created in the town of Morgan City, Louisiana.[51]

Senator Barry Goldwater (R–AZ) took the floor next. He saw the battle lines regionally, between the water-rich East and the water-poor West. He conceded that sometimes these programs were excuses for pork-barrel appropriations, but he assured the chamber—and McIntyre specifically—that his local project was not just pork. For his case, the funding went to a viable project: a valuable investment in the infrastructure of America and not as "donations to the State."

> When I hear people talk on this floor as if somehow these projects were gifts to the State, it does not amuse me; it concerns me. These are good investments on the whole. I will admit that there has been pork barreling in the past; but the average project, such as my friend from Louisiana is talking about, are absolute musts in this country, and we cannot ignore these musts if the country is to be fed.

Goldwater staunchly defended the two seemingly contradictory positions. The Chamber should scrutinize water projects but at the same time defer to individual senators such as himself about the efficacy of their local projects. Similar sentiments came from other senators about their home projects, but the amendment ultimately failed.[52]

Amidst the myriad of NIMBY defenses for local pork projects, one levelheaded analysis stood out. Representatives Jim Tucker (D–AR) and Romano L. Mazzoli (D–KY) defended their local projects while applauding John B. Oakes' exposé about the "Pork Barrel Challenge." Oakes scathingly criticized Congress for their graft and limited support for water project reform. "For what the old-timers in Congress have done has been to scrape the bottom of the pork barrel once again, just as though there was no inflation and no budgetary squeeze on federal expenditures to meet urgent social needs." Oakes wrote specifically about the bill as it worked its way through the Senate Appropriations Committee.

> Of the nine projects that the Senate is now trying to push through for full funding over Carter's objection, no less than eight are located in states whose senators happen to be on the Appropriations Committee (seven of them on public works subcommittee), which gives a pretty good idea of the criterion of judgment used by the Senate in making its evaluation.

Without mincing words, Oakes accused the senators of putting pork before good government. Carter faced a tough battle to review these water projects and Oakes suspected the president would end up swallowing a bitter pill.

> To keep the peace with Congress, President Carter will doubtless be asked by his political advisers to accept the bill containing these and similar extravaganzas. If

4. Water Project Cancellations

he does so, it will be a sad and crippling retreat. For he is the first President in generations to have faced up to the political and moral corruption inherent in so many of these projects. To back down now would be a severe defeat for the public, the economy and the environment, not to mention the surprisingly large number of members of Congress (especially the younger ones) who are sick and tired of pork-barrel venality and who are looking for a way to escape from it.[53]

A heavily modified version of the House and Senate bills eventually passed and went to the president for his signature. The bill added scrutiny to water projects but many of the questionable water projects remained funded in full. Carter found a bill for water reform on his desk, but it was not the bill he anticipated.

On August 7, 1977, Jimmy Carter signed HR 7553, the Public Works Administration bill, into law. After months of debate, various incarnations of back and forth, some water projects were discontinued. On paper, Carter claimed success.

> This bill is a precedent-setting first step in trimming spending on unnecessary, expensive, and environmentally damaging construction projects. In response to administration review of construction projects and recommendations to the Congress, nine unsound projects have been deleted and four modified. This is unprecedented progress. In addition to this action, the Congress has refrained from funding unbudgeted new construction starts.[54]

Though Carter declared the law a "positive step," his signing statement revealed his true feelings. The statement conveyed reserved enthusiasm for the bill in the form that made it to his desk. Carter's initial goal had been scrutinized, modified, and then sent through the grinder that is the legislative process. The bill accomplished three of Carter's big goals—deauthorization of deleted projects, continued close scrutiny of all projects, and institution of lasting reforms in water policy—and contained some project cancellations.[55] On one hand, Carter's signing statement—and the official position of the White House—declared victory even if the goalposts had moved. However, in reality, the final bill sent to Carter was the tough pill Oakes had warned about. Carter ended up with a choice between a half-a-loaf solution that did not disrupt the pork-barrel system or veto the bill and risk a likely override. In that event, pork would still continue, and Carter would be severely weakened. Carter fought and won some battles, but the process story of the fight was a loss in the end. Carter spoke publicly that his relations with Congress were improving. "I think the Congress now understands much more clearly what I am, what I stand for, what proposals we put forward, and the priorities accruing to those proposals. I think we've had good success with the Congress already."[56] In reality, Carter learned a lesson in how to work with Congress. He also learned the extent to which the power structure in Congress favored the *status quo* and how pork-barrel spending is sacrosanct.

With Carter's signature, the fight over 1978 appropriations closed. There would be future fights over impoundments of the budget and the FY 1979 budget. Carter's team reframed their loss as one battle in a larger fight. Carter learned many lessons in the process, both about water resource policy and especially about the true machinations of the legislative process. Indeed, insofar as Carter's fight threatened pork projects across the nation, the new president learned how the sausage got made.

5

Jimmy Carter and the Reinstatement of Draft Registration

By 1978, debate had stopped about Carter's pardon and his discharge review program. All reconciliation measures had run their course and Carter ended a long debate over the draft and what to do with those who avoided service. Five years after Richard Nixon switched military procurement to an all-volunteer force, the draft issue finally became moot. However, three years later, the same president who pardoned draft dodgers called for the resumption of draft registration. While registration is not the same as active draft calls, for the past three decades signing up with the government meant an inevitable call from the government for some of those young men to serve. How does the same president who let draft dodgers come home from Canada ask the next generation to sign up again, implying another draft might happen? Representative Robert Michel (R–IL) asked this question on the floor of Congress. In light of Carter's "very first official act ... why is he asking young Americans to register under penalty of law in 1980 when little more than 3 years ago he in effect told the nation's young people that if you yell long enough and loud enough you do not have to do your duty[?]"[1] Though Michel's statement smacked of election season posturing, the question still had merit. The answer involves an understanding of the context of Carter's decision and of the Cold War in the late 1970s. It also involves an understanding of the White House's position on Carter's decision and how the debate played out on the floors of Congress.

When Carter announced his pardon plans in the 1976 campaign,

Jimmy Carter and the Restoration of Presidential Dignity

he never claimed to be against the draft, though his pardon would resonate within the anti-draft community as a victory. From the beginning, Carter framed his actions in terms of reconciliation, not conscription. Carter pledged, "I do not favor a blanket amnesty, but for those who violated Selective Service laws, I intend to grant a blanket pardon." Carter later added,

> If I am President, I will issue a pardon for all those who are outside our country or in this country, who did not serve in the Armed Forces. I am going to issue a pardon—not an amnesty. I think those kids who have lived in Sweden and Canada or who have avoided arrest have been punished enough.

Carter's technical distinction reflected his belief that amnesty carries a connotation of moral absolution. A pardon cleaned the offender's slate, but Carter believed amnesty cleaned the slate and implied the offender was justified in doing what they did. Carter did not endorse their actions and he did not oppose the draft they dodged.[2]

Additionally, while Nixon adopted the all-volunteer force in 1973, in reality draft registration did not lapse until 1975. Ford ceased draft registration pending a review of the Selective Service System.[3] This review outlasted Ford's time in office, and by 1979, the Selective Service presented President Carter with proposals as to how he could reorganize the agency and how to renew registration. Coinciding with Carter's larger reorganization efforts, in the winter of 1979, new Selective Service Director Bernard Rostker outlined his proposal on how to reorganize the branch of government he oversaw in the best manner. His plan allowed the Selective Service to maintain the level of readiness required should Congress call for a draft while minimizing its infrastructure and budget during times of dormancy. At the time, Carter hoped to avoid registration, lest it renew the draft debate; Carter did not want to open old wounds. White House Domestic Policy Staff Advisor Stu Eizenstat assured Congress that year that Carter had "adequate authority to require registration if circumstances warrant" but that he opposed a return to registration. Within months, Carter and Eizenstat would eat those words.[4]

The proposals might not have garnered much attention, but for the December 27, 1979, Soviet invasion of Afghanistan. Carter sought bold countermeasures to combat Communist bravado; however, not

5. Jimmy Carter and the Reinstatement of Draft Registration

willing to commit American troops or other military actions, Carter opted instead for symbolic gestures. Committed to détente and reflecting his strong moral attitude toward peace, Carter's would not risk another Vietnam War–style engagement. Among the symbolic acts the president put forth to allay crumbling détente included a call to renew draft registration. (The other prominent measures were a grain embargo and a boycott of the 1980 Summer Olympics held in Moscow.) Carter saw registration as a gesture of military posturing and indicators of a tough foreign policy. In his view, it demonstrated that the United States would be ready should hostilities in Afghanistan continue.[5]

When Rostker gave Carter his report, he suggested the president insert language into his State of the Union Address calling for reorganization of the Selective Service. However, in light of Soviet aggression, Carter's staff pushed for a stronger position. Specifically, White House Counselor Lloyd Cutler feared another Burke-Wadsworth Act fiasco, a reference to the debacle in 1940 when Franklin Delano Roosevelt lobbied Congress to pass the Selective Training and Service Act, also known eponymously for its two lead sponsors, Senator Edward Burke (D–NE) and Representative James Wadsworth (R–NY). However, the Burke-Wadsworth Act required a renewal one year later and that extension passed by a single vote. Cutler argued that the perceived weakness, months before the bombing of Pearl Harbor, encouraged the Japanese. Cutler called for more than just a subtle allusion.[6] Having worked so hard to take the word draft out of the political lexicon, the decision to bring it back did not come lightly. Nonetheless, the strong and bold decision to bring the word "debate" back into the conversation was precisely Cutler's recommendation. Even if Carter disagreed with Cutler's *post hoc ergo proctor hoc* logic about the Burke-Wadsworth Pearl Harbor connection, Carter understood that the Soviet Union needed to understand the United States would implement a draft if necessary.

On January 23, 1980, speaking to Congress and the nation, Jimmy Carter announced his response to the Soviet invasion as part of his annual State of the Union Address. In addition to a boycott of the Summer Olympics to be held in Moscow and spearheading a grain embargo, Carter called for the renewal of draft registration:

> The men and women of America's Armed Forces are on duty tonight in many parts of the world. I'm proud of the job they are doing, and I know you share that pride. I believe that our volunteer forces are adequate for current defense needs, and I hope that it will not become necessary to impose a draft. However, we must be prepared for that possibility. For this reason, I have determined that the Selective Service System must now be revitalized. I will send legislation and budget proposals to the Congress next month so that we can begin registration and then meet future mobilization needs rapidly if they arise.[7]

Following up the next month with a report to Congress, Carter explained that, in order to implement his plan, Congress needed to fund "catch-up" measures as well as continuing registration. (A catch-up measure funded the registration of all young men who were not signed up in the mid–1970s.) Later that year, President Carter signed Proclamation 4771, "Registration Under the Military Selective Service Act," retroactively reestablishing the Selective Service registration requirement. Carter's actions sparked a debate in Congress over defense spending, Cold War policy, and conscription policy. Carter knew his proposal would be controversial. A majority would have to vote for Carter's plan in the House and, in light of a filibuster threatened by Senator Mark Hatfield (R–OR), a supermajority (sixty votes) would need to support it in the Senate.[8] Carter might have preferred consensus, but certainly he welcomed healthy debate. The latter was still preferable to the presidential fiat exercised by his predecessors. Every time a controversial issue made its way through the normal means of constitutional separation of powers, Carter's larger message of fairness in government shined through.

Congress Re-Fights the Vietnam War Draft Debate

Carter's fears from 1979 proved to be true. The registration proposal reopened the conscription debate. Though some members of Congress supported reforming the all-volunteer force and saw a return to draft registration as a plausible contingency, often partisanship influenced members' positions. Most Democrats rallied behind Carter, while most Republicans rallied to stop him. For example, the conservative and well-respected Senate Majority Whip Harry Byrd (D–VA) quoted Joseph A. Califano, Jr., a veteran of the John F. Ken-

5. Jimmy Carter and the Reinstatement of Draft Registration

nedy and Lyndon Johnson administrations, who was then currently working for the Carter administration. To Califano and Byrd, Carter's move was a way to replace what he saw as the "weakest weapon in [the American] our military arsenal" namely the all-volunteer force. Califano cited research by Senator Sam Nunn (D–GA) that American defense readiness had declined ever since Nixon started the all-volunteer force. The information exchange went both ways. Nunn supported his position in the debates with evidence from the White House. For example, he quoted Secretary of the Defense Harold Brown to Senator John C. Stennis (D–MS), chairman of the Committee on Armed Services. Brown argued the measure would significantly improve mobilization time and would send a dramatic signal to the Soviets. Brown called upon the Senate to pass the same bill that passed the House. He argued that opposition on principle of conscientious objection is best saved for debates about classification and draft commencement, not preparedness and preregistration.[9]

On March 13th, Patricia Schroeder extended her remarks in the House to point out a *New York Times* article written by Richard Halloran that noted that the Senate was reacting with more skepticism to Carter's plan than the House was. The article pointed out the strong opposition of Mark Hatfield. The senator lambasted the plan as a waste of money and a diversion of resources better spent to improve volunteer pay. Representative Robert Eckhardt (D–TX) supported the bill, though he wished the president had not broached the issue. He opposed drafts and draft registration but did not want the United States to appear weak because a symbolic gesture—or the nation's president—fell flat. "[O]nce the issue has been raised, I cannot fail to support the President." Eckhardt supported registration "as a token of support of national unity" but not "as a commitment to a course." Byrd, Eckhardt, and the others mentioned represented the gamut of Democratic positions. Some agreed with Carter entirely, others did not, but in general Democrats supported their president and his larger Cold War message.

On the other side of the aisle, most Republicans were skeptical, if not openly critical. Senator Harrison H. Schmitt (R–NM) called the proposal a "smokescreen," diverting attention from the more pressing problems with the military. Senator John Heinz (R–PA) argued that preregistration should only happen if proven to be a necessity, but that the Carter administration had not met this burden of proof. Representative Stewart McKinney (R–CT) conflated registration and conscription. He opposed registration because he felt it was not clear what kind of draft America was getting into. His quandary implied Carter's plan meant more than draft registration—he viewed it as a harbinger of an inevitable resumption of active draft calls. McKinney thought the legislation would neither solve any problems nor send a successful message. A notable hawk, Representative Jack F. Kemp (R–NY), supported registration but lamented that Carter's actions were only a gesture. He hoped the president would do more in terms of national defense and foreign policy to stand tall against the Soviets. While the arguments differed, most Republicans opposed Carter's course of action.[10]

While party lines served as an indicator for most politicians' views on Carter's proposal, on the issue of soldier wages, pragmatism trumped politics. Both sides of the aisle lobbied for this one-sided issue. To be painted as opposing better compensation for military personnel is, of course, political suicide. Despite this, some legislators tried to capture the salary debate within the draft debate. Representative Parren Mitchell (D–MD) argued that draft registration made another draft inevitable. He argued that the money for another draft should instead be invested in better pay for military personnel. He argued that Carter's plan—by denying these pay increases—amounted to passing the burden of service once again to the poorer echelons of society. Those logical leaps set up a story about an E4 handler working on the USS *Nimitz* making less than a cashier at McDonald's. Representative Bill Green (R–NY) concurred on another occasion, adding, "An E4 handling a $25 million jet aboard an aircraft carrier puts in about 100 hours a week without overtime and winds up with a per-hour wage less than a cashier at McDonalds." Though the salary comparison ignored some major perquisites of the job—most notably the food and board offered by the Navy (to say nothing of the benefits)—these sensational anecdotes carried great rhetorical power. The story questioned whether a pay raise would be a better allocation of money than the draft.[11]

The majority of Americans supported Carter's program in some form, though Democrats touted the statistics more often than Repub-

5. Jimmy Carter and the Reinstatement of Draft Registration

licans. For example, Representative Edward Boland (D–MA) offered some favorable numbers to show the president's plan had public backing: "An NBC poll concluded that 76 percent of the American people support pre-mobilization registration. An ABC poll found 74 percent of the American people favored registration and as a matter of fact in both a majority favored a draft." The specific breakdown varied from poll to poll and week to week but prevailing consensus favored a draft should it come and overwhelmingly favored registration in the meantime.[12]

For all the partisan jabs, some members of Congress genuinely believed that politics stopped at the water's edge—that Cold War logic transcended party lines. Both Democrats and Republicans supported sending a signal to the Soviets. Representative William Boner (D–TN) supported the bill because he believed it would send the right message. "I believe the final passage of this bill by Congress will send a clear signal to the Soviets and our allies that the United States is willing and able to counter Soviet aggression in Asia and Africa." Similarly, Senator Robert Byrd (D–WV) believed registration sent a clear message to American allies and enemies alike that America will defend its principles: "A display of American resolve in having our young men register with the Selective Service is not 'empty symbolism.'" Across the aisle, Senator Howard Baker (R–TN) distinguished between preregistration and a draft.

> I agree that this is not the resumption of the peacetime draft, nor would I support the resumption of the peacetime draft at this time. But I believe this step, this simple step, is a prudent caution in a time of international stress and tension, and in anticipation of even worse times which might disintegrate into a time of peril.[13]

Democrat or Republican, neither side wanted to look weak before the Soviets or to appear soft on communism. Once Carter suggested a course of action, an understanding emerged that backing down was not an option. Right or wrong, these members of Congress respected that the president, regardless of party, represented the voice and the face of the nation. They also realized that contradiction or undermining the president on foreign policy—even nominally—could be construed as a sign of weakness.

Another issue that crossed party lines was the fear that draft

Jimmy Carter and the Restoration of Presidential Dignity

registration guaranteed a draft. Some in Congress saw registration as a self-fulfilling prophecy; their fears were fueled by doomsday hyperbole. No sooner than Carter announced his plans, stories began to surface. For example, the Associated Press wire reported young Americans were already contacting the Canadian embassy—at the rate of about fifteen a day—for information about how to emigrate. They wanted to hedge their bets in case another Vietnam War draft situation arose.[14] Representative Leon Panetta (D–CA) specifically used the phrase "self-fulfilling prophecy." By his logic, "once we begin registration, we should be honest in acknowledging that it is a first step on the road toward the draft." In theory, he is correct so far; registration is *ipso facto* a precursor to a draft. However, Panetta's next line—and many similar sentiments uttered by members of Congress like him—proved less sound. "By reviving registration, we may be guaranteeing the need to revive the draft, whether during peacetime or during wartime." The word "may" in that sentence cemented his speculation as blind. Representative John Seiberling (D–OH) calculated that even if only 5 percent failed to register, that meant about 40,000 resisters and he concluded that such figures doomed the nation to "more Kent States" and a recurrence of "the trauma of the 1970s."[15]

Leading the charge of these claims was Senator Mark Hatfield (R–OR). In between quoting prominent draft resistance scholars Lawrence M. Baskir and William Strauss, the noted dove and anti-draft advocate read excerpts of Martin Luther King, Jr.'s, speeches into the record, most notably excerpts from his Riverside Church speech, in which King announced his change in stance on the Vietnam War, coming out against it and the draft that supported it.[16] As important as these scholars and activists are, Hatfield's tactics were part of the filibuster that Carter had feared. Hatfield opposed preregistration because he felt it would tacitly endorse a return to a draft. He conceded the proposal might have been a good symbolic gesture at the outset, but he concluded the act would ultimately send the opposite message. Former presidential candidate and dove Senator George McGovern (D–SD) supported Hatfield's position that a vote for registration is a vote for an inevitable future draft. He pointed to the Rostker report, arguing that it had been taken out of context. He argued that the post-mobilization plan was better than the pre-mobilization alternative. He called upon Carter to "have a firm for-

5. Jimmy Carter and the Reinstatement of Draft Registration

eign policy response based on substance, not on symbols." He wanted improvements to military readiness. Ultimately, only one member of Congress, Representative Edward Boland (D–MA), cut through the presumptions, pointing out that it is moot to presume that registration guaranteed a draft since the decision to enact a draft required a congressional vote anyway.[17]

Women—To Draft or Not to Draft

In the decade that saw Americans on the Left and the Right fight over the Equal Rights Amendment (ERA), the issue of draft parity sparked a lot of concern, especially on the floors of Congress. For all of the other issues and old wounds Carter raised by his proclamation reinstating draft registration, equally contentious was his decision that women would be drafted next to men. "There is no distinction possible, on the basis of ability or performance, that would allow me to exclude women from an obligation to register." *United Press International* reported that Stop Taking Our Privileges Equal Rights Amendment (STOP ERA) leader Phyllis Schlafly said, "Carter has stabbed American womanhood in the back in a cowardly attempt to get back the election-year support of the radical feminists." Senator Henry "Scoop" Jackson (D–WA) noted that any proposal to draft women would be the death knell for ERA. He noted that ERA opponents claimed drafting women as one of the negative consequences mandated by the amendment. Though the National Organization for Women (NOW) opposed peacetime registration, the organization agreed that if registration happened, both men and women should be expected to register.[18]

No member of Congress or West Wing staff—including Carter himself—said in 1979 that women should be drafted to serve in combat roles. However, some members of Congress, like Senator Barry Goldwater (R–AZ), shared Carter's position to draft women into noncombat roles. Others, like Representative Les AuCoin (D–OR), argued that draft registration would have the opposite effect than Carter desired because it would incite more hostility and proliferation rather than send the symbolic message Carter intended. Representative Joseph

Jimmy Carter and the Restoration of Presidential Dignity

Addabbo (D–NY) argued there were fundamental differences inherent between the sexes and for that reason women should not be drafted. Most troops are drafted for combat and Addabbo pointed to studies that concluded women could not handle that role. Representative Stephen Neal (D–NC) argued against registration of women, seeing as there is no reason to draft women. Neal accepted women's place in the military—though he tacitly endorsed their exclusion from combat roles—but he argued until the military decides to draft women, the registration of women was impractical. Like Addabbo, most members of Congress equated a draft with filling combat roles. Thus, as long as women did not serve in combat roles, there was no point in drafting them. Some members of Congress defended their stance as the extant result of the technicalities of the law, while others took a more subjective stance on the efficacy of women in combat.[19]

There were even more extreme positions, too. The first witness, at the first hearing before the House Armed Services Committee, was Iron Eagle Forum member Mrs. Eidson of Haleyville, Alabama. She predicted that more often than not, female recruits would be like her daughter. After two days of basic training, she figured her daughter would say, "Oh, you have got mud on my pants. I can't fix my hair." She did not claim to have any military experience, only experience with a teenage daughter.[20] Representative Marjorie Holt (R–MD) concurred with Eidson, asserting the majority of women wanted to stay out of the military. Though Carter would have preferred to draft women into noncombat positions, that was not the bill Congress put forth and Carter was not willing to abandon registration on this principle.

Drafting women ultimately was left out of the bill; however, the issue resurfaced the next year, not on the basis of women's rights, but on the basis of men's. In 1981, the Supreme Court heard the case of *Rostker v. Goldberg*. Robert Goldberg and his lawyers alleged that drafting men and not women violated his equal protection under the law. In his ruling on the case, Chief Justice William Rehnquist not only upheld the exclusion of women from the draft but implicitly ruled they should be excluded from combat roles as well.[21] Thirty-five years later, the restrictions were finally lifted, enabling equal service in combat and any other role in the military.[22]

5. Jimmy Carter and the Reinstatement of Draft Registration

Implications for the 1980 Presidential Election

Carter's case for congressional funding of his program played into election year politics. During the 1980 campaign, Republican contender Ronald Reagan came out against Carter's registration proclamation. Also vying for the Republican nomination, Representative John Anderson (R–IL) opposed the plan too. Even Democratic leader and presidential hopeful Senator Ted Kennedy (D–MA) called the plan "ill-conceived." He claimed the "military value" of Carter's proposal had "never been substantiated." All three wrote letters to Mark Hatfield expressing their position. Hatfield read all the letters on the floor of the Senate as part of his filibuster. Reagan did not see a return to registration as the answer. Specifically, he objected on moral grounds to registration.

> But perhaps the most fundamental objection to draft registration is moral. Only in the most severe national emergency does the government have a claim to the mandatory service of its young people. In any other time, a draft or draft registration destroys the very values that our society is committed to defending.

Anderson had similar letters with similar sentiments. Even former President Gerald Ford wrote Hatfield. Ford encouraged the funds to be used to boost the pay of volunteers. Hatfield concluded on the House floor that a vote for Reagan—who opposed the bill—was a vote against draft registration or a return to a draft, while a vote for Carter endorsed both. Hatfield claimed that Carter's draft registration proponents had clear intentions to push for a draft in the future. He concluded that the best way to voice the will of public opinion would be for more Americans to turn out and vote in that November's general election.[23]

In light of Reagan's position, when Carter left office reports began to surface that the next Congress would ask Reagan to rescind Carter's preregistration program. Nonetheless, Reagan, once ensconced in the Oval Office, not only retained the registration system but actively prosecuted those who failed to register. Reagan's secretary of defense, Caspar Weinberger, argued that Reagan did not change his opinion and abandon his principles but rather that the world had changed. The year 1982 was a "more dangerous world" compared to 1980, when Reagan made those anti-registration statements. Speaking on ABC's *Good Morning America*, he then claimed that Reagan's statements during the

Jimmy Carter and the Restoration of Presidential Dignity

election were based on faulty information coming out of the Selective Service System. While the 1980 data Reagan used to lambaste Carter's program claimed a mobilization expediency of a couple days, Reagan's 1982 numbers assessed the speed up at over six weeks faster. Senator Hatfield did not accept the flip-flop. "I am dismayed by the president's complete reversal of his position on this issue." Hatfield held up Reagan's 1982 statement in stark contrast to the personal letter Reagan wrote to him in 1980. As the Republican candidate, Reagan based his opposition in moral terms, not the statistical difference of days versus weeks.[24]

The reports were fueled in part by defection from within Carter's own ranks. By late 1980, Chief Naval Officer Admiral Thomas B. Hayward broke with President Carter and called for a return to a military draft. *Washington Post* staff writer George Wilson reported that Hayward became the first Joint Chiefs of Staff member to break with the administration line and call for a return to a draft. Hayward was quoted as saying that, "The all-volunteer force was slipping into failure mode." He argued that the all-volunteer force numbers were only strong because of a weak economy, and when the economy rebounds, the armed forces would run short on people to fill its ranks. Wilson reported that Hayward's remarks found support from the Senate Armed Services Committee chairman, John C. Stennis (D–MS), as well as House Armed Services Committee member Sonny Montgomery (D–MS).[25] Technically Hayward's position characterized the all-volunteer force as failing. He did not specifically call for a return to the draft but rather advocated for modifications and fixes.

In the end, both chambers passed the registration bill and Carter tried to parlay his victory into votes on the campaign trail.[26] Speaking at the Democratic Congressional Campaign Committee Victory Luncheon in the Grand Ballroom at New York's Plaza Hotel on August 14, 1980, Carter couched his decision to reinstate draft registration as a reaction to the Soviet invasion of Afghanistan. He also couched it as one action among many, including pushing for a trade embargo and calling for a boycott of the Moscow Olympics.[27] At a question and answer town hall meeting on September 15, 1980, in Corpus Christi, Texas, Danny Kucera asked if the Olympic boycott or grain embargo had any effect on the Soviet position. Of course, Carter answered yes,

5. Jimmy Carter and the Reinstatement of Draft Registration

though his explanation pivoted more to international solidarity for the symbolic gestures rather than real changes in Soviet aggression. In a follow-up, the next question came from seventeen-year-old Tony Martinez, a senior at Foy Moody, a local high school. As someone about to turn eighteen, he wanted to hear Carter talk about the draft. Carter clarified:

> I have been strongly in favor, as you know, of registration for the draft in case we do have to mobilize our forces in the future. We want to be ready to move rapidly, and this sends a clear signal to our allies and friends, to the American people, and to our potential opponents in the future that Americans are willing to take patriotic action for their country.[28]

There are other examples, too, of Carter on the campaign trail, but they were more of the same. Carter spoke out against the Soviets while defending that a draft was neither imminent nor inevitable.

Selective Service System Director Bernard Rostker announced that 93 percent of eligible youth successfully registered for the draft under Carter's registration plan. Youth signed up in the 1980s and had been registering ever since. Some presidents tried to cancel Carter's program—most notably Ronald Reagan in 1982 (a shift from his campaign position) and Bill Clinton in 1994—but despite their best efforts, draft registration continues today and for the foreseeable future. In the short term, Carter's actions might seem contradictory to conscription history and his reconciliation actions. However, his actions fit well in the 1970s détente Cold War narrative and with Carter's leadership style.[29] Carter did not need to force his position through executive orders and imperial tactics. Symbolism and comity proved an equally effective method. Carter consulted Congress and respected their role in the process. He acted within the scope of his powers while still asserting the leadership and gravitas demanded of the office.

6

Jimmy Carter and Foreign Intelligence Surveillance

In the 1976 campaign, Governor Jimmy Carter often repeated that Watergate taught the lesson that "[s]ecrecy in government is cancerous." In a campaign statement, Carter added, "After our recent experiences with Watergate, it is important that national government once again become a government of the people. Accountability is an elementary principle of democratic government." In 1976, Carter campaigned on a platform grounded in a commitment to transparency.[1] A direct line can be drawn from this campaign promise to the debate over wiretapping law and foreign intelligence surveillance. Carter's campaign and agenda coincided with the "Watergate Window," the time period following the Watergate crisis that political momentum rallied toward reform. Six years after Nixon's plumbers were caught fixing illegal wiretaps at the Democratic National Committee's Watergate headquarters, President Carter signed the Foreign Intelligence Surveillance Act (FISA) into law. FISA represented a clear response to the imperial presidency. Carter did not see any place for subterfuge in government. It would have no place in his administration and, to the extent that he could, Carter would fight for transparency. Sunshine and openness were his preferred method.[2]

Background

Though wiretapping technology progressively become more sophisticated during the course of the twentieth century, legislation to

6. Jimmy Carter and Foreign Intelligence Surveillance

regulate wiretapping lagged behind. By the 1960s, the American Civil Liberties Union (ACLU) warned that the lag was significant.

> [U]ntil 1968 there was no federal statute authorizing the use of electronic surveillance for law enforcement purposes. In fact, from 1934 until that time, federal law flatly prohibited electronic interception of communications and no wiretap evidence was admissible in court.[3]

The lag was not new. The first regulatory measure, the 1934 Communications Act, came six years after the Supreme Court's decision in *Olmstead v. United States,* in which it held that wiretaps did not require a warrant. Wiretaps did not impinge on the Fourth Amendment's protection against illegal searches and the Fifth Amendment's protection against self-incrimination. The Communications Act provided "for the regulation of interstate and foreign communication by wire or radio, and for other purposes." At a 1976 hearing on intelligence surveillance reform, Representative Robert Kastenmeier (D–WI) explained the context and extent of Franklin Delano Roosevelt's action.

> Presidents since Franklin Roosevelt have asserted that their responsibilities as Commander in Chief under article II of the Constitution give them the power to conduct electronic eavesdropping without regard to the restraints of the Fourth Amendment. On May 21, 1940, President Roosevelt issued a memorandum to the Attorney General asserting that electronic surveillance would be proper under the Constitution in cases of "grave matters involving the defense of the nation." The exact nature of "grave matters" involving the defense of the nation was never fully explained. However, it is known that national security was used as a reason or a pretext to eavesdrop on the communications not only of foreign spies but also of law-abiding American citizens who had no connection with a foreign power but whose views were considered subversive by the Director of the Federal Bureau of Investigation or by some other person high in government.[4]

As World War II unfolded, President Franklin Delano Roosevelt came to understand the Communications Act more broadly, interpreting legal wiretaps to include those on "persons suspected of subversive activities against the government of the United States, including suspected spies." By the end of World War II, President Harry Truman expanded that interpretation to permit wiretapping in "cases vitally affecting the domestic security or where human life is in jeopardy." By Lyndon Johnson's presidency, the executive branch of government simply endorsed all wiretaps in "investigations related to the national security."⁵ Over time, the language of the 1934 law had become outdated and, absent clarification, presidents ignored the law and proceeded without significant oversight.

Two 1967 Supreme Court decisions revisited the debate over surveillance warrant requirements. In *Berger v. New York* 388 U.S. 41 (1967), the Court established that a "wiretap is a 'search' governed by the requirements and limitations imposed by the Fourth Amendment." Later that year, the Court overturned *Olmstead* in *Katz v. United States,* holding that warrantless wiretaps do violate the Fourth Amendment. However, the Court specifically dodged the question of "national security" interests, stipulating that the *Katz* decision did not apply.⁶ The Supreme Court's decisions prompted Congress to pass the Omnibus Crime Control and Safe Streets Act of 1968. Clarifying the 1934 statute, the 1968 law further defined wiretap warrant procedure and began defining standards for foreign intelligence surveillance; however, the law divested all responsibility and acquiesced to executive discretion. It stipulated that neither the 1968 law nor its 1934 antecedent "shall limit the constitutional power of the president." The law restricted law enforcement but it extended *carte blanche* to presidents.

Four years later, in 1972, the Court held warrantless wiretaps to be unconstitutional in the case of *United States v. United States District Court for the Eastern District of Michigan,* better known as the *Keith* case.⁷ District Court Judge Damon Keith ruled against warrantless wiretaps. The Supreme Court agreed but held that there might be an inherent presidential power to wiretap. *Washington Post* reporter John M. Goshko explained:

> In 1972, the Supreme Court ruled that a warrant is required for wiretaps in security cases where a purely domestic threat is involved. But it left unanswered the question of whether the president's "inherent powers" permits the use of warrantless wiretaps against foreign agents.⁸

The Department of Justice responded to the *Keith* decision by limiting warrantless wiretaps to only foreign intelligence matters. Liberal groups such as the ACLU parsed a victory from the muddled decision, pointing in particular to Justice Lewis F. Powell, Jr.'s, opinion:

> Different standards may be compatible with the Fourth Amendment if they are reasonable both in relation to the legitimate need of government for intelligence information and the protected rights of our citizens. For the warrant application

6. Jimmy Carter and Foreign Intelligence Surveillance

may vary according to the governmental interest to be enforced and the nature of citizen rights deserving protection.

When defending their position and condemning warrantless wiretaps, the ACLU maintained that neither the Court nor Congress nor any president in between had clarified the limits of presidential authority and wiretap jurisdiction. In fact, it was the Omnibus Crime Control and Safe Streets Act of 1968 that set the stage for the wiretap debates of the 1970s because the 1968 act did not fully resolve the issue of wiretap legislation, the standards for and judgment of wiretap warrants, and the extent of inherent presidential power to wiretap without warrants.[9]

In an ominous coincidence, two days before the Supreme Court announced its decision in *Keith*, five men were caught breaking into the Watergate Hotel in Washington, D.C., to repair illegal wiretaps on the Democratic National Convention headquarters. The nation progressively became more and more aware of the perils of wiretapping over the course of the next two years as the Watergate scandal unfolded. By August 1974, that scandal forced Richard Nixon's resignation and three months later Americans elected the "Watergate class" of legislators into Congress. These new legislators were elected on a mandate to undo the imperial presidency and prevent future Watergate–style debacles. In 1975, Senator Frank Church (D–ID) chaired the Senate Select Committee to Study Governmental Operations with Respect to Intelligence Activities. Tasked with conducting "an investigation and study of governmental operations with respect to intelligence activities and of the extent, if any, to which illegal, improper, or unethical activities were engaged in by any agency of the federal government," the eponymously nicknamed Church Committee deliberated for fifteen months before it released an extensive report on its findings in 1976.[10]

President Ford supported wiretap and intelligence surveillance reform but he struggled to turn his advocacy into action. Ford issued an executive order that restructured the management of intelligence agencies and began to set limitations on their jurisdiction: "I think a president ought to be accountable. And what we have sought to do in this case is to make the process and the decision-making fall on the shoulders of the president and he will be held accountable by the American people." Ford prohibited foreign intelligence agencies from the "collection of information, however acquired, concerning the domestic activities of the United States persons." However, Ford's executive order stipulated various exceptions—what critics would call loopholes—that allowed some surveillance to continue.[11] Ford followed up his executive order by coveting bipartisan support for a comprehensive foreign intelligence bill. S 3197, the Foreign Intelligence Surveillance Act (FISA) of 1976, required judicial authorization for surveillance. A sign of Ford's shortcomings, the bill never made it to a final vote in Congress.

Carter-Mondale '76—A Campaign Position

In the 1976 general election campaign, Governor Carter contrasted his resolve with Ford's attempts at wiretapping reform. Carter and his campaign staff worked hard to define a position that respected the legislative effort in Congress (or at least the members of Congress supporting it) while explaining why he would do better. Carter convinced members of Congress that wiretap legislation would fare better in a Carter administration than in a Ford one. The subject of intelligence reform allowed the Carter campaign to remind the voters subtly that neither he nor his party orchestrated Watergate or pardoned Nixon. Carter's running mate, Senator Walter Mondale (D–MN), was an outspoken critic of Ford's bill. His vocal record made him a natural mouthpiece for direct criticism of Ford's position. Mondale criticized the bill for failing to resolve two important issues, "inherent presidential power and requiring probable cause of criminal activity as a predicate to initiating electronic surveillance." Carter campaign team member Michael Mullen noted that both arguments "were key recommendations of the Church Committee and the Subcommittee on Domestic Intelligence, which Senator Mondale chaired." On issues of surveillance and intelligence, Mondale proved to be an excellent running mate.

Mondale often quoted James Madison (*Pubulis*) in *Federalist #51*, reminding voters that government is necessary since men are not angels. Mondale campaigned in opposition to a liturgy of abuses. For example, when speaking to the University of Missouri Law School on October 5, 1976, his nefarious list ranged from the CIA's "operation

6. Jimmy Carter and Foreign Intelligence Surveillance

CHAOS" (surveillance on American citizens) to IRS "Special Services Staff" ordered to selectively audit targets, to FBI and CIA "black bag jobs," to the worst of all, what the FBI called COINTELPRO:

> It meant illegal investigations targeted against law-abiding individuals and groups—and punishment administered not by a court, but by a government agency—through harassment and tactics designed to break up marriages, destroy reputations, terminate employment, sabotage political campaigns and even encourage violent retribution by falsely and anonymously labeling intended victims as government informers.

Under COINTELPRO, the FBI famously bugged, wiretapped, and conducted surveillance on Martin Luther King, Jr. Mondale spoke about how the FBI created a "Do Not File File" so that incriminating evidence was destroyed rather than filed, thus avoiding "flap potential," i.e., the chance that someone might get caught.

Mondale went on to talk about his time on the COINTELPRO Committee uncovering malicious knowledge of these activities by presidents, including Nixon. Mondale claimed that Nixon only objected to these unconstitutional measures because the public might find out, not because it was illegal. "President Nixon himself admitted that he had cancelled his prior approval of this plan—not because it was illegal—but because the risk of a leak to the press was too great." Mondale quoted Nixon,

> There has been and will be in the future circumstances in which presidents may lawfully authorize actions in the interests of the security of this country, which if undertaken by other persons or even by the president under different circumstances would be illegal.

Mondale argued this doctrine reduced the president's discretion to break the law to a matter of fiat. He dubbed it the "doctrine of inherent illegality," noting that, driven to the extreme, the doctrine condones murder. He cited an exchange during the Watergate hearings where Senator Herman Talmadge (D–GA) asked John Ehrlichman if murder was included in Nixon's rubric. Ehrlichman answered that he could not say for sure. In short, Mondale argued there had been a breakdown of the basic "principle of telling the truth and obeying the law." The Carter-Mondale victory, the Minnesota senator argued, would rein in these abuses; a Carter presidency would undo these abuses of power. Carter would roll back the imperial presidency.

Jimmy Carter and the Restoration of Presidential Dignity

Mondale conceded that while both parties were guilty of abuses, and while the Ford administration was not specifically to blame, there were instances where Ford and Bob Dole acted sympathetically to the Nixon administration. Mondale cited the two congressmen's support for the Saturday Night Massacre and Ford's efforts as minority leader to quash the initial Watergate investigation by the House Banking Committee. More bluntly, Mondale noted that Ford continued to defend Nixon to the bitter end: "Long after it was obvious to many members of his own party, as well as most of the American people, that the Nixon administration was obstructing justice." Mondale argued that the Ford administration failed to "heed the lessons of Watergate and the abuses of the intelligence agencies." Ultimately, Mondale framed Ford's pardon of Nixon as tying Ford's fate to Nixon's legacy.

Ford's bill required judicial warrants, but it contained a caveat allowing for exceptions in "unprecedented situations ... beyond the contemplation of Congress in passing this legislation" for the president to order wiretaps without consultation. Mullen objected to the vague phrase "unprecedented"; the broad caveat created the potential for abuse:

> In any event, two things are clear: first, there is no clear line to determine what constitutes an unprecedented situation, and lacking such a clear line, its meaning can be stretched and abuse can occur; and second, there is no reason ... for not seeking a judicial warrant, nor have any situations been suggested in which seeking a judicial warrant would frustrate the President's exercise of his duties.

The issue of presidential power addressed "whether or not the President has the inherent authority to conduct warrantless electronic surveillance overseas which is targeted against Americans." The Church Committee found that, in fact, the president did not have this authority. Typically, overseas wiretaps involve intercepting radio transmissions, a job that had traditionally been the purview of the National Security Agency (NSA). Muller concluded Carter should oppose the "unprecedented" clause and that overseas surveillance always be preceded by a judicial warrant.

The other main critique regarded "Congressional oversight." The language of the bill stated that Congress shall not be denied author-

6. Jimmy Carter and Foreign Intelligence Surveillance

ity or information, yet there is no language positively asserting their power. This had some in Congress frustrated. Mullen warned Carter "not raise this as an issue because it involves internal House-Senate politics." Carter's camp knew members of Congress wanted more oversight to check the attorney general's discretion, much to the chagrin of the Ford administration. The Carter camp tried to stay on the sidelines as much as possible.[12]

Similar to Mullen, Political Strategist Burt Wides critiqued Ford and his executive order:

> Consistent with a desire not to attack the president's or Levi's integrity, any criticism of the executive order, and other present polices of controlling the intelligence agencies can be couched in terms of needing controls for the next time of stress and for leaders who might be tempted in the future, rather than insisting we can't trust Levi and Ford now without more express, biding restraints.

Wides concluded that along with the SHAMROCK program, Ford's executive order would not have prevented or precluded the CHAOS or MERRIMAC programs either.[13] Wides ended by suggesting Carter might tactfully attack the order. He joked that Carter ought to say it was so "riddled with loopholes" one could "drive a Ford truck" through it.[14]

The ACLU also shaped Carter's position. The organization labeled Ford's bill a "sham," warning that it would not safeguard against invasions of privacy.[15] The bill (S 3197)—at the behest of the Department of Justice—left "room for an executive claim of 'inherent constitutional authority' to disregard the bill's limitations if a sufficiently serious situation should ever arise." The ACLU elucidated,

> The Church Committee was unequivocal in its treatment of claims of inherent executive authority. In its first two recommendations—those it felt of primary importance—it flatly denied the existence of any such power and condemned the pernicious effect, government lawlessness, that such a doctrine embraced. Yet S 3197 implicitly recognizes the possibility of the executive's power to ignore the law in the name of national security—a doctrine that should be resoundingly denounced rather than accepted through a stance of passive neutrality.[16]

The ACLU strongly opposed wide latitude clauses couched in National Security claims if it meant compromising the Fourth Amendment and other individual rights.

Jimmy Carter and the Restoration of Presidential Dignity

Governor Carter's Rhetoric Becomes President Carter's Actions

Eager to pick up where Ford left off, Carter moved quickly once in office to issue his own executive order while pushing for comprehensive reform legislation. Carter's order rescinded previous rules, effectively removing the questionable latitude afforded to past presidents in issues of foreign intelligence surveillance. Carter's stopgap measure created an oversight board to review intelligence gathering while Congress renewed its debate over comprehensive reform. Carter remained committed to transparency and comity. He cleared the way for substantive debate and effective change. Equally important, though his initial steps were an executive action, it was a legal presidential instrument that placed the power with Congress. Carter could have written his own rules but that was not his style.[17]

Reform advocates in Congress proved equally eager to resume discussions of how to improve surveillance oversight. By March 1977, Robert Kastenmeier (D–WI) had already sought out Attorney General Griffin Bell regarding wiretap bills. Kastenmeier intended to introduce a new and improved bill later on in the session but he wanted to work in conjunction with the Carter administration. The Wisconsin representative recommended that all wiretaps should require judicial warrants and he opposed "any statutory recognition of inherent presidential power to initiate [surveillance] outside the procedures established by law." He believed judges should be "empowered to evaluate the facts supporting any application for a warrant rather than simply being required to accept the governments certification as to those facts." As chair of the Judiciary Subcommittee on Courts, Civil Liberties, and the Administration of Justice, Kastenmeier had become an expert on wiretapping law. He noted the biggest obstacle to real reform stemmed from the White House. Nixon and Ford did not appreciate the reform he had in mind. Carter and his staff were more receptive.[18]

Carter's proposal incorporated the recommendations of cabinet members like Attorney General Griffin Bell, as well as members of Congress like Kastenmeier. House Judiciary Committee Chairman Peter Rodino (D–NJ) advised that the president and Congress:

6. Jimmy Carter and Foreign Intelligence Surveillance

> ... had to walk a fine line between assuring that [they] would be free from the abuses that [they] had seen in the past whereby the rights of individuals were violated, the constitutionally protected rights, and the responsibility of government to assure that it would be free from the terroristic attacks that we have seen from espionage and from the theft of information that is necessary for the security of our nation.[19]

Carter's proposal struck that balance. It provided oversight with deference, accountability with flexibility, leadership with comity. Carter's bill moved beyond Ford's bill, requiring "a judicial warrant for all electronic surveillance within the United States conducted for foreign intelligence purposes."[20] President Carter had the national stage and national momentum on this issue of intelligence reform while embracing comity and respect for his legislative counterparts and the constitutional separation of powers.

However, for all the efforts by Carter, Bell, and the rest of his administration, one scandal emerged that significantly undercut Carter's position of reconciliation. While the president pushed for congressional definition of inherent powers with regard to wiretapping and while Carter removed the claim to "inherent power" from the bill, Carter went ahead and authorized warrantless wiretaps in the investigation of Ronald Louis Humphrey and Truong Dinh Hung. Bill McAllister and Christopher Dickey of *The New York Times* reported the controversy:

> Carter personally approved of secret television surveillance of Humphrey, who worked in the U.S. Information Agency's tightly guarded operations center in Washington. The president also authorized the FBI to tap the private telephone and place a listening device in the apartment of Trueng [sic], a Vietnamese national whose father once ran for president of the Southeast Asian country before it fell to the Communists.[21]

Past administrations had asserted this as a right and privilege, but Carter made no such claim. He did, however, argue that while he has the power—i.e., before Congress passes legislation to the contrary—he should be able to use this power. *The Washington Post* added,

> [T]he executive branch insisted there was a constitutional difference between searches for intelligence data and those for evidence of a crime. And the White House, under Richard Nixon and Gerald Ford as well as earlier occupants, argued that every president has an inherent right to order whatever kind of surveillance he thought necessary to protect the national security. Although the Carter administration is still arguing in a current espionage case that presidents

Jimmy Carter and the Restoration of Presidential Dignity

have an inherent power to act on their own, it has withdrawn the Nixon-Ford insistence that Congress specifically recognize that power.[22]

In fact, this is precisely the strategy adopted by the Department of Justice:

> Every president since Franklin D. Roosevelt has asserted the power under Article II of the Constitution, to authorize warrantless electronic surveillance to protect national security from foreign powers or agents of foreign powers. Article II outlines some of the Executive Branch's powers to conduct the United States' relationships with foreign powers and to protect the security of the United States.[23]

Time magazine framed Carter's decision as a litmus test of the president's right. Carter wanted the courts to rule on whether or not the president had this discretion in wiretapping. On the other hand, Senator Ted Kennedy (D–MA) pointed out that "the recent prosecution against Humphrey and Trueng [sic] point out the need for this legislation."[24] Kennedy did not say Carter was wrong *per se*, but rather that he should not have the power.

Ultimately, the Department of Justice decided not to use the wiretap evidence in prosecution but maintained they could have if they wanted to.[25] By the letter of the law, the Department of Justice was in the right. However, the scandal emboldened reform proponents. After standing with and speaking after President Carter at the May 18, 1977, press conference, Senator Ted Kennedy (D–MA) introduced S 1566 into the Senate.

> The legislation, which has broad bipartisan support, requires that a judicial warrant be secured before the government may engage in electronic surveillance in the United States for purposes of obtaining foreign intelligence information. I view it as the first step in the ongoing effort of this administration and the Congress to place meaningful restrictions on the largely unchecked power of the intelligence community.[26]

Kennedy boasted that the bill reflected six years of efforts by himself, along with Senators Gaylord Nelson (D–WI) and Charles Mathias (R–MD). It improved upon Ford's bill that failed to reach a vote in the previous session. Kennedy said, "Unfortunately, despite this overwhelming show of support last year by two Senate committees, time ran out before the full Senate could act on the legislation." Kennedy added,

6. Jimmy Carter and Foreign Intelligence Surveillance

> [T]he legislation introduced today improves S. 3197 in a number of important respects. Most importantly, the bill repeals the so-called executive "inherent power" disclaimer clause currently found in Section 2511(3) of Title 18 of the United States Code, and provides instead that the statutory procedures of this legislation, and Title 18, "shall be the exclusive means" for conducting electronic surveillance in the United States.

Kennedy also noted that the bill strengthened executive branch certification oversight and encompassed the jurisdiction of the National Security Agency—two things the last bill did not do. Kennedy ended by noting that (Judiciary Committee) hearings were already set, implying the importance of the bill and momentum residual from last year's bill and present for this year's bill. Perhaps also, Kennedy wanted to emphasize—and make extra certain—that this year's bill did not run out of time before it could make its way through the natural progression of the legislative progress.[27]

Senators James Eastland (D–MS), John McClellan (D–AR), Gaylord Nelson (D–WI), Daniel Inouye (D–HI), Charles Mathias (R–MD), Birch Bayh (D–IN), and Strom Thurmond (R–SC) all joined with Senator Ted Kennedy (D–MA) as cosponsors of the bill. These Senators, in addition to being from different parties and ideological backgrounds, happened to also be the ranking members on the Judiciary Committee. Senators Walter Huddleston (D–KY) and Jake Garn (R–UT) were added the next day as cosponsors as well. That same day, Representative Peter Rodino (D–NJ) introduced the same bill in the House as HR 7308. Introduced with broad bipartisan support, the bills quickly went off to committees for review, including the newly created Permanent Select Committee on Intelligence (the permanent replacement for the Church Committee).

During the Judiciary Committee hearings, specifically the Subcommittee on Criminal Laws and Procedures, many members of Congress spoke their mind and many witnesses testified about various aspects of wiretapping and foreign intelligence surveillance. While interesting and relevant to the development of the legislation—and often telling important reminders about the perils of illegal surveillance and Watergate—the vast majority of these sentiments are beyond the scope of this discussion of presidential power. However, one issue that recurred throughout the debates, both on the floors of Congress and

Jimmy Carter and the Restoration of Presidential Dignity

in their hearings, was the notion of "inherent power." More broadly, members of Congress—and the administration officials that testified before them—dealt with the sticky situation of how to resolve cooperation and consultation between the branches after the nadir of the imperial presidency (Watergate) and forty years of foreign intelligence being the sovereign and inalienable inherent power of the president. Speaking in his opening statement about the difficult balance between the necessity of foreign intelligence and respecting rights and liberties along the way, Attorney General Griffin Bell noted:

> Past administrations and this administration have confronted this problem daily in dealing with particular cases without the aid of legislation to authorize what is proper, to prohibit that which is not, and to effectively draw the line between the two. This bill is the first step in what will be for me and many others a continuing effort to fill that void. We in the executive branch are well aware of the abuses of the past. Internal measures have been taken both by the prior administration and by this administration to assure that those abuses cannot recur.[28]

In light of this opening and this shift in attitude of the Carter administration, the following exchange between the ranking member of the Senate Judiciary Committee, Senator Strom Thurmond (R–SC), and Attorney General Griffin Bell takes on added significance. Rather than stonewalling members of Congress or peppering them with evasive answers, the nation's top lawyer engaged the senior Senator from South Carolina directly and with comity:

> **THURMOND:** Judge Bell, S. 1566 differs from last year's S. 3197—by eliminating an express reservation of the president's inherent powers to engage in electronic surveillance in matters outside the definition of electronic surveillance and, also, for matters that could not be reasonably said to have been within the contemplation of Congress. Is it your position that even though this language is deleted from the bill, the inherent presidential power is preserved as interpreted by the courts?
>
> **BELL:** Yes. Because we can't change the Constitution. But this is an accommodation between the legislative and executive branches of the government where the president has agreed that he will follow the provisions of this statute in matters inside the United States. I repeat: We can't change the Constitution by agreement.[29]

It is impressive that two members from opposite parties engaged in a cordial exchange. The issue of comity transcends party lines. Beyond partisanship, these two politicians engaged in a conversation that would have been unheard of five years earlier when the Supreme

6. Jimmy Carter and Foreign Intelligence Surveillance

Court's *Keith* ruling first broached the question of warrantless wiretaps. By extension, a conversation that would seem shocking during the Nixon administration would have been anathema any further back, all the way to the inception of that interpretation of inherent powers during Franklin Delano Roosevelt's administration. Indeed, Bell's comment represented a shift in the attitude of the White House and reified the Carter administration's commitment to cooperation and transparency.

Later in the hearings, another exchange ensued, further emphasizing this nuanced attitude toward openness that was one of the hallmarks of the Carter campaign and a theme of the Carter administration. Continuing the conversation and emphasizing that this issue should transcend party lines, Senator Ted Kennedy (D–MA), the second-highest-ranking majority member of the committee, put Bell in a position to deliver a gesture of openness and cooperation from the Carter administration:

> **KENNEDY:** We had in the bill last year that you would notify the Congress concerning the application of this bill.
> **BARON:** In this year's bill, Senator, we did not include the full range of reporting provisions that we had in last year's bill, feeling that it was presumptuous of the executive branch to lay out what the Congress did or did not need.
> **KENNEDY:** You have no objection to provisions which would require you to report to the Congress?
> **BELL:** We will be glad to report it.[30]

Attorney General Griffin Bell, along with Special Assistant to the Attorney General Frederick D. Baron, not only positioned the administration as willing and enthusiastic of cooperation and consultation but did so while simultaneously not dictating terms. In this exchange, Bell and Baron were harbingers of Carter's new attitude toward cooperation and an indication that Carter was beginning to find niches to turn election slogans and promises into legislative practice.

Later, during the Senate floor debate, Senator James Abourezk (D–SD) confirmed the change in attitude Carter ushered into the White House.

> For 40 years, Presidents have engaged in electronic surveillance for foreign intelligence purposes in the United States. Their common justification for these

Jimmy Carter and the Restoration of Presidential Dignity

activities has been some claimed "inherent constitutional power" which somehow superseded the warrant requirements of the fourth amendments.

Abourezk then concluded "if enacted today, S 1566 will end this pattern."[31] Bell and Carter emphasized that the administration was not defending the inherent powers doctrine and that they were willing to defer to Congress and the courts—or at least to consult with them. In both cases, this reflected Carter's commitment to Congress' desire to move away from the Watergate era of presidential-congressional relations and the imperial presidency's attitude toward expansive interpretations of inherent president powers, such as in the realm of foreign intelligence surveillance.

The bill emerged from Senate committee and made its way through the legislative process, passing on the floor ninety-five to one. As the bill made its way through the House, debate continued regarding the elimination of the inherent power clause in the bill. However, when the dust settled, the House passed its own version and the differences were quickly resolved.[32] President Carter signed the bill into law. Senators from both sides of the aisle—e.g., Kennedy, Bayh, and Thurmond—praised each other for their collaborative and cooperative efforts. This reflects bipartisanship, though many representatives—especially conservative Republicans who opposed limits on executive power—felt they were caving more than their Senate counterparts.[33]

In the early 1970s, between the revelations of Watergate and the *Keith* case, among other events, average Americans and politicians alike came to be aware of the perils of unchecked wiretapping and the abuse associated with foreign intelligence surveillance gathering. Richard Nixon brought the Watergate scandal upon himself, but his attitude toward foreign intelligence surveillance reflected a trend amongst presidents that dated back to Franklin Delano Roosevelt. This is precisely one of the trends of the "imperial presidency" about which Schlesinger cautioned.

However, Carter made great strides toward stymieing and, in fact, reversing this trend. Carter campaigned on a platform of openness and reform and continued to reform the presidency during his term in office. Speaking on the perils of Watergate and other wiretapping imbroglios, Carter's Attorney General Bell elucidated Carter's goal in a speech at the 1978 *Yale Law Journal* banquet:

6. Jimmy Carter and Foreign Intelligence Surveillance

> These revelations, through their shock to the national conscience, have produced a consensus among the Executive and Legislative Branches, as well as among the American people, that an effective and Constitutionally-sensitive control system must be developed to avoid any recurrence of this history. The Carter Administration took office committed to this goal.

In closing, Bell added, "It is our duty as Americans to demonstrate that we can conduct intelligence activity successfully and vigorously while maintaining absolute respect for our Constitutional commitment to individual rights. That is the spirit in which we are moving forward."[34] Bell touted the administrations' record on transparency in governance as well as cooperation and consultation with the other branches of government, especially Congress. These were qualities that had dissipated in previous years and in recent administrations.

However, while the majority of Congress and the American people understood the context of Carter's actions, there were those that felt Carter was giving up too much. For example, Representative Henry Hyde (R–IL) opined on the House floor that:

> President Ford was reacting to a deplorable situation in which he found himself following Watergate. As far as President Carter is concerned, I am really at a loss to understand his action except that he campaigned against the "imperial Presidency." I am certainly not defending the "imperial Presidency," but I am defending the institution. I think the President has constitutional duties that we ought not to take away from him.

Hyde's call for presidential discretion and constitutional privilege proved to be too tough a sell in post–Watergate America.[35] The 1978 Foreign Intelligence Surveillance Act systematically changed the way the American government—particularly the Department of Justice—conducted surveillance. The law revised the Omnibus Crime Control and Safe Streets Act of 1968 and was targeted to prevent future Watergate–type abuses of presidential discretion and authority.[36] The bill set up a "wall" between foreign and domestic surveillance, cracking down on the potential for abuse and preventing the recurrence of some of the most egregious dirty tricks of the Nixon administration and flamboyant incarnations of the imperial presidency.

Though Carter's successor, Ronald Reagan, issued his own executive orders, restoring a bit more of the Ford model of executive discretion, for almost thirty years, this bill was the standard for intelligence gathering.[37] However, in the wake of the September 11, 2001, attacks, the restrictions and limitations of FISA implemented in the 1970s to prevent abuse were now looked at as constrictive bureaucracy that impeded national defense. Whitfield Diffie and Susan Landau explain:

> FISA came under intense scrutiny after the attacks of September 11, 2001 because post-hoc consensus was that the civil liberties restrictions and bureaucratic complexities of the law prevented adequate surveillance and detection of the plot. This caused a change in the law. Now foreign intelligence need not be the *primary* reason for a FISA wiretap, merely a *significant* one. This change, along with rest of the USA PATRIOT Act package, emerged within six weeks after the September 11th attacks. Other amendments and modifications the way the FISA court handled wiretaps would come in 2002 in light of the enhanced focus on terrorism and the war on terror.

Initially, scrutiny after 9/11 focused on the law-enforcement branches and the agents themselves but recently there has been a revision to that conclusion, arguing that the bureaucracy set up under FISA to prevent abuse was to blame.[38]

In the wake of the attacks, public outrage over how the plot developed unnoticed by federal officers brought intense scrutiny on the means and regulation of foreign intelligence surveillance. Critics such as Lawrence White note that the intelligence community almost stumbled on the plot. FBI investigator Steve Bongardt, the agent who investigated the 2000 bombing of the USS *Cole*, had suspicions about al-Qaeda member Khalid al-Mihdhar. However, when Bongardt came to know in August 2001 that Mihdhar had entered American soil, he was ordered to "stand down" because the "wall" prevented FBI surveillance. Bongardt infamously exclaimed, "If this guy is in the country, it's not because he's going to fucking Disneyland." Weeks later, Mihdhar and four other men hijacked American Airlines Flight 77 and flew it into the Pentagon as part of the 9/11 attacks.[39]

In response to public outrage and law-enforcement frustration about the restrictive nature of the "wall" and the inadequacies exposed by recent terrorist acts (such as 9/11), President George W. Bush interpreted the outrage as a mandate for sweeping reform and promptly pushed for revisions to rules for intelligence gathering. From this platform, the USA PATRIOT Act of 2001 amended 1978's FISA.[40] Bush ensured that American intelligence agencies—e.g., the Central Intel-

6. Jimmy Carter and Foreign Intelligence Surveillance

ligence Agency and the National Security Agency—had wide latitude and broad discretion to pursue agents of terror and prevent future attacks. Nearly two decades after these attacks, the effectiveness of Bush's actions and the legacy of the USA PATRIOT Act are still being debated.[41]

7

Jimmy Carter and the Legislative Veto

Fighting an Encroachment on Federal Comity

When Herbert Hoover reorganized the federal government in 1929, he balanced his request for executive discretion with a concession. Calling for dramatic change, more power and deference to the presidency, and more discretion to the federal bureaucracy, as a compromise the president conceded to Congress the ability to nullify regulations by a one-house vote that was subject neither to approval of the other branch of Congress nor to presentation to the president for signature or veto. Thus, Hoover conceded to Congress the power to veto presidential action. At the time, Hoover acknowledged that this legislative veto represented a new check on presidential power. He believed it could be used in moderation and tolerated as a facet of the larger framework of federal checks and balances. When Franklin Delano Roosevelt took over the presidency in 1933, he viewed the legislative veto as a fair price for leeway in executive power. Preoccupied with consensus building and drumming up support for his New Deal, Roosevelt accepted Hoover's compromise.[1]

Though every president from Franklin Roosevelt to Lyndon Johnson dealt with legislative vetoes, their encounters remained infrequent and occasional. Political scientists Joseph Cooper and Patricia A. Hurley wrote that, "One of the most significant institutional developments in Congress during the past half-century has been the emergence of the legislative veto as a prime oversight weapon." However, as the arrogance and bravado of the imperial presidency peaked in the early

7. Jimmy Carter and the Legislative Veto

1970s under Richard Nixon, members of Congress fought back with the full arsenal at their disposal. This included a proliferation of legislative veto clauses as an exogenous check on federal power. Cooper and Hurley later noted that, in the 1970s, "use of the veto ... accelerated rapidly." Arthur John Keeffe similarly noted, "Congress fell in love with the device." Frustrated by the growing abuse of presidential power, the number of legislative veto clauses passed by congresses during Richard Nixon's presidency—including the Gerald Ford interregnum—was almost triple the number during the time of Lyndon Johnson. By 1970s, Congress had become so concerned with control that the bipartisan House leadership nicknamed the Ninety-Sixth Congress (1979–1981) the "Oversight Congress."[2]

Representative Elliott Levitas (D–GA) championed the device's cause in Congress, a crusade that earned him the nickname "Mr. Legislative Veto." One of the many freshman members of Congress—especially Democrats—of the "Watergate class," Levitas firmly believed additional congressional oversight would check abusive presidents and runaway federal regulations. Though only starting his second term when Carter took office, Levitas had already made a name for himself promoting the cause and sponsoring legislation, which in and of itself is impressive for a freshman representative. More than just voting for legislative vetoes, Levitas' adamant participation in the debate over the device reflects what Richard Hall calls "legislative participation," i.e., actively promoting an issue.[3]

Amidst the scandals of Watergate and the Vietnam War, Nixon proved unable to muster the political capital to fight the proliferation of legislative vetoes; his actions may have even contributed to the proliferation. Ford's pardoning of Nixon weakened his credibility in Congress, limiting his chances for reform. In this context, Jimmy Carter emerged as the first president with a real chance to walk back the congressional power grab. Elected in 1976 on a platform of government cooperation and government reform, and against the backdrop of the presidential sins of the last decade, Carter entered office with a clean slate and a desire to bring comity back to Washington.

Carter's efforts started small and cordially.[4] Initially, his opposition amounted to polite requests for alternate solutions and stern signing statements admonishing the legislative device. However, as the congressional debate over legislative vetoes stalled, Carter followed up with a sterner message, sent directly to Congress, presenting his case against legislative vetoes and why he felt they were unconstitutional. When this still failed to get movement from Congress, Carter's administration moved to outright defiance of the legislative veto authority. Carter's administration refused to acknowledge the authority of congressional rulings stemming from legislative vetoes. Carter demonstrated his prowess as a leader who would not be abused by Congress but would not use abusive tactics to achieve his goals. Carter's leadership laid a foundation for a constitutional challenge to legislative vetoes that culminated with the Supreme Court's 1983 ruling in *Immigration and Naturalization Service v. Chadha*.[5]

Constitutionalism

In December 1976, having secured victory in a close election against an incumbent president, the Carter-Mondale transition team moved quickly to get the president-elect apprised of the current status of a variety of issues. One of Vice President-Elect Walter Mondale's legislative assistants, Robert B. Barnett, helped out with various issues during the transition, including a profoundly influential memo about legislative vetoes. Barnett, a respected partner at the prestigious firm of Williams & Connolly, made a persuasive case as to why the incoming president ought to fight the device. Barnett emphasized that, no matter how "legalistic and intricate" the arguments may seem and how "minor and esoteric" the issue might appear, he assured the incoming administration that the issue was of the utmost importance. "You are not only making choices which will influence the success of your efforts to get reorganization authority from the Congress. You are also making choices which could restrict your ability to resist the inclusion of legislative veto provisions in future legislation." Barnett urged the incoming administration to take a hard stance against legislative vetoes, for their unconstitutional grounding, for the threat they represented to presidential prerogatives, and because they ran counter to Carter's plans to promote balance in government.[6]

The debate over the constitutionality of legislative vetoes reduces

7. Jimmy Carter and the Legislative Veto

to interpretations of two paragraphs of the United States Constitution (Article 1, Section 7, Clauses 2[7] and 3[8]). The founders defined the normal means by which bills—as well as orders, resolutions, and votes—are to be passed by both branches of Congress and presented to the president before they can be law. Barnett suggested—and the Carter administration adopted—an interpretation of the Constitution based on the original intent, arguing that normal means preclude the use of legislative vetoes. However, proponents of the device tended toward a looser and more progressive interpretation of the Constitution. Calling for judicial activism, they interpreted the Constitution more dynamically, not viewing the document as exclusively written. This clause and this debate eventually came to be at the heart of the Court's ruling in the *Chadha* case.

Moving beyond general descriptions of the history of the legislative veto and the segments of the Constitution from where the debate arose, Barnett summarily broke down the main constitutional arguments that backed his position. Most prominently, he argued that legislative vetoes violated the separation of powers envisioned by the framers. Barnett added that there are two tests to see if a law or action violates separation of powers. The first method is called the "Inherent Functions" test. The legislature passes the laws, the executive branch enforces the laws, and the judicial branch interprets the laws. By this standard, the legislative veto is unconstitutional because Congress is encroaching upon judicial authority to interpret law. By reserving the right to nullify, Congress is usurping judicial duty. Alternately, if it is to be viewed as oversight—extra regulation on executive agencies—then it is encroaching upon the executive branch's job to enforce the law as it sees fit. The second test to see if a law or action violates the separation of powers is the "balance of power" analysis. This test determines if the law or action seeks to shift power between the branches of government. Legislative vetoes reduce executive discretion to be "exercised only at the pleasure of the Congress." Normally, legislative acts are implemented by executive discretion constrained by the regulations established by the legislature. Congress takes over a role of the executive branch with legislative vetoes and hence its power is expanded at the executive branch's expense.[9]

Even if the legislative veto is defined as a legislative function, other problems arise. One-house vetoes invoke the bicameralism argument, while two-house vetoes invoke the veto clause argument. Citing the Connecticut Compromise that provided the United States with a bicameral legislature, Barnett presented the constitutional concept of bicameralism—that laws must be passed by both houses of Congress before they can become law. One-house vetoes allowed a single branch of Congress to act unilaterally, bypassing the Constitution. One-house acting—either to approve law or negate executive regulation—denies the other house its constitutional right to weigh in and perhaps negate the first house. Two-house vetoes respect bicameralism but still violate the veto (or presentment) clause as defined by Article I, Section 7 of the Constitution, i.e., that every law passed by Congress shall be presented to the president for approval or disapproval. Barnett noted that the presidential veto acted not to check "unwise legislation" but rather to check congressional encroachment on executive power. The framers envisioned veto power as presidential self-defense. Furthermore, the Constitution included no provision for transferring the power to veto. The veto power could be delegated to Congress and Congress could take legislative action without presenting it to the president for approval or disapproval.

Legislative vetoes allowed Congress to make laws that were untouchable by presidential action. Rather than have to resort to a two-thirds override, Congress retained power and avoids the threat of a presidential veto. The founders' intent of this clear-standing rule checking legislative power was further evidenced by the fact that the founders specified the only instances when exceptions can be made.

1. "The House of Representatives alone was given the power to initiate impeachments." (Article I, Section 2, Clause 5)
2. "The Senate alone was given the power to conduct trials following impeachment on charges initiated by the House and to convict following trial." (Article I, Section 3, Clause 6)
3. "The Senate alone was given final unreviewable power to approve or to disapprove Presidential appointments." (Article II, Section 2, Clause 2)
4. "The Senate alone was given unreviewable power to ratify treaties negotiated by the President." (Article II, Section 2, Clause 2)

7. Jimmy Carter and the Legislative Veto

The clarity and universality of any rule—including bicameralism and presentment—were strengthened when a limited set of exceptions were already defined. Legislative veto proponents' contention that the founders intended unicameral action to check federal regulation waned in light of the reality that the founders specifically outlined rules and exceptions to the contrary. The founders specified when their rule could be broken, and legislative vetoes were not one of those instances.

Barnett conceded that it could be argued that legislative vetoes were not traditional or constitutional legislative acts and therefore not confined or bound by the bicameralism or veto clauses. "Yet the policy decisions and legal consequences of a legislative veto are indistinguishable from the policy decisions and legal consequences of ordinary legislation." Barnett refuted the argument that legislative veto simply reversed the process of legislative action. He considered it a tough sell to equate congressional inaction with the deliberation and "detailed process" of congressional consideration that precludes any bill's vote.

Barnett balanced his legal and constitutional arguments with what he called "political and practical considerations." Often, presidents accepted legislative veto provisions attached to legislation that the president needed to be passed or that the president simply lacked the political capital to fight. Barnett also noted that members of Congress generally favored legislative vetoes, not only because they provided an exogenous check on presidential power but also because they allowed Congress to reassess legislation post-passage and post-implementation. Legislative vetoes, in other words, allowed legislative oversight to operate as a "fall-back" measure for Congress:

> With the legislative veto as a fall-back, oversight device, Congress need not undergo the often-painful process of anticipating contingencies, specifying boundaries, and controlling delegations of power. Because it can always use the legislative veto, Congress escapes the necessity for careful consideration of statutory enactments.

In essence, Barnett argued that legislative vetoes gave Congress a second bite at the apple, causing sloppy lawmaking and increased backlog. If Congress faced less pressure to get everything right the first time, Barnett predicted, there would be a growing deference to pass it first and fix it later. Subsequently, vaguely written bills would be passed, and members would actually spend more time monitoring existing regulations than they currently spent drafting and debating potential legislation.

Barnett's blueprint of how to confront this issue proved close to the strategy Carter later employed vis-à-vis legislative vetoes. For example, Barnett urged Carter to use "report-and-wait" clauses as a palpable alternative. Under this scenario, once adopted by the Carter administration, federal regulations were sent to Congress for comment before implementation. However, Congress could not unilaterally rescind actions once put in place. Ultimately, Barnett recommended that Carter do everything in his power to avoid legislative veto clauses. This included trading to get the clauses out of bills or acquiescing to other oversight mechanisms. He added that this give-and-take was easier in the Senate than in the House because of staunch legislative veto advocates like Levitas.

Further confirmation about the challenge Carter faced in Congress came a month after the new president took office. In February 1977, the Senate's Government Operations Report entitled "Study on Federal Regulation" devoted an entire chapter to the legislative veto issue. The report outlined the benefits of the provision, primarily citing excerpts by Levitas as evidence. For example, the report noted that,

> Proponents of the legislative veto argue that current oversight mechanisms are inadequate to control bureaucratic excesses. The veto mechanism is also needed, it is contended, because passing an act of Congress is too cumbersome and time consuming a tool to effectively control the regulatory bureaucracy.

The report also quoted Levitas as arguing that Congress was too lax with delegating legislative authority to the executive without guidelines. Elsewhere, Levitas added that legislative vetoes provide "the people, through their elected representatives, an input into and a control over the rules that govern their lives." He argued legislative vetoes put more regulatory control back into the hands of elected representatives and out of the hands of unelected bureaucrats. This refuted the accusation that legislative vetoes act as a fallback mechanism and lead to laxity in Congress. The report concluded that legislative veto provisions—as with any oversight mechanism, even ones used sparingly—could lead to better legislation. However, the report also concluded that legislative vetoes would most likely not solve laxity of delegation or advance more stringent regulations.¹⁰

Despite the one-man show defending the legislative veto, Levitas' arguments faced a strong bombardment in the committee's report from the arguments against the device. The report acknowledged the problems of the legislative veto, including the increased delay in the regulatory process and the increase in pressure on Congress. Agency records would matter less, and agencies would be discouraged from rulemaking. Even the Senate's own report acknowledged that there might be a substantial increase in congressional workload. The report concluded that, "the across-the-board legislative veto approach embodied in some proposals is undesirable. Equally undesirable is the routine addition of a Congressional veto to every bill that Congress considers." In general, the Senate Committee on Government Affairs and its chairman, Senator Abraham Ribicoff (D–CT), concluded the legislative veto may "[h]ave an adverse effect on the entire regulatory process." Ultimately, the report confirmed Barnett's findings and his prediction that legislative vetoes had stronger support in the House than in the Senate.¹¹

Early Battles

In 1977, as Carter settled into Washington, when initially confronted with legislative veto clauses Carter reacted with calm, and a complacency that would evaporate later on in his term of office. HR 186, "A bill to implement the Convention on the International Regulations for Preventing Collisions at Sea," best demonstrates this initial spirit. On July 12, 1977, when the bill came to the House floor, bill sponsor Representative John Murphy (D–NY) moved to pass and implement the bill, including a section allowing for a legislative veto. "HR 186 preserved Congressional participation in this process while still expediting adoption of regulation revisions through the mechanisms of a legislative veto, here in the form of a concurrent resolution initiated by either House." Representative Mario Biaggi (D–NY) noted that President Gerald Ford had pocket-vetoed this bill when it was last proposed on account of a one-house veto clause. Murphy proposed

Jimmy Carter and the Restoration of Presidential Dignity

a concurrent resolution this time in hopes of preventing future presidential vetoes. His efforts paid off. These were the only two people to speak on the bill and their speeches only lasted twenty minutes. It breezed through votes in both chambers and four days later it went to the president for approval.[12]

On July 28, 1977, Carter signed HR 186 into law, but in a signing statement, he expressed "clear constitutional reservations" about a section of the law that allowed "Congress, by concurrent resolution, to disapprove a proposed amendment to the convention." Carter added that he believed this provision "may violate" Article I, Section 7 of the Constitution. By using a presidential signing statement, Carter respectfully criticized congressional methods for legislative oversight while not rejecting what he considered to be an otherwise strong bill. Intent to try and put comity before conflicts, Carter tried at every turn to exhaust cordial means to thwart the use of legislative vetoes. However, patience would only go so far.[13]

By his second year in office, Carter recognized the adamancy of Congress—especially the House—on the legislative veto issue. Carter began to fight back with more tenacity and fervor. Moving beyond subtle and polite commentary, the White House began actively campaigning to quash legislative veto legislation. On March 23, 1978, Assistant Attorney General John M. Harmon sent a memo to White House Counsel Robert Lipshutz and Chief Domestic Policy Advisor Stu Eizenstat noting that on February 23, 1978, "Mr. Legislative Veto"—Elliot Levitas—introduced HR 11112 that would require all rules to be submitted to Congress for review. It would add a legislative veto clause to every bill. Determined to be the champion of the legislative veto in Congress and in the eyes of the press, this bill encapsulated Levitas' "crusade" to make every rule subject to the device. As with past bills, the Carter administration objected. The consensus in the West Wing remained that the bill was unconstitutional; it violated Article I, Section 7. Harmon argued that the likely congressional support for the bill created a "concomitant need for an early Administration response." He worried the bill would delay the legislative process, decrease public participation, and distort the relationship between rulemaking and judicial review of rulemaking.[14]

Three weeks later, on April 13, 1978, Domestic Policy Staff (DPS)

7. Jimmy Carter and the Legislative Veto

Associate Director for Government Reform Simon Lazarus sent a memo to Office of Management and Budget (OMB) Deputy Director Bo Cutter and Executive Associate Director Harrison Wellford regarding Harmon's memo, soliciting their thoughts as the administration formulated its response. Given how much Levitas' bill presented a "continual source of vexation" for them all, Cutter replied with a memorandum from OMB Assistant Director for Budget Review Dale McOmber, arguing that legislative vetoes "would impose an enormous burden on both the Congress and the President." Congress would have a barrage of added issues, thousands of regulations and rules to pass judgment on annually. Meanwhile, the president would need to be ready to fight Congress on each and every issue should the legislature so desire. On the other hand, he conceded that if Congress saw the sheer volumes of regulations out there, they might have second thoughts about passing some of the bureaucracy. He concluded that Levitas must be convinced to drop the legislative veto clause for an alternative form of legislative oversight.[15]

Though HR 11112 never reached a vote on the floor, another bill made it much further through the legislative process. In addition to trying to push the legislative veto as an independent bill granting universal oversight, as a second option and a compromise, Levitas pursued legislative veto clauses as amendments to other bills. On January 24, 1978, Levitas pushed hard for the legislative veto to be retained when HR 3816, the Federal Trade Commission Amendments of 1978, went to conference, noting that the legislative veto amendment had passed in the House by a 2–1 majority.[16]

Four days later, DPS General Counsel Richard Neustadt sent a memorandum to Stu Eizenstat, incoming OMB Director Jim McIntyre, and Congressional Liaison Frank Moore regarding the status of HR 3816. He predicted that the bill would likely leave conference without a legislative veto and at worst a thirty-day report-and-wait clause. McIntyre responded, expressing the views of his agency on HR 3816. His concerns with the Senate-passed bill focused on substantive issues, while his concern with the House-passed bill centered on inclusion of a legislative veto statute. McIntyre expressed opposition to the provision for its violation of Article I, Section 7. The bill made no provision for presidential veto or other checks on congressional action.[17]

Jimmy Carter and the Restoration of Presidential Dignity

On February 9, 1978, Neustadt reported to Eizenstat, McIntyre, and Moore that they were successful and HR 3816 left conference without any legislative veto language.[18] However, while Neustadt knew that his staff, along with the help of members of Congress such as Representative Robert Eckhardt (D–TX), kept the legislative veto out of the conference report, Levitas would likely still try to reinsert the clause when the bill returned to the floor. Both Eckhardt and Neustadt called upon the leadership to block Levitas, noting that the Senate would stand firm in their position (keeping the legislative veto clause out of the bill) and that Carter would veto the bill if it came to him with a legislative veto. Irwin B. Arieff reported in *Congressional Quarterly* that the legislative veto provision "dogged" the Federal Trade Commission (FTC) bill throughout House debate. Elsewhere, *Congressional Quarterly* reported the strong indication that Carter "would veto the bill if it contained the legislative veto provision."[19]

While Levitas did reintroduce a legislative veto clause amendment, he offered what he considered a compromise. Not prepared to concede defeat, on March 6, 1978, Levitas switched his plans (though Simon Lazarus called it more of an "ambush"), converting his one-house veto into a veto by joint resolution. The catch is that the president can veto joint resolutions. Lazarus explained,

> Hence, this resolution would give the legislative veto nuts on the Hill a significant piece of what they want, but satisfy Justice's constitutional anxieties about protecting the veto power (and in the process, give the President new power over the independent agencies, or at least this particular one).

The one-house veto now became a two-house veto. Lazarus' memo touted the differences of this incarnation, such as how it expedited challenges and prevented a single branch of Congress from subverting regulations.[20]

Beyond his changed plans, Levitas also realized that he should avoid direct conflict with the White House. The congressman requested a sit-down with Neustadt and Eizenstat to try and reach a compromise. On March 22, 1978, Levitas vetted his compromise bill with these three elements: (1) a one-house veto (with the potential for override from the other house); (2) report-and-wait provisions for some executive agencies; and (3) a sunset provision for the whole bill after three to five years. Levitas argued that the president currently

7. Jimmy Carter and the Legislative Veto

had no control over independent regulatory commissions and hence this change would not be a loss of power. Furthermore, Levitas said he would not accept the bill without a one-house veto. However, Neustadt informed Levitas that FTC counselors Michael Pertschuk and Michael Sohn stood firmly against the idea, stating they would rather lose the improvements in HR 3816 than accept a legislative veto.[21]

Though the meeting was both respectful and cordial, it was clear that neither side planned to budge. Deference to federal comity requires the respectful interaction between the branches of government but not necessarily a confluence of opinions. In a follow-up memo, Neustadt explained why Levitas' compromise solution should be rejected. He felt the legislative veto clause would be counterproductive, causing deadlock and legislative logjam. Also, should Carter sign into law any incarnation of a legislative veto, it might impair any future efforts by the administration to pursue their legal challenges.[22]

As the bill came up for final debate and vote in September, Neustadt told Eizenstat to warn the leadership that, though not a major piece of legislation, the FTC bill might be vetoed. Neustadt also convened a meeting with FTC, Justice, and others to discuss the FTC bills impending return to the floor.[23] On September 6, 1978, Pertschuk asked Neustadt if the president or vice president would call Levitas about the FTC authorization conference report (slated for House action the following week). Pertschuk thought that Levitas would go along with the conference report if he received a call from a "high-level person" from the White House. However, Neustadt told Pertschuk that in light of the president's obligations and seclusion at Camp David, such a scenario might not be possible but that he would try to get Eizenstat to make the call instead.[24]

The conference report passed the Senate without debate, but as the Carter administration expected, the same could not be said of the reports' fate in the House. Representative Robert Eckhardt (D–TX) argued that, despite Levitas' best efforts, even the Senate rejected across-the-board legislative vetoes. Eckhardt pushed for what he saw as an acceptable compromise—both houses vote, and presidential signature is required. He argued that, without compromise, no bill would pass and hence no oversight at all. This was the same Eckhardt who—in line with the administration—tried to get all legislative veto language out of the bill. Hence, his compromise, complete with presentment to the president, read more like a victory for the Carter administration. Representative Henry Waxman (D–CA) concurred, rationalizing that a compromise beats no bill and hence no FTC oversight at all. Representative Don Edwards (D–CA) added that while he had reservations about the legislative veto from a policy standpoint, he considered the compromise a fair middle ground. "I support this provision, because it is a fair compromise between the strong positions of the two Houses and, most important, because I believe it is constitutional, unlike the so-called 'one-House veto.'" These members saw this diminutive legislative veto as a middle ground between Levitas and Carter.[25]

Countering Eckhardt's compromise solution and siding with Levitas, Representative Henson Moore (R–LA) defended the legislative veto on different grounds, arguing that the vote came down to whether or not members of Congress supported "regulatory reform and a strong legislative veto." Those who did would vote against compromise and those who were not concerned would vote for it. He argued that the compromise represented a restatement of the *status quo.* If the point of the bill is to resolve problems with the *status quo,* then passing a do-nothing bill seems useless. The chairman of the full committee, Representative Harley Staggers (D–WV), flipped Moore's critique, suggesting that if the bill was the *status quo,* there was no reason not to pass it. Moore responded by noting that this bill is designed to give a check on the FTC just as the Congress currently checks the president. Put bluntly, he added,

> But I have a sneaking suspicion, from what many of you have said in the last few months, that we have got to get a control of the bureaucracy, and the mindless regulations which come out of there have to be controlled by elected representatives responsible to the people. Now is your chance. You can put up or shut up, or maybe get out.

Moore's rejoinder reflected the subtle genius of Eckhardt's compromise. By presenting an alternative that has all the symbolism of congressional oversight but none of the constitutionally questionable teeth of Levitas' amendment, Eckhardt allowed members to vote for oversight while still endorsing a bill they knew Carter might actually sign. Eckhardt's compromise mitigated the encroachment on presidential power represented by Levitas' amendment.[26]

7. Jimmy Carter and the Legislative Veto

Ultimately on a vote of 174 to 214 (with thirty-four not voting), the House rejected the conference report. The Carter administration stood its ground and rallied enough support in Congress to carry its position on the legislative veto. Carter's efforts on the legislative veto resulted in a definitive victory without sacrificing his moral authority. Carter took strong stands and acted commandingly, yet he did so in a way that respected Congress and the Constitution.[27] Carter followed up on these victories in 1978 with an even clearer statement of opposition to legislative vetoes. In June of that year, Carter sent a formal message to Congress presenting his case against the contested device.

Message to Congress

Amidst the continued debate over the legislative veto and especially due to Levitas' universal legislative veto bill (HR 11112), by April 1978, Carter and his White House staff realized a clear yet firm stance needed to be transmitted to Congress outlining his views and his administration's formal position on legislative vetoes. As Neustadt and other White House staffers met to begin to work out the details, they realized that the gesture could only succeed if they proceeded with caution and invited frequent consultation from Congress. This mindset tied directly to the larger attitude of the White House. Even when taking a harsh and divisive stance, respect for the legislative body of government and its members remained crucial. Though this logic may sound ubiquitous in politics, the imperial presidencies of years past defied this rule and spurned cooperation. For example, Neustadt told Congressional Liaison Bill Cable to set up a meeting with Speaker of the House Tip O'Neill (D–MA) to discuss the administration's plan. Beyond being the leader and the most powerful Democrat in the House of Representatives, O'Neill represented the epitome and prominent face of the northern liberal Democratic contingent. Meetings with O'Neill and various other Washington insiders begat early drafts of the speech. Neustadt called for suggestions and advice from anyone and everyone in the White House and Congress. He knew that if this message did not come across exactly as designed, it might destroy Carter's political capital in Congress.[28]

Jimmy Carter and the Restoration of Presidential Dignity

The next week, Office of Legal Counsel Attorney-Advisor Larry Simms sent a memo to Lipshutz and Eizenstat with his draft of the memorandum for the president. Endorsing a formal statement outlining the president's views on legislative vetoes, he supported the idea of sending a message to Congress because the administration's policy needed to be clearly established in a way that could be "uniformly implemented by all agencies of the Executive Branch which are subject to your control." Simms and Lipshutz also contributed suggestions, arguing that the message should lay out the constitutional objections to the legislative veto, yet also recognize "the legitimate interest Congress has in oversight of executive branch activities." Beyond making the case for why he objected to legislative vetoes, they suggested Carter needed to define a universal response that he could apply to all current and future legislative veto bills. While noting that the presidential veto was often a useful tool in subverting legislative vetoes, they suggested the more respectful alternative was that the president push for "report-and-wait" provisions and joint resolutions, which were, in and of themselves, subject to presidential veto.[29]

By June, the message—still in draft form—began to take shape. Commenting on the draft, Harmon gave the following recommendation to Neustadt and Eizenstat: "We recommend that any Presidential statement be of general applicability rather than oriented towards a specific piece of legislation such as the Housing and Community Development Amendments of 1978. We see no need for the President to speak definitively more than once on this issue."[30] This comment was matched by many others, though perhaps none more poignant than one from Attorney General Griffin Bell. Bell sent a handwritten note to Neustadt with pointed concern about the language of the latest draft of Carter's speech and how it would fit in with his larger political message.

Rick—

If our objective really is "to work together to restore trust between the branches" (p. 6), I question whether we are wise to take such a hard line against the legislative veto, which is the only realistic mechanism Congress has to restrain bureaucratic abuses in an age of Administrative Law.

That is an objection to our policy. The other main objection I have on this is the unpersuasiveness of saying these vetoes are bad because they are such an imposition on Congress (pp. 3, 5). If Congress thought they were an imposition they wouldn't enact them, and they don't need JC to tell them that.

7. Jimmy Carter and the Legislative Veto

> I've edited the draft, which, considering the policy framework Stu apparently wants to pursue, seems OK to me. I did dig up a surviving draft from the work I did on this last December, which I pass along just for your information in case there is something in it you want to use.
>
> Cheers—
> Griffin[31]

Bell laid out one of the largest gambles of the message to Congress. He bluntly told his friend and colleague that Carter could not afford to appear as being discourteous or disrespectful to Congress. Carter wanted to get his point across, but he did not want to burn bridges, and he knew support in Congress would neither be automatic nor universal.

By mid–June, Neustadt sent Eizenstat a revised draft of the message to take to the president, reflecting input and changes from a myriad of outside sources.

> The message incorporates comments from Congressional Liaison, NSC, W.H. Counsel, the speechwriters, and Justice. Frank Moore's people have run the main points by the House and Senate leadership and the Judiciary Committee chairmen, and I checked it with Muskie. None of them have any objections.

The former vice-presidential candidate Senator Edmund Muskie (D–ME) was a trusted voice in the Carter administration. In fact, in 1980 Muskie replaced Cyrus Vance as secretary of state while Carter campaigned for reelection. After seeing the draft, Carter wrote back to Eizenstat regarding this draft noting, "ok—on a message to Congress the language should be more formal—'Violation of historical precedent' not adequately emphasized." At every step of this process, White House leaders and staff solicited congressional advice and respected congressional dignity in an effort to ensure Carter's message reflected the larger good government goals of his administration. Carter recognized what Griffin Bell and others were saying. This was a moment for Carter to tell Congress and the nation his position, but it was also a time to connote clear signs of respect. The entire nation was an audience to his speech. Better they should hear the commanding yet respectful speech of their leader than the arrogant and forceful tirade of an imperial president.[32]

Given the nature of Carter's impending letter, it is an even greater testament to Carter's commitment to federal comity that his staff took great efforts to get the opinion of the chief legislative veto proponent, Representative Elliott Levitas (D–GA). Of course, consultation does not guarantee support. On June 20, 1978, after meeting with Levitas, Eizenstat reported what was to be expected: that Levitas "does not agree with the thrust of the message and would prefer that we at least exclude independent regulatory agencies from its coverage." Eizenstat reminded the president that they do not agree with this exclusion. Levitas asked to meet or speak with Carter personally but the president declined. While Carter meant no disrespect to the member of Congress, he knew what the legislator planned to say, and he had heard it before.[33]

After all the revisions and consultations, Carter delivered his message to Congress on June 21, 1978. Carter accepted stronger and more proactive congresses. He respected their level of engagement but called for constructive—and more constitutional—use of their efforts. Laying out his views on the legislative veto, he encouraged his congressional counterparts to pursue other means for oversight, ones that resided more clearly within the constitutional separation of powers and the purview of federal comity.

> In recent years, the Congress has strengthened its oversight of Executive Branch decisions. I welcome that effort. Unfortunately, there has been increasing use of one oversight device that can do more harm than good—the "legislative veto." This proliferation threatens to upset the constitutional balance of responsibilities between the branches of government of the United States. It represents a fundamental departure from the way the government has been administered throughout American history.

Carter briefly told his audience the history of legislative vetoes and how they had come into greater use in recent times. However, Carter cautioned Congress against treating legislative vetoes as panaceas for past presidential sins.

> The desire for the legislative veto stems in part from Congress' mistrust of the executive, due to the abuses of years past. Congress responded to those abuses by enacting constructive safeguards in such areas as war powers and the budget process. The legislative veto, however, is an overreaction which increases conflict between the branches of government. We need, instead, to focus on the future. By working together, we can restore trust and make the government more responsive and effective.

He welcomed congressional oversight and encouraged Congress to keep working toward the constitutionally dictated separation of pow-

7. Jimmy Carter and the Legislative Veto

ers, no more and no less. Carter nevertheless maintained, "It is my view, and that of the Attorney General, that these legislative veto provisions are unconstitutional."[34] Carter added that legislative vetoes actually slow the pace of reform because they overburden an already full congressional agenda.

Carter proposed a conciliatory and congenial "report-and-wait" alternative to legislative vetoes. Respecting Congress and the Constitution, Carter offered solutions and alternatives, not just rejections and defiance.

> I urge Congress to avoid including legislative veto provisions in legislation so that confrontations can be avoided. For areas where Congress feels special oversight of regulations or other actions is needed, I urge the adoption of "report-and-wait" provisions instead of legislative vetoes. Under such a provision, the Executive "reports" a proposed action to Congress and "waits" for a specified period before putting it into effect. This waiting period permits a dialogue with Congress to work out disagreements and gives Congress the opportunity to pass legislation, subject to my veto, to block or change the Executive action. Legislation establishing "report-and-wait" procedures has been introduced. Even these procedures consume resources and cause delays, however, so they should be used sparingly.

Carter came to office to restore the balance of power. True to his nature and his campaign promises, Carter's message to Congress reflected his overall persona and larger political message. Even when Carter felt the need to send a stern and formal message to Congress, the thirty-ninth president made every effort to do so in a way that conveyed dignity and respect.[35]

The day after the message went to Congress, Neustadt told Eizenstat to follow up to help prevent a row with Congress over the message. This included communication with the congressional liaison, Frank Moore, and a media blitz, in an attempt to get articles printed in *The Washington Post* or *The New York Times* that crystallized Carter's perspective and downplayed any friction. He also suggested that Eizenstat attend the Friday legislative liaison meeting to urge lobbyists to discuss the issue with the representatives with whom they work. Neustadt added, "A massive lobbying effort is needed because the issue will be decided on the House floor."[36] Neustadt's follow-up campaign won an early victory when Speaker of the House Tip O'Neill (D–MA) concurred with Carter that Congress overstepped its bounds in its pursuit of legislative veto provisions. Responding to Carter's message to Congress, the leader of the House of Representatives did not officially endorse Carter's message, but he conceded that in some instances, Congress overstepped congressional duties.[37]

Too savvy to leave Carter's position to sell itself, White House staff took extra precautions to make sure the messages' meaning resonated clearly and to the right people. Neustadt knew he needed to win the perception battle to win the legislative veto war. However, despite Carter's message and the best efforts of Neustadt and other White House staff, legislative veto oversight clauses persisted in Congress, prompting the administration to resort to more drastic tactics.

GEPA (General Education Provisions Act)

The Department of Education (DOE)—formerly the Office of Education (OE)—became the first federal agency to be subjected to the congressional oversight of a legislative veto. By 1980, the cordial debate over education policy oversight devolved into defiance and a political showdown. Carter tried to be amicable and steer Congress toward alternate oversight solutions but when members became adamant about exercising their legislative veto power, Carter and his administration reacted with stronger tactics. On May 4, 1980, the newly created DOE officially assumed control of education regulations (including those dictated by GEPA), and just two weeks later Congress vetoed four of the new agencies' regulations (two on May 15th and two on May 21st).[38]

On June 5, 1980, Attorney General Benjamin Civiletti sent a memorandum to the newly empowered Secretary of Education Shirley Hufstedler. Her office had only been created the previous year and she had assumed bureaucratic control a month earlier.[39] Despite the recent congressional vetoes of GEPA regulations, and for a long list of logistic and constitutional reasons, Civiletti concluded that Hufstedler was "entitled to implement the regulations in question in spite of Congress' disapproval." GEPA, as amended, gave Congress the right to disapprove (veto) federal regulations. In this case, Congress revoked four federal regulations. The head of the Department of Justice explained

7. Jimmy Carter and the Legislative Veto

to the head of the Department of Education why it was administration policy to ignore the congressional action respectfully but willfully.

The attorney general cited the same constitutional arguments presented previously by White House staff and discussed elsewhere in this chapter. Civiletti told Hufstedler that the administration did not recognize this right as legitimate and hence the regulations should still be treated as in full effect. The attorney general told the secretary of education to disavow the congressional decision. Respecting the balance of power was not always the same as respecting Congress. In this case, Congress had stretched its power too far. Civiletti added,

> ... to regard these concurrent resolutions as legally binding would impair the executive's constitutional role and might well foreclose effective judicial challenge to their constitutionality. More important, I believe that your recognition of these concurrent resolutions as binding would constitute an abdication of the responsibility of the executive branch, to preserve the integrity of its functions against constitutional encroachment.

Despite previous cordial efforts by Carter to pursue alternative oversight mechanisms and the fact that there were court cases then under review challenging the constitutionality of the legislative veto, Congress insisted on continuing to exercise a power it knew would cause political strife. On this issue, members of Congress placed a desire to check presidential power above a desire for a balance of power. Unwilling to compromise and rather than wait for judicial rulings, Congress proceeded with its questionable measures.[40]

The next day, Hufstedler drafted a memorandum to her assistant secretaries regarding recent congressional activity and forwarded the letter she received from the attorney general. She informed her assistants that, despite congressional disapproval of Education Department regulations, in concurrence with the president and the attorney general, said regulations would still be treated as "final and effective rules." Hufstedler tried to balance this harsh stance toward Congress by adding that despite this situation, the executive branch and the Education Department would continue to respect congressional opinion when said input referenced flaws or imperfections in departmental policy.

Civiletti's memo read like a history lesson on the legislative veto and might be perceived as redundant had Hufstedler not been so recently appointed to her new post. However, the clear and certain terms by which Hufstedler was told to ignore that the congressional action mattered more than the memorandum's tone. These sentiments were reiterated in the July 1980 edition of *Federal Focus,* the "interpretative report for school administrators on federal education programs," reiterating the general statement made by the attorney general that no matter their form, all legislative vetoes were unconstitutional. Quoting the memo to Hufstedler, "I believe that your recognition of these concurrent resolutions as legally binding would constitute an abdication of the responsibility of the Executive Branch." If actions are not subject to presidential approval or veto, then they are outside the boundaries of the Constitution.[41]

Later that month, Hufstedler sent a memo to the president laying out the course of action she—in concert with White House Counsel Lloyd N. Cutler and Civiletti—believed best. She noted that when she followed the attorney generals' recommendation to ignore the congressional decisions, she received much criticism for an "arrogant defiance of legitimate congressional powers." However, while she did not propose any action that would undermine the administration's position in the fight with Congress, she suggested middle ground on the affected DOE regulations that "reflect our sensitivity to specific Congressional objections to the technical features of these … regulations." Her suggestions respected congressional input but in no case overtly deferred to it. Carter approved.[42]

This conflict came to a face-to-face showdown on September 18, 1980, when the House Committee on Education and Labor's Subcommittee on Elementary, Secondary, and Vocational Education held a hearing to vet all sides of this confrontation. The subcommittee convened the entire hearing solely to discuss this application of GEPA Section 431. As written, it allowed Congress to "disapprove final regulations for education programs, within 45 days of publication and transmission, if Congress finds they are inconsistent with the authorizing statute." Specifically, the subcommittee convened the hearing to discuss the four disapproved regulations that had come into controversy. The members of the subcommittee sought to "provide a forum for a discussion of the status of these four specific sets of regulations and also the general issue of congressional disapproval of regulations."

7. Jimmy Carter and the Legislative Veto

Though only a day long, it provided ample time for all sides to voice their opinion and answer to congressional inquiry.[43]

Representative William Goodling (R–PA)—a member elected in the wake of Watergate, like Levitas—asked Harmon if his bosses, the attorney general and the president, were "seeking a court test." Harmon replied that there was a case—with congressional representation—currently awaiting verdict from the Ninth Circuit. He clarified that the administration sought a ruling but not a confrontation.[44] Freshman Representative Arlen Erdahl (R–MN) continued, asking Harmon if the administration sought to deny congressional power, "Unless I misheard you, you seem to say that since Congress delegated the power, we do not have the right to come back and reclaim it. In layman's terms, once the cat has escaped from the bag, we in the Congress can't stuff it back in again." Harmon replied that the administration recognized the congressional power to reconsider and redo legislation but that this power is restricted to constitutional means including, amongst other things, presentment to the president for approval. He argued that the president and his delegate—in this case the secretary of education—have an obligation to apply the law as passed by Congress. If an individual disagrees with a law, they can take the secretary to court and if the Congress disagrees with a law, it can write new superseding laws. He concluded that those are the only legitimate ways to oppose the secretary's actions.

Despite Harmon's frank and crisp answer, Representative William Ford (D–MI) disagreed with this interpretation, arguing the legislative veto was only another check in the founder's vision of checks and balances.

> You are fascinating me with that kind of argument. What you're saying would sound really great at a cocktail party. It doesn't make any sense in this city, because a lot of things have happened since Mr. Madison did his writing. The balance of power between the branches of government exists with checks.

Ford argued that Harmon erred when he and the president believed that Levitas "had invented something new" when he presented the legislative veto as a clause in congressional legislation. The Michigan congressman concluded that Harmon, Civiletti, and Carter all misinterpreted the Constitution and "what Madison really meant." He argued that the provision sought to check executive regulations that distort the congressional intent of legislation, a practice he noted that happened all too often during the Nixon administration.⁴⁵

Representative Ford conceded that the GEPA legislative veto manifested as a reaction to Nixon's imperial tendencies. "We threw the regulation review amendment at a President when he was under threat of being impeached and he accepted it when he was asserting executive privilege for everything you could possibly imagine." He argued that, since the law took effect, three succeeding congresses came to accept the rule as their own—and not just as "Mr. Levitas' baby." Ford further purported that the DOJ had long since accepted the clause before this fight. He argued that oversight regulation is like atomic weapons. In both cases, the threat of use served as a sufficient deterrent. In his view, the clauses prevented (rather than incited) conflict. To this end, Ford questioned how resistance to legislative vetoes reconciled with Carter's larger "good government" approach. Ford accused the president, who campaigned on a platform of good government and federal comity, of picking fights that eschewed the opposite image.⁴⁶

Following the DOJ case made by Harmon, Levitas, Mr. Legislative Veto himself, issued a prepared statement and then testified. Levitas thanked the committee for the opportunity to speak, noting that he had previously spoken often with the attorney general, the president, and Harmon. He also commended Ford and his committee for taking the lead in "the practical utilization of this mechanism." Levitas proceeded to deny the premise of the Carter administration's constitutional question. He argued that the issue was not one of constitutionality or legality. He argued that because a president had signed the clause into law it was not the prerogative of any president—the same or future—to decide not to obey said law.⁴⁷

The final major witness provided a rejoinder for the White House position. The secretary of education, Shirley Hufstedler, issued a statement and then spoke extemporaneously on the subject. Her interrogation revolved mostly around her willingness to work with Congress and ways to avoid future confrontations. The conversations dealt with the legislative veto, but they dealt more with the general understanding of the DOE relationship with the Committee on Education. Hufstedler responded to the claim that this issue was dropped on her doorstep.

7. Jimmy Carter and the Legislative Veto

> It would have been a fine and happy day if I hadn't been confronted within 10 days after the Department was formed, finding myself in the middle of a long-time constitutional match, to use—and I don't mean it at all frivolously—I was just flying by and suddenly found out I was the birdie in the middle of a constitutional badminton game which is a little unnerving.[48]

Though technically the defiance was her action, and though she supported Carter's position, her testimony minimized her role in the imbroglio. She framed the debate as a battle between Congress and the White House (via the DOJ), where the DOE was just a means to the fight.

After the GEPA showdown, Hufstedler continued to follow White House policy with regard to congressional oversight of DOE regulations. For all newly signed regulations, administration policy followed the report-and-wait model. On November 12, DOE General Counsel Betsy Levin and Cutler informed Secretary Hufstedler regarding two legislative veto provisions Carter signed into law with the Education Amendments (Act) of 1980. Levin and Cutler informed the secretary that, as per Carter's message to Congress, these clauses should be treated as "report-and-wait" provisions. The next week, Chairman of the Committee on Education and Labor's Subcommittee on Elementary, Secondary, and Vocational Education Representative Carl Perkins (D–KY) sent a letter to Hufstedler commending her department's progress in improving educational regulations. However, Perkins still offered suggestions. She replied to Perkins, the same chairman who had presided over the GEPA hearings two months earlier, assuring the congressman that her department would consider his suggestions thoroughly and reply to him when they transmitted the regulations for publication.[49]

However, while Hufstedler and Perkins were having this cordial exchange, Representative Ken Kramer (R–CO) issued a statement regarding a lawsuit that was about to be filed against Hufstedler. He and his coplaintiffs filed suit against Hufstedler because of her disregard and failure to comply with the GEPA regulation vetoes. The suit sought judgment on the constitutionality of the legislative veto. Kramer, seventeen other representatives, and four senators brought suit against her for her actions. Seeking declaratory and injunctive relief, they hoped to force compliance. The court action bore none of the redeeming hallmarks of logical argument; it was based squarely in the realm of partisan politicking and election-year shenanigans. Twenty of twenty-two plaintiffs were Republican (freshman Senator Carl Levin (D–MI) and freshman Representative Larry McDonald (D–GA) being the only Democrats), making the gesture seem more akin to an election-year ploy than a legitimate challenge (especially because the suit was later withdrawn). Beyond Carter's impending challenge from California Governor Ronald Reagan, all of the representatives faced reelection as well.[50] Reduced to stunts and gimmicks, members of Congress had exhausted all available political capital on the issue. Unable to outflank Carter on the merits of the device, some members resorted to weaker tactics.

Carter's tenure in office marked a major shift in the history of the legislative veto. When Herbert Hoover accepted the measure, he had no idea how it would proliferate in the future. Though previous presidents had voiced their opinion of the measure, none had been as adamant or forthright as Carter. His implementation of report-and-wait interpretations, coupled with his formal message to Congress and the respectful defiance by his staff, constituted a turning point in the legislative veto history. Carter tried polite and respectful tactics, but when they proved insufficient to deter the staunch proponents of legislative vetoes, the thirty-ninth president shifted to more aggressive measures. Carter's fight against the legislative veto put federal comity first. Carter valued the cooperative presidency over the imperial one. Carter proved presidents could lead with respect and not resort to positions of arrogance.

One of the clearest legacies of Carter's action and major proofs of his success manifested in the Supreme Court case *Immigration and Naturalization Service v. Chadha* (1983). In 1966, Jagdish Chadha entered the United States on a student visa. In 1972, when the visa expired, Chadha remained in America illegally. When ordered to leave the country, he appealed to the Immigration Court for a stay in his deportation. In 1974, after an Immigration and Naturalization Service (INS) inquiry, a judge ordered Chadha's deportation suspended; however, the immigration law, as written, gave Congress legislative veto authority over the immigration court and hence the power to reinstate Chadha's deportation. On December 12, 1975, Chairman of the Judi-

7. Jimmy Carter and the Legislative Veto

ciary Subcommittee on Immigration, Citizenship, and International Law Representative Joshua Eilberg (D–PA) introduced HR 926, a "resolution opposing the granting of permanent residence in the United States to [six] aliens," including Chadha. Approved by the House Committee on the Judiciary, it returned to the House, where it was passed by consent.[51]

Chadha appealed the legislative veto of the INS decision on grounds that such congressional action was unconstitutional. His case rested on the logic that his deportation, or more accurately the legislative veto of the stay in his deportation hearing, constituted an unconstitutional encroachment of power by Congress on the jurisdiction of the executive. Carter's administration followed and supported Chadha's case as he appealed defeats until he reached the penultimate victory before the Supreme Court, where, by a vote of seven to two, the highest court in the land agreed with his and Carter's position. On June 23, 1983, Chief Justice Warren Burger affirmed Chadha's right to stay in the United States seventeen years after he first entered the country.

The Court's decision had implications far greater and broader than the fate of Jagdish Chadha. The Court struck down the legislative veto, a tool used by congresses since the time of Herbert Hoover and Franklin Delano Roosevelt, but one that had come under intense scrutiny in recent years. Bruised and marginalized by Lyndon Johnson and Richard Nixon, members of Congress in the late 1970s acted with a conviction to make sure no president ever amassed that much power again. To some, most notably Elliott Levitas, this included legislative vetoes to check the president and the executive branch where they otherwise had sovereign jurisdiction. Jimmy Carter made great efforts to move congressional oversight elsewhere, arguing that legislative vetoes hurt government and violated separation of power, doing more harm than good.[52]

Though the Supreme Court heard and ruled on the *Chadha* case during Ronald Reagan's presidency, the major showdown over the device occurred during Carter's time in office. Despite the gestures of Ford and the presidents before him, the major battle occurred on Carter's watch. While the Court's ruling formally struck down legislative vetoes, informal oversight mechanisms—*de facto* legislative vetoes—persisted in some instances. However, these mechanisms operated in

Jimmy Carter and the Restoration of Presidential Dignity

ways that respected the constitution and the presidency. The *Chadha* decision proved to be the epilogue to the story of Carter's fight for comity in government. While the practice of legislative vetoes dated back to the Hoover presidency, by Carter's tenure in office the device violated the separation of powers. Carter fought to restore the constitutional imbalance.

Conclusion

On February 13, 2016, the Republican National Committee held one of many debates in hopes of winnowing down the wide field of contenders for the 2016 Republican nomination. A common theme in any presidential election is the nonincumbent party firing up their base by criticizing the incumbent administration. Republicans interspersed their jabs at each other with jabs at Barack Obama's administration. When moderator John Dickerson of CBS News asked Senator Marco Rubio (R–FL) what he might ask a former president, the candidate's response quickly spun to the dyad of lauding Ronald Reagan, at the expense of Jimmy Carter.

> Well, I think one of the presidents—well, the president I grew up under was Ronald Reagan. And if you think about what Ronald Reagan inherited, it's not unlike what the next president is going to inherit.
>
> The American people were scared about the future. They were scared about what kind of country their children were going to live in and inherit. And yet somehow Ronald Reagan was able to instill in our nation and in our people a sense of optimism.[1]

Rubio's language fed off a caricature perpetuated by Republicans, particularly in light of their reverence for Carter's successor. To paint Reagan as America's savior, Rubio and others needed to paint Carter as a failure. The underlying implication is that Carter failed America in his four years in office. Rubio and others like him never mention what Carter inherited or what he achieved. Their criticisms fail to contextualize his tenure in office relative to where he started from.

Four decades ago, Jimmy Carter entered office after a string of presidents who expanded presidential power, some in questionable ways. In 1970, Lyndon Johnson's press secretary, George Reedy, described the dangers of extreme presidential power.

Conclusion

> [N]o one is going to act to interfere with the presidential exercise of authority unless the president drools in public or announces on television that he is Alexander the Great. And even in these extreme cases, action would be taken hesitantly indeed.

Carter took office after the twin scandals of the Vietnam War and Watergate. The first strained American patience and faith in government, as a limited foreign engagement devolved into a quagmire with no clear exit strategy and dwindling chances for victory. The later scandal fractured public faith in government further as *Washington Post* reporters Bob Woodward and Carl Bernstein uncovered a botched attempt by Richard Nixon's operatives (the plumbers) to repair surveillance equipment at the Democratic National Committee headquarters during the 1972 election cycle. Reedy later added, "So long as a man stands without peers at a summit of power, he can be removed from office only by what amounts to a *coup d'état*."[2] Though there was no *coup*. Nor was there even an impeachment trial, only because Nixon resigned days before an impeachment vote was scheduled for the House floor.

On August 9, 1974, Richard Nixon became the first president to resign from office. His resignation represented the culmination of a disturbing trend. Only under threat of imminent impeachment did Nixon concede he was not above the law. Gerald Ford assumed office at a nadir in American political history. Less than a decade after ratification of the Twenty-Fifth Amendment, its protocols were called upon twice, promoting the Michigan congressman to vice president and eventually president. Ford made great strides for reconciliation in his two and a half years in office, but economic woes and a lingering distaste for Watergate—exacerbated by Ford's pardon of Nixon—lowered his political stock and soured his reelection prospects. Campaigning on his outsider status and a squeaky-clean peanut-farmer image, Jimmy Carter pledged to further reconcile the nation. Carter provided a viable alternative; he provided redress from the imperial presidency.[3]

The phrase "imperial presidency" comes from the title and subject of Arthur M. Schlesinger, Jr.'s, seminal 1973 book. He argued that the gradual expansion of presidential power since the nation's inception inched the nation toward a monarch in the White House. As mentioned in the introduction, Schlesinger called for strong presidents

Conclusion

within the Constitution; he should be "neither a czar nor a puppet" and certainly "no larger than the law."[4] Carter shaped his presidency along these lines, balancing strength and collaboration. Carter acted to reconcile the nation and restore domestic comity. He worked to restore the separation of powers and boundaries of power between the president and Congress. After the twin traumas of Vietnam and Watergate, the image and reputation of the American presidency left much to be desired.

This book examined two types of solutions sought by Carter. Some redress focused on primarily symbolic gestures, while other actions were more directly tied to legislation. Symbolic gestures began with Carter's campaign: How he painted himself and how he framed his narrative set the stage for how he would serve as president. Beyond ubiquitous rhetoric of an opposition party promising a change from the incumbent, Carter sought to remind the nation that they could do better than the party of Watergate. Carter wanted to restore that grace and respect to the presidency. Once in office, symbolic gestures, such as the sale of the *Sequoia*, showed that Carter's focus would be the business of state and not the trappings of office. Carter's frugality stood in stark contrast to the apotheosis of past presidents. There would be no gold tunics on Carter's White House guards.

Carter's legislative style followed a similar vein. Adamant about restoring comity to government, Carter's actions operated within the scope of executive powers and with the consent of Congress to the extent possible. Carter solicited the opinions and feedback from his legislative counterparts on everything from draft reinstatement to FISA reform. Even when the topics invited fierce debate, such as water projects and legislative vetoes, Carter always made time to value the opinions of the other branch of government, even if their opinions would not sway or change his own.

In both cases, Carter stressed acting legally and with constant and commensurate respect for Congress. Comity did not require agreement; it only demanded respect. Carter did not shy away from battles with Congress, but he always welcomed their advice and opinions, even when in dissent. From Carter's first action as president, pardoning draft dodgers, he made friends and enemies in Congress. Opposition and debate are important to governance, but Carter would make

Conclusion

sure civility and respect were not lost along the way. Carter's strategy had limitations. Threatening congressional pork with his water projects plan proved a costly defeat in his first year in office. However, even in legislative defeat, Carter won the symbolic victory of showing how a president could operate within the scope of the law and with respect for other politicians.

When Carter ran for reelection in 1980, a strong outsider once again courted America. All the reconciliation and restoration of comity did not stack up against the critique of a failing economy and Carter's inability to bring home the hostages held in Iran. Supply-side economics and tough talk wooed many swing voters to the movie star turned politician. In November 1980, an electoral and popular vote majority limited Jimmy Carter to one term. However, for some, Ronald Reagan represented a return to the policies and practice that had plagued the White House a decade before. Americans later learned about the Iran–Contra crisis and found themselves once again asking what did the president know and when did he know it? In the wake of the 1980 election, Carter joined the ranks of other presidents who failed to win reelection. Four years after Jimmy Carter took the oath of office, he watched a new president thank him for him for what he had done. Though Carter has proven to be an exemplary ex-president, the legacy of his time in office is still disputed. The peanut-farmer-turned-president was not perfect, but he brought America to a better place. The country was better off for his efforts.

Postscript

*Donald Trump and New Questions
of Presidential Dignity*

In 2016, Donald Trump promised to "Make America Great Again."[1] As a campaign slogan, the short quip rallied enough Americans to his bandwagon. Many Americans found Trump's narrative persuasive. In his view, America reeled from eight years of Barack Obama's presidency. More than just a nonincumbent candidate attacking the record of the incumbent party, Trump's criticism seemed a bit more personal. Some of this owes to Trump's unique dialect and a background in business, not in politics. However, some of Trump's promises focused specifically on undoing Obama's legacy. The candidate who spent years purporting falsely that Obama was born in Kenya (not Hawaii), and thus should be ineligible for the presidency, became the candidate who made the repeal of Obamacare a priority. Campaign promises are not new nor is political mudslinging during a campaign. However, the 2016 campaign raised questions of what a Trump presidency might look like. Between comments at rallies that seemed to condone, if not encourage, violence, and the Billy Bush tape, where Trump lewdly described his seduction tactics during an appearance on the television show *Access Hollywood* in 2005, Trump's path to the presidency created new challenges to comity. Even if those statements are out of context, the fact that they were uttered at all still raises questions about presidential decorum.

This postscript considers Donald Trump's presidential dignity. To the extent possible, I am trying to divorce this postscript from questions of impropriety and impeachment. I leave the questions of whether

Postscript

Trump committed crimes to future historians. Likewise, I leave the predictive question of whether Trump will be impeached to prognosticators like Nate Silver.² Impeachment is a big term to toss around; no president has ever been convicted and few ever had formal charges voted up. Beyond Andrew Johnson and Bill Clinton (each impeached), and Richard Nixon (resigned when impeachment was a *fait accompli*), who else came close? Even at the height of the Iran–Contra scandal, there was no significant push to impeach Ronald Reagan. Silver quoted Representative Gerald Ford (R–MI), who cynically said in 1970, "an impeachable offense is whatever a majority of the House of Representatives considers [it] to be at a given moment in history."³ Ford's statement reinforces that impeachment is unlikely as long as party loyalty remains strong in Congress. Impeachment requires enough Republicans in both chambers to turn on the sitting president.

Since his inauguration, Trump maintained his victory gave him *carte blanche* to implement his agenda. Ignoring his popular vote minority—or perhaps the weak turnout on the mall for his inauguration—Trump expected lockstep from his party and cooperation from Democrats. Susan J. Douglas argued that all Trump's talk about a rigged election and his claims that he actually won the electoral college were attempts to refute the implication that a minority popular vote/majority electoral vote win means he has no mandate.⁴ Julia Azari argued that mandates are apocryphal, at best. In reality, regardless of the margin of victory, a mandate is only as legitimate as the president who takes charge.

Official portrait of President Donald J. Trump (courtesy Library of Congress).

Postscript

Trump's power resonated not from electoral momentum but in the words of Richard Neustadt, presidential power being the "power to persuade." Trump himself seemed to prefer the language of George Reedy. Speaking about presidential power in the mid–twentieth century, he observed that elections had become tantamount to coronations; an "apotheosis," elevating the victor to divine rank.[5]

Trump's confidence is not the issue. The bigger question regards the extent to which Trump carried himself and represented his office with the dignity demanded. Jimmy Carter struggled to avoid an imperial presidency and to paint the president as austere and above petty disputes. Azari and others argue that these are some of the very factors that define Trump as different. To suggest a president conducts himself differently in office does not necessarily imply that difference is unprofessional. Donald Trump is different from the forty-three men who served before him in many different ways. Azari argued that some of these deviations from the norm had more consequential implications; they "can undermine democratic values" and "damage public trust in the press." Trump's actions as president often flew in the face of precedent and at times spurned respect for legislators and the press. Azari framed the issue in terms of norms and customs. I use a different word: comity. Trump's disparaging remarks toward fellow politicians, even those from his own party, are the anti-comity. Trump is not above circumventing Congress to promote his signature policies; he does not treat the legislature with respect as individuals nor does he respect their power. Azari referenced Speaker of the House Nancy Pelosi's (D–CA) decision to temporarily rescind Trump's State of the Union invitation in 2019. A bold move based on partisanship in the middle of a government shutdown, it also highlighted Pelosi's position as the leader of a "coequal" branch of government. "Norms have long protected the presidency-centric nature of the government—no one expected Congress not to invite the president to speak—but by forgoing this norm, Pelosi dispelled the notion that Congress answers to the White House." Azari's discussion of norms in this regard suggests that presidency has once again crept toward imperial. The presidency has grown in importance and weight vis-à-vis Congress. While this trend is not something Trump started, his bold persona bolsters the trend.[6]

For example, nine months into his term in office, Senator Bob

Postscript

Corker (R–TN) accused President Trump of running the White House like a "reality show." In response, Trump called Corker "a fool."[7] *New York Times* reporter Peter Baker argued that Corker's critique boiled down to a question of dignity. How was Trump conducting himself in office and is that behavior appropriate for a president of the United States? Adam Serwer extended the criticism to an extreme. He compared Trump's disdain for comity to the antics of a toddler. Serwer added, "[t]he president is beginning to get wind of how his petulance is being perceived." Serwer quoted the president: "I don't have temper tantrums."[8] However, there is a fine line between perception of indignity and presidential style. Baker quoted Laurie Ouellette, an expert at defining reality television. "Reality TV is known for its humiliation tactics and its aggressive showmanship and also the idea that either you're in or you're out, with momentum building to the final decision on who stays and who goes." Baker concluded Ouellette's standard confirmed Corker's accusation.

James Fallows argued Trump continued to defy expectations and complicate his public perception. In other words, Trump was acting undignified, and his actions were the cause. For example, Fallows contrasted Trump's proclivity to escape for golf while Puerto Ricans reeled in the wake of Hurricane Maria in 2017. In Fallows' opinion, "Temperamentally, intellectually, and in terms of civic and moral imagination, he is not fit for the duties he is now supposed to bear." Fallows cited as evidence a thread of September 30, 2017, tweets by Trump:

> Such poor leadership ability by the Mayor of San Juan, and others in Puerto Rico, who are not able to get their workers to help. They want everything to be done for them when it should be a community effort. Federal workers now on Island doing a fantastic job.

Fallows concluded that Trump either instinctively felt the need to debase Puerto Ricans in their time of need, or it was a subtle dog whistle to embolden racists.[9] Either way, Fallows offered that the tweet thread is indicative of undignified behavior, actions not befitting the office.

David J. Cook put it more bluntly: "Donald Trump is sui generis. President Trump will go where no one has gone before. President Trump will upset every settled expectation." Cook argued that Trump "deigns to control his image and his message at nearly any cost."[10] Jef-

Postscript

frey Crouch, Mark J. Rozell, and Mitchel A. Sollenberger put Cook's argument into more scientific terms. They applied Stephen Skowronek's theory of the unitary executive to Donald Trump. Crouch, et al., illustrated how Trump followed a pattern that began with George W. Bush and did not recede with Barack Obama. Specifically, they applied Skowronek's theory of expanded presidential power to all of the twenty-first-century presidents. Though their analysis of Trump comes relatively early in his presidency, they point to campaign rhetoric and early executive orders—such as his immigration ban—as indicators of how his operational philosophy paralleled his predecessors and Skowronek's model. Skowronek's analysis "is that a new construction of the presidency gains currency when it legitimizes the release of governmental power for new political purposes." Elsewhere, he framed it more bluntly.

> The theory of the unitary executive promotes exactly what the earlier generation of conservatives feared. It is a brief for the President to act as the exclusive manager of all matters that fall within the purview of the instrumentalities of the executive branch.

Crouch, et al., concluded that Trump followed in the footsteps of those before him who sought to aggrandize the powers of the presidency by shifting the balance of power. Donald Trump's leadership challenges traditional notions of constitutional clauses such as the "take care" and "vesting" clauses.[11] Consolidating presidential power—usurping it from other branches—is the antithesis of comity. In this view, Trump does not need a mandate, or Congress, only a nuanced interpretation of presidential power and the confidence to implement it. More importantly to this book, Trump's actions—or his scuffle and derision of Corker—raise concerns about the degree of comity in Trump's White House. To what extent does he respect the legislature, its members, and its authority?

Amidst questions of his comity and dignity, there is one other comparison that warrants mention. Donald Trump entered office in 2017, campaigning as an outsider promising to bring dignity to an undignified Washington establishment. This is not new, though his promise to "drain the swamp" seemed a little blunter than his predecessors. Trump is a politician who does not fit the traditional mold of his party. Julia Azari argued that Trump represents a turn away from the mold

Postscript

of the Reaganite Republican. In terms of "political time" (with a nod to Steven Skowronek), Azari compared Trump to Jimmy Carter.[12]

> It's difficult to think of two modern political figures more different than Donald Trump and Jimmy Carter. Carter came into the White House with quiet style, downplaying the trapping of the office. His scandalous revelation was that he had "lusted in his heart," as he admitted in an interview with *Playboy* magazine. Revelations of the thrice-married Trump were, well, somewhat different.

"Somewhat different" is a polite euphemism. Azari is referring specifically to the Billy Bush tape, mentioned earlier. However, in terms of similarities, both Trump and Carter campaigned on promises of being an outsider and a technocrat. They promised to get things done.

Dylan Matthews also described similarities between Carter and Trump. He concluded that Trump squandered his congressional majority, just as Carter did. Both presidents entered office with united government—their party holding a majority in both chambers of Congress. However, Matthews reached a similar conclusion to Azari that Trump, like Carter, struggled to make legislative victories in his first year in office.[13] Trump's cabinet raised some eyebrows, as he brought in unconventional experience. Carter faced some similar criticism for his "Georgia mafia" that he brought on board. Trump entered office with grand promises to build a wall on the United States–Mexico border and to repeal the Affordable Care Act. Though Trump struggled to find success on either venture (or others), Carter also struggled during his first year in office. Both men promised a dignified solution that would rise above politics. Both men were wrong. Matthews pointed specifically at Carter's water projects efforts as the moment at which the squandering began. "The original sin of his presidency was his handling of a water bill—boring, run-of-the-mill legislation that turned into an utter catastrophe. A month after taking office, Carter decided to eliminate 19 water projects in 17 states from the budget." Matthews concluded, as do I in my chapter, that Carter threatened congressional pork and asked members of Congress to put party loyalty over their own political future and reelection prospects. Carter eventually signed a bill that was, at best, a compromise measure. In retrospect, Carter agreed it was a problematic strategy so early in his presidency. In comparison, so far Trump has expressed no such remorse beyond the con-

Postscript

tention that "nobody knew that healthcare would be so complicated."[14] Perhaps Trump will think differently in retrospect too.

In chapter three, I wrote about Richard Nixon's imperial move to have the White House guard don frilly tunics. While Trump has not made any changes, as of this printing, to the uniforms at the White House, he does have one habit that has raised concerns. At no point would anyone label Trump as austere, and ostentatious seems hardly a strong enough term to describe his lifestyle before taking office. Still, while the presidency has changed him in some ways, it has not affected his penchant for golf, despite what his pre-office tweets might have suggested. Numerous times while campaigning, Trump lambasted Obama for his occasional rounds of golf.[15] Trump's characterization of Obama's golf habits carried connotations that it was a superfluous habit—a distraction from carrying out the duties of the office. Now, as president, Trump has made frequent official trips to golf courses, and there are rumors of more time spent at one of his privately owned resort properties. My issue here is not accusations of hypocrisy but the implications for the dignity of the office. Jimmy Carter railed against frivolities of the presidency. He sold the *Sequoia* and cut down on limousine usage. He limited flag cordons and reduced the use of "Hail to the Chief." The notion of spending so much time—to say nothing of taxpayer money—golfing while president is antithetical to the vision for the office Carter promoted.

The dignity of a president is not based on popularity of electoral results. Jimmy Carter served one term in office. The nation resoundingly chose Ronald Reagan in 1980. However, despite the electoral landside, Jimmy Carter conducted himself in office with dignity. Donald Trump's record is still being cast. Whether he drains the swamp or leaves his own variant of murk behind has yet to be seen.

Chapter Notes

Introduction

1. Jimmy Carter, "Inaugural Address," January 20, 1977. Online by Gerhard Peters and John T. Woolley, *The American Presidency Project*. Available online at http://www.presidency.ucsb.edu/documents/inaugural-address-0.

2. Historian Joan Hoff Wilson argued that Herbert Hoover predicted the imperial presidency as the logical extension of the buildup of presidential power beginning with the New Deal in the 1930s. See Joan Hoff Wilson, *Herbert Hoover: Forgotten Progressive* (Boston: Little, Brown and Company, 1975), 213. For the history of expanding presidential power from America's inception through the Nixon administration, see especially Arthur M. Schlesinger, Jr., *The Imperial Presidency* (Boston: Houghton Mifflin, 1973, 1989). For other accounts of the broader trend of aggrandized presidential power, see, for example, Michael A. Genovese, *The Power of the American Presidency: 1789–2000* (New York: Oxford University Press, 2001); David Gergen, *Eyewitness to Power: The Essence of Leadership Nixon to Clinton* (New York: Simon & Schuster, 2000); Fred I. Greenstein, *The Presidential Difference: Leadership Style From FDR to Clinton* (New York: The Free Press, 2000); Ann Van Wynen Thomas and A. J. Thomas, Jr., *The War-Making Powers of the President: Constitutional and International Law Aspects* (Dallas: Southern Methodist University Press, 1982); Christopher Capozzola, "'It Makes You Want to Believe in the Country' Celebrating the Bicentennial in an Age of Limits," *America in the 70s*, Beth Bailey and David Farber, eds. (Lawrence: University Press of Kansas, 2004), 36.

3. For more discussion of the founders' intentions, see, for example, Charles L. Black, Jr., "The Presidency and Congress," *Washington and Lee Law Review* 32:4 (Fall 1975), 841–54; W. Taylor Reveley III, *War Powers of the President and Congress: Who Holds the Arrows and Olive Branch?* (Charlottesville: University of Virginia Press, 1981); David Gray Adler and Larry N. George, eds., *The Constitution and the Conduct of American Foreign Policy* (Lawrence: University of Kansas Press, 1996).

4. George E. Reedy, *The Twilight of the Presidency* (New York: New American Library, 1970), 5.

5. Arthur M. Schlesinger, Jr., *The Imperial Presidency* (Boston: Houghton Mifflin, 1973, 1989), xxviii. Though the initial edition of the book was published as the Watergate scandal was still unfolding, in the second edition of the book Schlesinger reflected on Nixon.

6. Deep Throat's identity was kept secret until 2005, when Felt chose to make his secret identity known. Felt died in 2008 with an epitaph as one of the most famous whistleblowers in history. See Tim Weiner, "W. Mark Felt, Watergate Deep Throat, Dies at 95," *The New York Times* (December 19, 2008), 1. For the Haldeman quote, see Sherri Cavan, *20th Century Gothic: America's Nixon* (San Francisco: Wigan Pier Press, 1979), 168–69.

7. Since its occurrence over thirty years ago, the nadir of aggrandized presidential power, Watergate, has been the subject of a myriad of books. There is a wealth of scholarship on the abuses of

Chapter Notes—1

Watergate, from the hotel break-in to the fight over ownership of Nixon's audiotapes. See Stanley I. Kutler, *The Wars of Watergate: The Last Crisis of Richard Nixon* (New York: A. A. Knopf, 1990); Carl Bernstein and Bob Woodward, *All The President's Men* (New York: Simon & Schuster, 1974).

8. For a subject where perception is as relevant as reality, there exists a more fitting and symbolic transitional moment. As Ford took office, Nixon flew home to San Clemente, California, from Washington, D.C. When President Nixon took off, he was aboard Air Force One. However, the clock struck 12 p.m. midflight, over Jefferson City, Missouri, and the Air Force pilot radioed the local tower to change the plane's call sign to SAM 27000. Air Force One is the Federal Aviation Administration's designation for any fixed wing aircraft carrying the president of the United States. At that moment, the president of the United States was no longer on board that airplane. No longer the proverbial leader of the free world, Nixon was—once again—just an ordinary citizen. Thus it was that moment that the imperial presidency ended. This information is available in many places. One such site is "Air Force One: Facts and History of 707 as Air Force One." Available online at http://www.707sim.com/air-force-one.html. (Accessed March 27, 2007.) See also online, "VC-137B/C Stratoliner." Available online at http://www.globalsecurity.org/military/systems/aircraft/vc-137.htm. (Accessed March 27, 2007.) (The VC-137 is the version of the Boeing 707 modified for use by presidents and other high-ranking officials. For more discussion of Nixon's exit flight, see "Exit Nixon," *Time* (August 19, 1974), 13B–14.

9. Gallup polling in August 1974 showed 65% of Americans supported impeachment. They believed he should be brought before a trial in the Senate. A September 2, 1974, poll found that number at 56%, and on September 18, right before the pardon was announced, the number was 58%. In that same poll, 53% of Americans said they did not feel Nixon should be pardoned. See *The Gallup Poll Cumulative Index: Public Opinion, 1935–1997* (Lanham: Rowman & Littlefield, 1999), 331–36, 349–51, 354–58.

10. The quote is the title of Kriner's dissertation. See Douglas L. Kriner, "Taming the Imperial Presidency: Congress, Presidents and the Conduct of Military Action," PhD Dissertation, Harvard University, 2006; "Trust in Government," Gallup. Available online at http://www.gallup.com/poll/5392/trust-government.aspx. (Accessed January 5, 2016.)

11. Eric M. Uslaner, "Comity in Context: Confrontation in Historical Perspective," *British Journal of Political Science* 21:1 (January 1991), 47–53; Eric M. Uslaner, *The Decline of Comity in Congress* (Ann Arbor: University of Michigan Press, 1993). For the quote, see page 1 of Uslaner's book.

12. A draft dodger is anyone accused or convicted of Selective Service System violations. A military resister is anyone accused or convicted of nonviolent crimes under the Universal Code of Military Justice. The latter category includes but is not limited to deserters. Clemency is the legal opportunity to earn one's way back into society. Pardon removes the legal barriers and expunges the criminal records but does not lend moral credibility to those who committed the absolved offenses. These terms will be discussed in more detail in chapter one.

13. Charles O. Jones, *The Trusteeship Presidency: Jimmy Carter and the United States Congress* (Baton Rouge: Louisiana State University Press, 1988), 3–9; Garland A. Haas, *Jimmy Carter and the Politics of Frustration* (Jefferson: McFarland & Company, Inc., 1992); Clark R. Mollenhoff, *The President Who Failed: Carter Out of Control* (New York: The Free Press, 1980); Edwin C. Hargrove, *Jimmy Carter as President: Leadership and the Politics of the Public Good* (Baton Rouge: Louisiana State University Press, 1988), xxiii.

Chapter 1

1. Stanley I. Kutler, *The Wars of Watergate: The Last Crisis of Richard Nixon* (New York: A. A. Knopf, 1990), 571; Memorandum, Stu Eizenstat to Jimmy Carter,

Chapter Notes—1

November 14, 1976, "Memoranda—In—Organization 10/31/76–11/14/76" Folder, Box 4, Powell, Staff Press Offices, Jimmy Carter Library. Similar recommendations were made a couple weeks later by Harrison Wellford. See Memorandum, Harrison Wellford to Jimmy Carter, December 1, 1976, "White House Organization 12/1/76–1/6/77" Folder, Box 6, Powell, Staff Press Offices, Jimmy Carter Library.

2. For a more in-depth discussion of Carter's campaign for the presidency, see, for example, Jeffrey Bloodworth, "Jimmy Carter's 1976 Presidential Campaign: The Saint, the Sinner, and the Hopeless Dreamer" in *A Companion to Gerald R. Ford and Jimmy Carter*, Scott Kaufman, ed. (Malden: John Wiley & Sons, 2016).

3. Adriana Bosch, producer, "Jimmy Who?" *Jimmy Carter*, American Experience (Alexandria: PBS Video, 2002); Lloyd Bitzer and Theodore Rueter, *Carter vs Ford: The Counterfeit Debates of 1976* (Madison: University of Wisconsin Press, 1980), 17; Burton I. Kaufman and Scott Kaufman, *The Presidency of James Earl Carter, Jr.* (Lawrence: University of Kansas Press, 2006), 16.

4. Jimmy Carter, *White House Diary* (New York: Farrar, Straus and Giroux, 2010), 5.

5. The election results are a matter of public record. See also David Wilma and Kit Oldham, "State voters elect Dixy Lee Ray as first woman governor of Washington, re-elect Senator Henry Jackson and House incumbents, and prefer Ford to Carter on November 2, 1976," *HistoryLink.org Essay 5611*. Available online at http://www.historylink.org/File/5611. (Accessed November 5, 2016.)

6. In Gallup polling, for example, Carter was not polled as the Democrats top choice until late May. By February, Carter at least had enough name recognition to poll in double digits. See Scholarly Resources, *The Gallup Poll: Public Opinion, 1935–1997*, CD-ROM edition.

7. Kutler, 578.

8. Issue Statement: Secrecy, no date "Position Papers" Folder, Box 230, Simon File, Office of Staff Secretary, Jimmy Carter Library.

9. Patrick Anderson, *Electing Jimmy Carter: The Campaign of 1976* (Baton Rouge: Louisiana State University Press, 1994), 22.

10. Jimmy Carter's Code of Ethics, "Position Papers" Folder, Box 230, Simon File, Office of Staff Secretary, Jimmy Carter Library.

11. Though not dated, the document's location in the archives suggest it was published about the same time. See Issue Statement: Secrecy, no date "Position Papers" Folder, Box 230, Simon File, Office of Staff Secretary, Jimmy Carter Library.

12. Wilma and Oldham; Carter, *White House Diary*, 5; Stephanie Smith, "Presidential Transitions," Congressional Research Service, 2008. Available online https://www.fas.org/sgp/crs/misc/RL30736.pdf. (Accessed November 22, 2016.)

13. Transcript, "A Standard Stump Speech," May 31, 1976 (Rapid City, South Dakota), Issue Statement: Secrecy, "Speeches—Addresses, Statements—1/76–11/76" Folder, Box 48, 1976 Campaign Files, Carter Family Papers, Jimmy Carter Library.

14. *Ibid.*

15. "A New Beginning," "Primary Campaign Statements" Folder, Box 231, Simon File, Office of Staff Secretary, Jimmy Carter Library; Richard Skinner, "Jimmy Carter changed presidential transitions forever," *Vox* (October 5, 2016). Available online at www.vox.com/mischiefs-of-faction/2016/10/5/13142390/jimmy-carter-changed-presidential-transitions. (Accessed November 17, 2016); John P. Burke, "The Transition" in *A Companion to Gerald R. Ford and Jimmy Carter*, Scott Kaufman, ed. (Malden: John Wiley & Sons, 2016).

16. Speech, "Address by Jimmy Carter to the American Bar Association, Atlanta, Georgia," August 11, 1976, "Speeches—Master File, 1976" Folder, Box 48, 1976 Campaign Files, Carter Family Papers, Jimmy Carter Library. For polling data similar to the ones Carter had access to, see, for example Scholarly Resources, *The Gallup Poll: Public Opinion, 1935–1997*, CD-ROM edition.

17. Patrick Anderson, *Electing Jimmy Carter: The Campaign of 1976* (Baton

Chapter Notes—1

Rouge: Louisiana State University Press, 1994), 94.

18. Speech, "Remarks by Jimmy Carter at Town Hall Forum, Los Angeles, California," August 23, 1976, "Speeches—Master File, 1976" Folder, Box 48, 1976 Campaign Files, Carter Family Papers, Jimmy Carter Library.

19. Interview, "Jimmy Carter/Congressional Quarterly," August 24, 1976, "Speeches—Master File, 1976" Folder, Box 48, 1976 Campaign Files, Carter Family Papers, Jimmy Carter Library.

20. Speech, "Democratic Party—Van Ryswyk Farm—Des Moines, Iowa," August 24, 1976, "Speeches—Master File, 1976" Folder, Box 48, 1976 Campaign Files, Carter Family Papers, Jimmy Carter Library.

21. For cautions against overconfidence, see for example Memorandum, Stu Eizenstat to Jimmy Carter, et al., July 1, 1976, "A New Beginning," "Memos" Folder, Box 4, Special Projects Stern, Staff Offices, Domestic Policy Staff, Jimmy Carter Library. For an example of conversations about Carter's transition theme of a commitment to transparency, see, for example, Carter-Mondale Transition Group Policy Guidelines; Conflicts of Interest; Financial Disclosure; and Restrictions Following Government Service, no date, "Carter Code of Ethics & 1/3/77 Financial Disclosure 12/30/76–1/4/77 [CF, O/A 751]" Folder, Box 1, Staff Offices, Press, Powell, Jimmy Carter Library; Smith; Laurence Stern "Transition Unit at Work For Carter," *The Washington Post* (August 9, 1976), A1.

22. Burke, 255–56; Jules Witcover, "Blueprint for Transition Going to Carter," *The Washington Post* (November 4, 1976), A18; Garland A. Haas, *Jimmy Carter and the Politics of Frustration* (Jefferson: McFarland & Company, Inc., 1992), 7.

23. Memorandum, Jack Watson to Jimmy Carter, November 3, 1976, "White House Organization, 11/76–1/77" Folder, Box 3, Office of Staff Secretary, Handwriting File, 1976 Campaign Transition File, Jimmy Carter Library; Memorandum, Stu Eizenstat to Jimmy Carter, nd, "White House Organization, 11/76–1/77" Folder, Box 3, Office of Staff Secretary, Handwriting File, 1976 Campaign Transition File, Jimmy Carter Library; Memorandum, Stu Eizenstat to Greg Schneiders, December 12, 1976, "White House Organization, 11/76–1/77" Folder, Box 3, Office of Staff Secretary, Handwriting File, 1976 Campaign Transition File, Jimmy Carter Library.

24. This quote is referenced in many places, such as Fred R. Shapiro, ed., *The Yale Book of Quotations* (New Haven: Yale University Press, 2006), 182.

25. Memorandum, Stu Eizenstat and David Rubenstein to Jimmy Carter, November 30, 1976, "Promises, Promises 12/76" Folder, Box 6, Special Projects Stern, Staff Offices, Domestic Policy Staff, Jimmy Carter Library; Smith, 15.

26. Memorandum, John Moore to Jimmy Carter, December 1976, "Code of Ethics, 12/76" Folder, Box 1, 1976 Campaign Transition File, Office of Staff Secretary, Jimmy Carter Library.

27. In the infamous *Playboy* interview, Carter admitted to lusting in his heart for other women. See Robert Scheer, "Playboy Interview: Jimmy Carter," *Playboy* (November 1976); Paper, "Internal Working Paper on Political Strategy," December 10, 1976, "Memoranda—Pat Caddell 12/10/76–12/21/76" Folder, Box 4, Powell, Staff Press Offices, Jimmy Carter Library. Another copy of this paper can be found in the "Election of 1980" Folder, Box 17, Robert Lipshutz Subject Papers, Jimmy Carter Library; Julia R. Azari, *Delivering the People's Message: The Changing Politics of the Presidential Mandate* (Ithaca: Cornell University Press, 2014), 128–29.

28. These quotes come from the same "Internal Working Paper on Political Strategy."

29. Kaufman and Kaufman, 28.

30. Memorandum, Walter Mondale to Jimmy Carter, no date, "White House Organization 12/1/76–1/6/77" Folder, Box 6, Powell, Staff Press Offices, Jimmy Carter Library.

31. Carter, *White House Diary*, 12.

32. Anderson, 59; Don Richardson, ed., *Conversations with Carter* (Boulder: Lynne Rienner Publishers, 1998), 63–64. Richardson reprinted an interview published in *Time* on January 3, 1977.

Chapter 2

1. Parts of this chapter were published previously in "Reconciling the Vietnam War: Draft Dodgers, Resisters and the debate over Amnesty" in *War Resisters in Retrospect: Papers from the 2007 Our Way Home Peace Event and Reunion,* Joseph Jones and Lori Olafson, eds. (Ottawa: National Research Council of Canada Press, 2009).

2. For Nixon's remarks, see Memorandum, Kenneth F. Bailey to Howard Kerr, March 4, 1974, "Amnesty—President Nixon's Statements" Folder, Box 2, John O. Marsh Files, Gerald R. Ford Library; Transcript, CBS Television Program "Conversation with the President," January 2, 1972, "Amnesty—President Nixon's Statements" Folder, Box 2, John O. Marsh Files, Gerald R. Ford Library. Nixon's opposition to amnesty left no room for debate but it did not come lightly. After some of the earliest calls for amnesty manifested in Congress, Nixon investigated his options and the history of presidential amnesty. In December 1971, White House advisor and speechwriter Pat Buchanan suggested that "Christmas Pardons" might be a compromise gesture to appease the amnesty doves in Congress while not totally alienating Nixon's hawk base. The pardons would target a select few conscientious objectors who had willingly gone to jail for their beliefs. This would demonstrate compassion by Nixon but would not abandon his "law and order" attitude. However, Buchanan's possibility never manifested into practice. Nixon later explained, "amnesty means forgiveness. We cannot provide forgiveness for them. Those who served paid their price. Those who deserted must pay their price; and the price is not a junket in the Peace Corps.... The price is a criminal penalty for disobeying the laws of the United States." There were no Christmas pardons, and by January, Nixon had reified his stance against amnesty in any form. See Memorandum, Patrick Buchanan to the President, November 18, 1971, "Vietnam—Follow up—Amnesty, 1971–73 (1)" Folder, Box A142, Melvin R. Laird Papers, Gerald R. Ford Library; Memorandum, Patrick Buchanan to the President, December 15, 1971, "Vietnam—Follow up—Amnesty, 1971–73 (1)" Folder, Box A142, Melvin R. Laird Papers, Gerald R. Ford Library; Note, J. F. Lehman to Bill Baroody, "Draft amnesty resolution," February 3, 1973, "Vietnam—Follow up—Amnesty, 1971–73 (1)" Folder, Box A142, Melvin R. Laird Papers, Gerald R. Ford Library; Position Paper, "AMNESTY," February 5, 1973, "Vietnam—Follow up—Amnesty, 1971–73 (1)" Folder, Box A142, Melvin R. Laird Papers, Gerald R. Ford Library.

3. Gerald R. Ford, "Program for the Return of Vietnam Era Draft Evaders and Resisters: Proclamation 4353. September 14, 1974," *Weekly Compilation of Presidential Documents* Volume 10, Number 38 (September 23, 1974), 1050; Jimmy Carter, Proclamation, "Presidential Proclamation of Pardon. Proclamation 4483. January 21, 1977," *Weekly Compilation of Presidential Documents* Volume 13, Number 4 (January 24, 1977), 90. In both cases, as in most proposals, the affected time period was defined as August 4, 1964, to March 28, 1973, from the Gulf of Tonkin incident through the removal of ground troops nine years later.

4. For a history of presidential pardoning, see, for example, *Congressional Record,* 93rd Congress, 1st Session, Volume 119, part 12:15558.

5. For a discussion of Carter's distinction between the two terms, see Sharon Rudy Plaxton, "To Reconcile A Nation: Gerald R. Ford, Jimmy Carter, and the Question of Amnesty 1974–1980," Doctoral Thesis, Queen's University, December 1995, 184–90. For examples of the competing views on the clemency issue—including historical precedents—see especially, Report, "The President's Pardoning Power," December 29, 1974, "Presidential Pardoning Power" Folder, Box 1, Robert J. Horn Files, Gerald R. Ford Library; Memorandum, General Lewis Walt to Charles Goodell, October 9, 1974, "Alternatives to Pardon" Folder, Box 1, Charles E. Goodell Papers, Gerald R. Ford Library; Memorandum, Captain John Euler to Presidential Clemency Board, October 29, 1974, "Alternatives to Pardon" Folder, Box 1, Charles E. Goodell Papers, Gerald R. Ford Library;

Chapter Notes—2

Jay French to Russ Rourke, July 28, 1975, "Amnesty—Presidential Clemency Board General" Folder, Box 2, John O. Marsh Files, Gerald R. Ford Library; Memorandum. Russ Rourke to Phil Buchen. July 24, 1975, "Amnesty—Presidential Clemency Board General" Folder, Box 2, John O. Marsh Files, Gerald R. Ford Library; Note, Lew [Walt] to Russ [Rourke], July 23, 1975, "Amnesty—Presidential Clemency Board General" Folder, Box 2, John O. Marsh Files, Gerald R. Ford Library.

6. *Brown v. Walker* 161 U.S. 591 (1896); Report, "The Power of Congress to Enact Amnesty Legislation," no date, "Amnesty—Power to Enact Legislation on, 1972" Folder, Box A53, Melvin R. Laird Papers, Gerald R. Ford Library.

7. *Congressional Record*, 92nd Congress, 2nd Session, 1974, Volume 118, part 13:16122; *Congressional Record*, 93rd Congress, 1st Session, 1973, Volume 119, part 8:9912; *Congressional Record*, 93rd Congress, 2nd Session, 1974, Volume 120, part 16:20815.

8. See, for example, *Congressional Record*, 92nd Congress, 2nd Session, 1972, Volume 118, part 1:71–2; *Congressional Record*, 92nd Congress, 2nd Session, 1972, Volume 118, part 6:7620; *Congressional Record*, 93rd Congress, 2nd Session, 1974, Volume 120, part 9:11459. For Abzug's quote, see Congress, Senate, Committee on the Judiciary, Subcommittee on Administrative Practice and Procedure, *Clemency Program Practices and Procedures*, 93rd Congress, 2nd Session, Hearing, 595–98. For examples of Koch and Abzug's politics, see, for example, Edward I. Koch and William Rauch, *Politics* (New York: Simon & Schuster, 1985); Suzanne Braun Levine and Mary Thom, *Bella Abzug: How One Tough Broad from the Bronx Fought Jim Crow and Joe McCarthy, Pissed Off Jimmy Carter, Battled for the Rights of Women and Workers, Rallied Against War and for the Planet, and Shook Up Politics Along the Way* (New York: Farrar, Straus and Giroux, 2007). For a discussion of Abzug's ideology, see chapter 2, page 18. For Koch, see Edward I. Koch with Daniel Paisner, *Citizen Koch: An Autobiography* (New York: St. Martin's Press, 1992).

9. *Congressional Record*, 94th Congress, 1st Session, 1975, Volume 121, part 12:14868. For explanation of his nickname, see Michael O'Brien, *Philip Hart: The Conscience of the Senate* (East Lansing: Michigan State University Press, 1995). For other proposals, see, for example, *Congressional Record*, 94th Congress, 1st Session, 1975, Volume 121, part 14:18775–6; *Congressional Record*, 94th Congress, 2nd Session, 1976, Volume 122, part 9:10609–11.

10. For an example of the derisive language, see *Congressional Record*, 93rd Congress, 2nd Session, 1974, Volume 120, part 10:12727–8.

11. *Congressional Record*, 93rd Congress, 1st Session, 1973, Volume 119, part 6:6752–3, 6793; *Congressional Record*, 95th Congress, 1st Session, 1977, Volume 123, part 1:926. For Derwinski's opposition to apologetic rhetoric, see Edward J. Derwinski, "Carter's Foreign Policy: Much Ado About Nothing," in *Can You Afford this House?*, David C. Treen, ed. (Edison: Caroline House Press, 1978), 146.

12. The armies raised for every major war since the Revolutionary War empirically disprove this precedent. This is because (as pro-amnesty advocates frequently noted) amnesty was offered after the Revolutionary War, as well as every other declared war in American history and even some of the undeclared ones. See, for example, *Congressional Record*, 95th Congress, 1st Session, 1977, Volume 123, part 1:412–3; *Congressional Record*, 93rd Congress, 1st Session, 1973, Volume 119, part 6:7341–3. For a discussion of Goldwater's politics, see Earl Black and Merle Black, *The Rise of Southern Republicans* (Cambridge: Harvard University Press, 2002), 33, 127, 225.

13. *Congressional Record*, 93rd Congress, 2nd Session, 1974, Volume 120, part 6:8022–3; *Congressional Record*, 95th Congress, 1st Session, 1977, Volume 123, part 1:908–9, 916–8, 1142–5.

14. *Congressional Record*, 93rd Congress, 2nd Session, 1974, Volume 120, part 5:6660 and *Congressional Record*, 93rd Congress, 1st Session, 1973, Volume 119, part 15:18802; *Congressional Record*, 95th Congress, 1st Session, 1977, Volume 123, part 10:12377. For talk of POWs, MIAs, KIAs, and other veteran categories, see,

for example, *Congressional Record*, 93rd Congress, 2nd Session, 1974, Volume 120, part 24:32479–80; *Congressional Record*, 93rd Congress, 2nd Session, 1974, Volume 120, part 24:32629–30; *Congressional Record*, 94th Congress, 1st Session, 1975, Volume 121, part 17:22449–50; *Congressional Record*, 95th Congress, 1st Session, 1977, Volume 123, part 1:912–4; *Congressional Record*, 94th Congress, 1st Session, 1975, Volume 121, part 27:35250–2.

15. Radio Address, "Script For Use By Fifth District Radio Stations The Weekend of March 24–25, 1973," March 24–25, 1973, "Fifth District Weekly Radio Reports, 1973" Folder, Box D36, Gerald R. Ford Congressional Papers, Gerald R. Ford Library.

16. Gerald R. Ford, Remarks, "Program For The Return of Vietnam Era Draft Evaders and Military Deserters: The President's Remarks Announcing The Program. September 16, 1974," *Weekly Compilation of Presidential Documents* Volume 10, Number 38 (September 20, 1974), 1149–150; Gerald R. Ford, "Society of Professional Journalists, Sigma Delta Chi: The President's Remarks in a Question-And-Answer Session at The Society's Convention in Phoenix, Arizona November 14, 1974," *Weekly Compilation of Presidential Documents* Volume 10, Number 46 (November 18, 1974), 1449; Gerald R. Ford, *A Time to Heal: The Autobiography of Gerald R. Ford* (New York: Harper and Row, 1979), 141.

17. Gerald R. Ford, Executive Order, "Presidential Clemency Board, Executive Order 11803. September 16 1974." *Weekly Compilation of Presidential Documents* Volume 10, Number 38 (September 20, 1974): 1051–052.

18. Letter, Edward Kennedy to the President, August 29, 1974, "Judicial Matters—Clemency Program" Folder, Box 26, Presidential Handwriting File, Gerald R. Ford Library.

19. Memorandum of Conversation, September 16, 1974, "September 16, 1974—Ford, Bipartisan Congressional Leadership, and Others" Folder, Box 5, National Security Adviser—Memoranda of Conversations, Gerald R. Ford Library. For the quote and description of Hébert, see Robert McG. Thomas, Jr., "F. Edward Hébert, Ex-Lawmaker, Dies," *The New York Times* (December 30, 1979), 14; F. Edward Hébert with John McMillan, *"Last of the Titans": The Life and Times of Congressman F. Edward Hébert of Louisiana* (Lafayette: Center for Louisiana Studies, 1976).

20. Similarly, the hawkish Senator John Tower (R-TX) urged the President "for God's sake... not to by-pass the military courts in dealing with deserters." Tower added, "If the President by-passes the military courts there will be a total collapse of military discipline and I hope he realizes this as he decides on this whole matter." Tower represented the conservative wing of the Grand Old Party. As the first Republican to crack the Southern Democratic juggernaut, he predated many of the conservative giants in the Republican Party, earning him added status and respect amongst his peers by the 1970s. *Congressional Record*, 93rd Congress, 2nd Session, 1974, Volume 120, part 23:31279; Memorandum, Tom C. Korologos to the President, September 10, 1974, "Judicial Matters—Clemency Program" Folder, Box 26, Presidential Handwriting File, Gerald R. Ford Library. For discussion of Tower's political views, see, for example, John G. Tower, *Consequences: A Personal and Political Memoir* (Boston: Little, Brown and Company, 1991); and Black and Black, 72, 88–91, 271.

21. *Congressional Record*, 93rd Congress, 2nd Session, 1974, Volume 120, part 22:28862–3, 30133; *Congressional Record*, 93rd Congress, 2nd Session, 1974, Volume 120, part 23:30893; *Congressional Record*, 93rd Congress, 2nd Session, 1974, Volume 120, part 24:31758; *Congressional Record*, 94th Congress, 1st Session, 1975, Volume 121, part 1:54; *Congressional Record*, 94th Congress, 1st Session, 1975, Volume 121, part 2:2415–6; *Congressional Record*, 94th Congress, 2nd Session, 1976, Volume 122, part 4:4718–9. For other references to the "half-a-loaf" talking point, see, for example, Article, "By Almost Any Standard, the Amnesty Plan Isn't Working," October 27, 1974, "News Clippings (2)" Folder, Box 8, Charles E. Goodell Papers, Gerald R. Ford Library; Phil Stanford, "By Almost Any Standard, the Amnesty Plan Isn't Working," *The New York Times* (October 27,

1974), E7; Garland A. Haas, *Jimmy Carter and the Politics of Frustration* (Jefferson: McFarland & Company, Inc., 1992), 67.

22. For the statistics on the clemency program, see Lawrence M. Baskir and William A. Strauss, *Chance and Circumstance: The Draft, The War and The Vietnam Generation* (New York: Alfred A. Knopf, Inc., 1978), 215. For Tropp's comments, see Memorandum, Richard Tropp to William Nicholson, September 8, 1975, "Amnesty—Presidential Clemency Board General" Folder, Box 2, John O. Marsh Files, Gerald R. Ford Library; Press Release, "Statement By the President," September 16, 1975, "9/16/75—Termination of Clemency Board" Folder, Box 23, Paul Theis and Robert Orben Files, Gerald R. Ford Library; Press Release, "Statement By the President," September 16, 1975, "9/15/75–9/20/75" Folder, Box 68 FG 6–28, White House Central Files Subject File, Gerald R. Ford Library; Briefing Paper, Philip W. Buchen to the President, September 16, 1975, "9/15/75–9/20/75" Folder, Box 68 FG 6–28, White House Central Files Subject File, Gerald R. Ford Library.

23. See, for example, *Congressional Record*, 93rd Congress, 2nd Session, 1974, Volume 120, part 25:33073–4; *Congressional Record*, 93rd Congress, 2nd Session, 1974, Volume 120, part 26:34526; *Congressional Record*, 93rd Congress, 2nd Session, 1974, Volume 120, part 24:32810; *Congressional Record*, 94th Congress, 2nd Session, 1976, Volume 122, part 14:16971–2.

24. Gerald R. Ford, Remarks, "The Presidents New Conference on February 8, 1976," *Weekly Compilation of Presidential Documents* Volume 12, Number 7 (September 20, 1974), 151–67; Gerald R. Ford, Remarks, "Vail, Colorado: The President's Remarks With Reports at Chairlift 6," *Weekly Compilation of Presidential Documents* Volume 13, Number 1 (January 3, 1977), 1–2.

25. "Recommendations For The Treatment of Civilian and Military Offenders of the Vietnam Era," no date, "Pardon, etc. Vietnam War, 01/1977–10/1978" Folder, Box 41, White House Counsel's Office Files, Jimmy Carter Library.

26. Speech, "Carter's Statement on Amnesty," September 23, 1976, "Amnesty" Folder, Box 3, James M. Cannon Files, Gerald R. Ford Library; Gerald R. Ford, Remarks, "Presidential Campaign Debate of September 23, 1976 held in Philadelphia, Pennsylvania," *Weekly Compilation of Presidential Documents* Volume 12, Number 39 (September 23, 1976), 1371; "Carter Quotes—Amnesty" Folders, Boxes H21 and H24, President Ford Committee Campaign Records, Gerald R. Ford Library.

27. Ford did not believe that Watergate or amnesty sealed his loss. Rather, Ford believed it hinged on his inability to carry New York State in the 1976 general election. Ford blames his shortcoming—in part—due to the fallout that developed in 1975 when Ford declined to bail out New York City. Many New Yorkers painfully remembered the infamous *New York Daily News* headline covering his decision: "Ford to City: Drop Dead." See Rachel Sklar, "Ford Coverage: Nixon, Chevy Chase And Football, But Something's Missing," *Huffington Post* (December 27, 2006). Available online at https://www.huffingtonpost.com/entry/ford-coverage-nixon-chevy_b_37218?guccounter=1&guce_referrer=aHR0cHM6Ly-93d3cuZ29vZ2xlLmNvbS8&guce_referrer_sig=AQAAAGO0-QUj8_fdy-0FQ6Zmk8n-RN5g4mlWIA2VQF79JRPh0JMfCojJrQ7x-ZgeUckCEZCjcDDxgRfP2-Oocg5Y-d7sb-kQ16BD_fWC2uR7iI-VPKgUr2PcA3Y-IWN6fFrDAPMIBGSXxklGu_LrvV51b-ZMP9LiTVqUVr40eni_0QergBGES. (Accessed January 17, 2009.)

28. Executive Order, Jimmy Carter, January 21, 1977, "Presidential Pardon of Draft Evaders, 1/21/77" Folder, Box 69, White House Press Office Files, Jimmy Carter Library; Jimmy Carter, Executive Order, "Executive Order relating to Proclamation of Pardon: Executive Order 11967. January 21, 1977," *Weekly Compilation of Presidential Documents* Volume 13, Number 4 (January 24, 1977), 90–91. For Kennedy's quote, see "Keeping His First Promise," *Time* (January 31, 1977), 15.

29. "Heroes Without Honor Face the Battle at Home," *Time* (April 23, 1979), 31.

30. "Senate Turns Down Funds to Carry Out Carter Pardon Plan," *The New York Times* (June 25, 1977), 1, 7; Plaxton, 205–08.

31. Ulman cited two Supreme Court cases, *Schick v. Reed* 419 U.S. 256 (1974) and *United States v. Klein* 80 U.S. 128 (1871). Ulman also argued the bill would interfere with resident aliens' Fifth Amendment right to procedural due process (and the amendment can be conceived as a bill of attainder). See Memorandum, Leon Ulman to Margaret McKenna, June 24 1977, "Pardon, etc. Vietnam War, 01/1977–10/1978" Folder, Box 41, White House Counsel's Office Files, Jimmy Carter Library.

32. Memorandum, Bob Lipshutz to the President, July 29, 1977, "Pardon, etc. Vietnam War, 01/1977–10/1978" Folder, Box 41, White House Counsel's Office Files, Jimmy Carter Library; Memorandum, Bob Lipshutz and Stu Eizenstat to the President, August 2, 1977, "Pardon, etc. Vietnam War, 01/1977–10/1978" Folder, Box 41, White House Counsel's Office Files, Jimmy Carter Library; Jimmy Carter, "Appropriations Bill Statement on Signing H.R. 7556 Into Law," *The Public Papers of Jimmy Carter 1977*, Book 2 (Washington, D.C.: Government Printing Office, 1977), 1409–410. For Carter's signing statement, see Remarks, "Appropriations Bill: Statement on Signing H.R. 7556 Into Law. August 3, 1977," *Weekly Compilation of Presidential Documents* Volume 13, Number 22 (August 8, 1977), 1163–164.

Chapter 3

1. Writing about the current Uniformed Division dress, Secret Service scholar Philip Melanson noted, "In sharp contrast to the tailored business suits worn by regular secret service agents, the Uniformed Division wear uniforms that are a cross between policy and military dress: distinctive black pants with bright gold striping, white shirts with gold trim, gold and blue badges, name tags that include the officer's home state, highly polished black shoes, police-style caps, and shoulder chevrons indicating rank." See Philip H. Melanson, *The Secret Service: The Hidden Story of an Enigmatic Agency* (New York: Carroll & Graf Publishers, 2002), 171–72; "The Palace Guard," *Time* (February 9, 1970), 8; Arthur M. Schlesinger, Jr., *The Imperial Presidency* (Boston: Houghton Mifflin, 1973), 218–23.

2. Congress, House, Committee on Appropriations, Subcommittee on the Treasury, Postal Service, and General Government Appropriations, *Federal Expenditures at San Clemente and Key Biscayne*, 93rd Congress, 1st Session, 1973, Hearing.

3. Jimmy Carter, *Keeping Faith: Memoirs of a President* (Toronto: Bantam Books, 1982), 26.

4. Other initiatives included turning down White House thermostats, the use of the Herald Trumpets, and the displaying of the National Flag Cordon. See, for example, Jimmy Carter, Remarks, "Swearing-In Ceremony for Members of the Cabinet," *Weekly Compilation of Presidential Documents* Volume 13, Number 5 (January 23, 1977), 96; Memorandum, Zbigniew Brzezinski to Rick Hutcheson, February 8, 1977, "1/20/77–1/20/81" Folder, Box FE-1, White House Central Files, Jimmy Carter Library; "Resisting the 'State and Pomp,'" *Time* (December 6, 1976), 19; "If You Can't Stand the Heat," *Time* (June 23, 1979), 21; "Warm Words from Jimmy Cardigan," *Time* (February 14, 1977), 18; "Just Call Him Mister," *Time* (February 21, 1977), 11–12; "Yacht Carter banished is coming back," August 25, 1983, "1/20/77–1/20/81" Folder, Sequoia Box, White House Vertical File, Jimmy Carter Library; Susan Farrar, "Yacht Carter banished is coming back," *Atlanta Constitution* (August 25, 1983), 12-A. For Carter's quote, see Carter, *Keeping Faith*, 27; G. H. Bennett, *The American Presidency 1945–2000: Illusions of Grandeur* (Thrupp: Sutton Publishing, 2000), 169. For Smith, see Gaddis Smith, "Carter's Political Rhetoric" in Kenneth W. Thompson, ed. *The Carter Presidency: Fourteen Intimate Perspectives of Jimmy Carter* (Lanham: University Press of America, 1990), 205.

5. Julia R. Azari, *Delivering the People's Message: The Changing Politics of the Presidential Mandate* (Ithaca: Cornell University Press, 2014), 126; "Just Call Him Mister," *Time* (February 21, 1977), 11–12. See also "The Ford-Carter Character Test," *Time* (October 4, 1976), 22; "Carter's Pollster," *Time* (August 6, 1979), 14.

6. Yanek Mieczkowski, *Gerald Ford and the Challenges of the 1970s* (Lexing-

ton: University Press of Kentucky, 2005), 43. Mieczkowski cited Mark J. Rozell, *The Press and the Ford Presidency* (Ann Arbor: University of Michigan Press, 1992), 7; *Time* (July 14, 1975), 7; John Robert Greene, *The Presidency of Gerald R. Ford* (Lawrence: University of Kansas Press, 1995), 191; Ford, *A Time to Heal*, 126; "Ford in Command," *Time* (July 28, 1975), 7-10; "President's Gridiron Song Is Booted by Peking Band," *The Wall Street Journal* (December 2, 1975), 3; "Fumble by Peking Band Brings on Punt by U.S.," *The Wall Street Journal* (December 3, 1975), 26; Henry Graff, "Hour and Man May Have Met," *Time* (August 19, 1974), 64-67; "Betty and Jerry Are at Home," *Time* (December 30, 1974), 9.

7. Ford, *A Time to Heal*, 217-18.

8. James Fallows, "The Passionless Presidency," *The Atlantic* 243:5 (May 1979), 40; Louis W. Koenig, *The Chief Executive* (New York, Texas: Harcourt, Brace & World, 1960). See page 13.

9. Draft Memo, Frank Moore to Bob Lipshutz, Richard Hardin, Hamilton Jordan, nd, "Memos to & from Frank Moore" Folder, Box 6, Frank Moore Collection, Subject Files, Jimmy Carter Library.

10. The "limousine issue" refers to the fleet reductions discussed later in this chapter and the "draft amnesty" referred to Carter's pardon of draft dodgers addressed in previous chapter. See Memorandum, Jody Powell to Jimmy Carter, January 22, 1977, "1/20/77-1/20/81" Folder, Box WH-9-2, White House Central Files, Jimmy Carter Library.

11. Jimmy Carter, Remarks, "Department of the Treasury," *Weekly Compilation of Presidential Documents* Volume 13, Number 7 (February 10, 1977), 177.

12. Carter, *Keeping Faith*,18.

13. Memorandum, Bill Gulley to Jack Watson, February 23, 1977, "Military Notebook—Military Personnel at White House—Sequoia" Folder, Box 46, Hugh Carter Files, Record of the White House Office of Administration, 1977-1981, Jimmy Carter Library; Article, "Reunion on the Sequoia," September 25, 1982, "1/20/77-1/20/81" Folder, Sequoia Box, White House Vertical File, Jimmy Carter Library; "Reunion on the Sequoia," *The New York Times* (September 25, 1982), 11; Joseph Kraft, "The Carter Style: Sincere or Phony?" *The Washington Post* (February 17, 1977), A19.

14. Memorandum, Bill Gulley to Hugh Carter, February 23, 1977, "Military Notebook—Military Personnel at White House—Sequoia" Folder, Box 46, Hugh Carter Files, Record of the White House Office of Administration, 1977-1981, Jimmy Carter Library.

15. Memorandum, Hugh Carter to Jimmy Carter, March 23, 1977, "Sequoia" Folder, Box 80, Hugh Carter Files, Record of the White House Office of Administration, 1977-1981, Jimmy Carter Library.

16. Memorandum, Hugh Carter to Jimmy Carter, March 23, 1977, "Sequoia" Folder, Box 80, Hugh Carter Files, Record of the White House Office of Administration, 1977-1981, Jimmy Carter Library; Note, Rick Hutcheson to Hugh Carter, March 28, 1977, "Sequoia" Folder, Box 80, Hugh Carter Files, Record of the White House Office of Administration, 1977-1981, Jimmy Carter Library; Memorandum, Jimmy Carter to the Secretary of Defense (Harold Brown), March 30, 1977, "Sequoia" Folder, Box 80, Hugh Carter Files, Record of the White House Office of Administration, 1977-1981, Jimmy Carter Library; Announcements, *Weekly Compilation of Presidential Documents* Volume 13, Number 14 (April 1, 1977), 482; Jimmy Carter, *The Public Papers of Jimmy Carter 1977*, Book 1 (Washington, D.C.: Government Printing Press, 1977), 557.

17. Article, "All the President's Yachts," April 2, 1977, "Sequoia" Folder, Box 80, Hugh Carter Files, Record of the White House Office of Administration, 1977-1981, Jimmy Carter Library; Judith Martin, "All the President's Yachts," *The Washington Post* (April 2, 1977), D1.

18. Article, "Carter Sold Yacht—Hill May Buy It Back," May 2, 1977, "Sequoia" Folder, Box 80, Hugh Carter Files, Record of the White House Office of Administration, 1977-1981, Jimmy Carter Library; Letter, Jim Purks to Hugh Carter, April 7, 1977, "Sequoia" Folder, Box 80, Hugh Carter Files, Record of the White House Office of Administration, 1977-1981, Jimmy Carter Library.

Chapter Notes—3

19. For an account of some of the famous and infamous bidders, see "Hustler, History, Et Al Bid On Sequoia's Presidential Past," May 12, 1977, "Sequoia" Folder, Box 80, Hugh Carter Files, Record of the White House Office of Administration, 1977–1981, Jimmy Carter Library; Judith Martin, "Hustler, History, Et Al Bid On Sequoia's Presidential Past," *The Washington Post* (May 12, 1977), D1.

20. Letter, John W. Jenrette, Jr., to Frank Moore, April 26, 1977, "Sequoia" Folder, Box 80, Hugh Carter Files, Record of the White House Office of Administration, 1977–1981, Jimmy Carter Library. Another copy of the letter was in the "1/20/77–1/20/81" Folder, Box WH-9-3, White House Central Files, Jimmy Carter Library.

21. *Ibid.* For a discussion of Jenrette's "pioneering," see Merle Black and Earl Black, *The Rise of Southern Republicans* (Cambridge: Harvard University Press, 2002), 183–84.

22. Letter, Herb [Upton] to Bill [Gulley], no date, "1/20/77–1/20/81" Folder, Box WH-9-3, White House Central Files, Jimmy Carter Library; Letter, William M. Fogarty to W. L. Gulley, May 18, 1977, "1/20/77–1/20/81" Folder, Box WH-9-3, White House Central Files, Jimmy Carter Library; Letter, Len Shupe to Bill Gulley, May 4, 1977, "1/20/77–1/20/81" Folder, Box WH-9-3, White House Central Files, Jimmy Carter Library; Letter, Ronna Friedberg to Bill Gulley, May 21, 1977, "1/20/77–1/20/81" Folder, Box WH-9-3, White House Central Files, Jimmy Carter Library; Letter, W. L. Gulley to John W. Jenrette, Jr., May 24, 1977, "1/20/77–1/20/81" Folder, Box WH-9-3, White House Central Files, Jimmy Carter Library.

23. This is not the only instance of Jenrette ire toward the White House. The following year, the second-term Congressman accused the Department of Commerce of "making announcements in the district that I represent without our office being notified." Jenrette noted that he had spoke with Carter about this problem specifically and that he expected to be notified of grant announcements before the general press was told. A formal response to Jenrette was not found but in the letter on file, Hamilton Jordan had written "I'm damn tired of this crap." See Letter, John W. Jenrette, Jr., to Juanita Kreps, April 12, 1978, "Memos to & from Frank Moore" Folder, Box 6, Frank Moore Collection, Subject Files, Jimmy Carter Library.

24. Article, "The Sequoia: The High Bid," "Sequoia" Folder, Box 80, Hugh Carter Files, Record of the White House Office of Administration, 1977–1981, Jimmy Carter Library; Judith Martin, "The Sequoia: The High Bid," *The Washington Post* (May 19, 1977), C1; Letter, Harold Brown to the President, May 24, 1977, "1/20/77–1/20/81" Folder, Box WH-9-3, White House Central Files, Jimmy Carter Library; "Navigation Regulations," *Federal Register* 42:189 (September 29, 1977), 51574.

25. Utley included the January 25, 1974, edition of the *Federal Register*, most recently updating their jurisdiction. Advisory Council on History Preservation, "Procedures for the Protection of Historic and Cultural Properties: Establishment of New Chapter and Part," *Federal Register* 39:18 (January 25, 1974), 3365–70; Letter, Robert M. Utley to Francis B. Rouche, April 21, 1977, "1/20/77–1/20/81" Folder, Box WH-9-3, White House Central Files, Jimmy Carter Library; Article, "Hustler, History, Et Al Bid On Sequoia's Presidential Past," May 12, 1977, "Sequoia" Folder, Box 80, Hugh Carter Files, Record of the White House Office of Administration, 1977–1981, Jimmy Carter Library; Judith Martin, "Hustler, History, Et Al Bid On Sequoia's Presidential Past," *The Washington Post* (May 12, 1977), D1; Letter, James A. Joseph to W. Graham Claytor, Jr., May 16, 1977, "Sequoia 4–5/77" Folder, Box 142, Margaret McKenna Files, White House Counsel's Office Files, 1977–1981, Jimmy Carter Library; Article, "The Sequoia: A Victim of Due Process," "Sequoia" Folder, Box 80, Hugh Carter Files, Record of the White House Office of Administration, 1977–1981, Jimmy Carter Library; Judith Martin, "The Sequoia: A Victim of Due Process," *The Washington Post* (May 20, 1977), B8.

26. Memorandum, Margaret McKenna to Joe Cornelison, April 25, 1977, "1/20/77–1/20/81" Folder, Box WH-9-3,

Chapter Notes—3

White House Central Files, Jimmy Carter Library; Memorandum, Joe Cornelison to Margaret McKenna, April 26, 1977, "1/20/77–1/20/81" Folder, Box WH-9-3, White House Central Files, Jimmy Carter Library; Richard Nixon, Executive Order, "Protection and Enhancement of the Cultural Environment," *Weekly Compilation of Presidential Documents* Volume 7, Number 20 (May 13, 1971), 757–58; 16 United States Code 470 (1966); Memorandum, Joe Cornelison to Margaret McKenna, April 26, 1977, "1/20/77–1/20/81" Folder, Box WH-9-3, White House Central Files, Jimmy Carter Library.

27. Leisurecraft agreed not to do any of the following without Navy approval: "First, change the configuration of the hull. Second, substantially modify the interior of the vessel. Third, change the vessel's colors, i.e., those parts of the vessel that are white will remain white, those that are varnished will remain varnished." See Memorandum, Robert Lipshutz and Margaret McKenna to Jody Powell, May 23, 1977, "Sequoia 4–5/77" Folder, Box 142, Margaret McKenna Files, White House Counsel's Office Files, 1977–1981, Jimmy Carter Library; Memorandum, Robert R. Garvey, Jr., to Hugh Carter, July 6, 1977, "Sequoia" Folder, Box 80, Hugh Carter Files, Record of the White House Office of Administration, 1977–1981, Jimmy Carter Library; Memorandum, Bob Lipshutz to Jody Powell, May 23, 1977, "Sequoia" Folder, Box 80, Hugh Carter Files, Record of the White House Office of Administration, 1977–1981, Jimmy Carter Library; Memorandum, Bob Lipshutz to Jody Powell, May 23, 1977, "Sequoia 4–5/77" Folder, Box 142, Margaret McKenna Files, White House Counsel's Office Files, 1977–1981, Jimmy Carter Library.

28. *Congressional Record*, 97th Congress, 1st Session, 1981, Volume 127, part 10:12629.

29. Article, "Search For Presidential Yacht Quietly Sails Onto Back Burner" and "No Reagan Yacht Now," "Sequoia" Folder, Vertical File, Jimmy Carter Library; "Search For Presidential Yacht Quietly Sails Onto Back Burner," *The Washington Star* (June 4, 1981), 1; "No Reagan Yacht Now," *The New York Times* (June 4, 1981); Article, "Yacht Enjoyed By Presidents No Ship of State," "Sequoia" Folder, Vertical File, Jimmy Carter Library; Jane Mayer, "Yacht Enjoyed By Presidents No Ship of State," *The Washington Star* (June 29, 1981); Article, "Sequoia Returns to Home Port," June 29, 1981, "1/20/77–1/20/81" Folder, Sequoia Box, White House Vertical File, Jimmy Carter Library; David Remnick, "Sequoia Returns to Home Port," *The Washington Post* (June 29, 1981), C1, C7.

30. For an explanation of the law of unintended consequences, see Steve M. Gillon, *"That's Not What We Meant to Do": Reform And Its Unintended Consequences in Twentieth-Century America* (New York: W. W. Norton & Company, 2000).

31. Article, "Ship of State Sails Out of the Past; Sequoia All Decked Out for Buyers," April 17, 1998, "1/20/77–1/20/81" Folder, Sequoia Box, White House Vertical File, Jimmy Carter Library; Ken Ringle, "Ship of State Sails Out of the Past; Sequoia All Decked Out for Buyers," *The Washington Post* (April 17, 1998), B1; "Camp David: A Palatial Retreat," *Time* (February 13, 1976), 10. Also, even Carter occasionally took vacations. See, for example, "Rafting in the Rockies," *Time* (September 4, 1978), 12–13. The *Sequoia* is currently still afloat and available as of 2016 for rent or visitation. For more information, see http://www.sequoiayacht.com/aboutus.htm.

32. Memorandum, Stu Eizenstat to Greg Schneiders, December 12, 1976, "White House Organization, 11/76–1/77" Folder, Box 3, Office of Staff Secretary, Handwriting File, 1976 Campaign Transition File, Jimmy Carter Library.

33. For the quotes, see Jimmy Carter, Address, "Report to the American People," *Weekly Compilation of Presidential Documents* Volume 13, Number 6 (February 2, 1977), 141–42; Carter, *Keeping Faith*, 26. For further discussion of the transportation ballet, see Memorandum, Jimmy Carter to H. S. Knight, January 21, 1977, "1/20/77–1/20/81" Folder, Box WH-9-2, White House Central Files, Jimmy Carter Library. Though Carter received much praise for his action in the press, his staff sometimes missed their perquisites. (Ultimately, though, they understood the nature of the measure.) See, for example,

"Just Call Him Mister," *Time* (February 21, 1977), 11–12; "Hannibal Astride the Potomac," *Time* (March 14, 1977), 14.

34. Proxmire noted there were five exceptions to this rule: (1) the President, (2) members of his cabinet, (3) physicians on outpatient duty, (4) officials on "field service" far from their home, and (5) ambassadors abroad. See Letter, William Proxmire to Hamilton Jordan, January 31, 1977, "1/20/77–1/20/81" Folder, Box WH-9-2, White House Central Files, Jimmy Carter Library.

35. Memorandum, Jimmy Carter to H. S. Knight, January 21, 1977, "1/20/77–1/20/81" Folder, Box WH-9-2, White House Central Files, Jimmy Carter Library; Note, [Elian] to [Millie D.], no date, "1/20/77–1/20/81" Folder, Box WH-9-2, White House Central Files, Jimmy Carter Library; Letter, Hugh Carter to William Proxmire, February 10, 1977, "1/20/77–1/20/81" Folder, Box WH-9-2, White House Central Files, Jimmy Carter Library; Letter, Hamilton Jordan to William Proxmire, February 4, 1977, "1/20/77–1/20/81" Folder, Box WH-9-2, White House Central Files, Jimmy Carter Library.

36. Letter, H. S. Knight to Jimmy Carter, February 10, 1977, "1/20/77–1/20/81" Folder, Box WH-9-2, White House Central Files, Jimmy Carter Library.

37. Letter, Jimmy Carter to Mike Blumenthal, February 15, 1977, "1/20/77–1/20/81" Folder, Box WH-9-2, White House Central Files, Jimmy Carter Library.

38. Letter, Jimmy Carter to Jim Maloney, October 21, 1977, "1/20/77–1/20/81" Folder, Box WH-9-2, White House Central Files, Jimmy Carter Library.

39. White House Press Release, June 22, 1977, "Sequoia" Folder, Box 80, Hugh Carter Files, Record of the White House Office of Administration, 1977–1981, Jimmy Carter Library.

40. Carter, *Keeping Faith*, 26–27.

41. Jimmy Carter, Remarks, "Conversation With the President," *Weekly Compilation of Presidential Documents* Volume 13, Number 53 (December 28, 1977), 1954; Interview, Robert MacNeil, et al., of Jimmy Carter, "Interview with the President," December 28, 1977, "Chronological" Folder, Box 12, Records of the Speechwriters Office, 1977–1981, Jimmy Carter Library. James Fallows also felt Carter's "style of thought" crippled him. "He thinks he 'leads' by choosing the correct policy; but he fails to project a vision larger than the problem he is tackling at the moment." However, Fallows did concede that Carter gradually became more adept at Congressional relations. See Fallows, 42–43.

Chapter 4

1. *Congressional Record*, 95th Congress, 1st Session, 1977, Volume 123, part17:21837; *Congressional Record*, 95th Congress, 1st Session, 1977, Volume 123, part 19:24331–2,24493–4; John B. Oakes, "The Pork-Barrel Challenge," *The New York Times* (July 21, 1977), 23.

2. David Mayhew wrote the seminal work on reelection as the driving force for senators and representatives. See David R. Mayhew, *Congress: The Electoral Connection* (New Haven: Yale University Press, 1974).

3. Letter, William Proxmire, et al., to Jimmy Carter, February 14, 1977, "Water Projects (2/77–3/77) and (Undated) [CF, O/A 46] [1]" Folder, Box 315, Eizenstat, Staff Offices Domestic Policy Staff, Jimmy Carter Library.

4. Letter, Jimmy Carter to Congress, no date, "Water Projects, 2/15/77–4/16/77 [O/A 6473]" Folder, Box 50, Office of Congressional Liaison Moore, Jimmy Carter Library; Note, Rick Hutcheson to Frank Moore, February 17, 1977, "Water Projects, 2/15/77–4/16/77 [O/A 6473]" Folder, Box 50, Office of Congressional Liaison Moore, Jimmy Carter Library; Memorandum, Stu Eizenstat to Jimmy Carter, February 16, 1977, "Water Projects, 2/15/77–4/16/77 [O/A 6473]" Folder, Box 50, Office of Congressional Liaison Moore, Jimmy Carter Library.

5. The nineteen projects were: Cache Basin (Arkansas); Richard B. Russell (Georgia/South Carolina); Freeport (Illinois); Grove Lake (Kansas); Dayton (Kentucky); Paintsville Lake (Kentucky); Yatesville Lake (Kentucky); Atchafalaya River and Bayous Chene, Boeuf, and Black

Chapter Notes—4

(Louisiana); Dickey-Lincoln School Lakes (Maine); Meramec Park Lake (Missouri); Lukfata Lake (Oklahoma); Central Arizona Project (Arizona); Auburn-Folsom South and Central Valley Project (California); Dolores (Colorado); Fruitland Mesa (Colorado); Garrison Diversion Unit (North Dakota/South Dakota); Oahe Unit (South Dakota); and Central Utah Project and Bonneville Unit (Utah). See, for example, White House Projects Meeting, March 10, 1977, "Water Projects, 3/77" Folder, Box 42, Plains File, Subject File, Transition: State and Defense Options, Jimmy Carter Library; *Congressional Record,* 95th Congress, 1st Session, 1977, Volume 123, part 4:4810. For the Graves memo, see Memorandum, Ernest Graves to Stu Eizenstat, February 20, 1977, "Water Project Briefing, 3/10/77 [O/A 6748]" Folder, Box 50, Office of Congressional Liaison Moore, Jimmy Carter Library; Charles O. Jones, *The Trusteeship Presidency: Jimmy Carter and the United States Congress* (Baton Rouge: Louisiana State University Press, 1988), 143.

6. Garland A. Haas, *Jimmy Carter and the Politics of Frustration* (Jefferson: McFarland & Company, Inc., 1992), 76; Press Release, February 21, 1977, "Water Projects, 1/77–4/77 [1]" Folder, Box 29, Eleanor Weaver's Subject Files, White House Press Office Media Liaison Office, Jimmy Carter Library. Colbert's original quote can be found in many places. See, for example, William Sharp McKechnie. *The State & the Individual: An Introduction to Political Science, with Special Reference to Socialistic and Individualistic Theories* (Glasgow: James MacLehose and Sons, 1896), 77.

7. Press Release, February 21, 1977, "Water Projects (2/77–3/77) and (Undated) [CF, O/A 46] [1]" Folder, Box 315, Eizenstat, Staff Offices Domestic Policy Staff, Jimmy Carter Library; Edwin C. Hargrove, *Jimmy Carter as President: Leadership and the Politics of the Public Good* (Baton Rouge: Louisiana State University Press, 1988), 93.

8. Memorandum of Call, John Hesse to Jim [Purks], February 23, 1976, Press Release, February 21, 1977, "Water Projects, 1/77–4/77 [1]" Folder, Box 29, Eleanor Weaver's Subject Files, White House Press Office Media Liaison Office, Jimmy Carter Library.

9. Burton I. Kaufman and Scott Kaufman, *The Presidency of James Earl Carter, Jr.* (Lawrence: University of Kansas Press, 2006), 35.

10. *Congressional Record,* 95th Congress, 1st Session, 1977, Volume 123, part 3:2792–2795; *Congressional Record,* 95th Congress, 1st Session, 1977, Volume 123, part 4:4939; *Congressional Record,* 95th Congress, 1st Session, 1977, Volume 123, part 5:5408.

11. *Congressional Record,* 95th Congress, 1st Session, 1977, Volume 123, part 5:5747–51, 6114; *Congressional Record,* 95th Congress, 1st Session, 1977, Volume 123, part 6:6946–8.

12. *Congressional Record,* 95th Congress, 1st Session, 1977, Volume 123, part 6:6456–7.

13. Memorandum, Stu Eizenstat to Jimmy Carter, February 24, 1977, "Water Projects (2/77–3/77) and (Undated) [CF, O/A 46] [1]" Folder, Box 315, Eizenstat, Staff Offices Domestic Policy Staff, Jimmy Carter Library; Letter, Edmund S. Muskie and William D. Hathaway to Jimmy Carter, February 22, 1977, "Water Projects (2/77–3/77) and (Undated) [CF, O/A 46] [1]" Folder, Box 315, Eizenstat, Staff Offices Domestic Policy Staff, Jimmy Carter Library; Letter, Edmund S. Muskie and William D. Hathaway to Jimmy Carter, January 17, 1977, "Water Projects (2/77–3/77) and (Undated) [CF, O/A 46] [1]" Folder, Box 315, Eizenstat, Staff Offices Domestic Policy Staff, Jimmy Carter Library; Memorandum, Dan Tate to Frank Moore, February 23, 1977, "Water Project Briefing, 3/10/77 [O/A 6748]" Folder, Box 50, Office of Congressional Liaison Moore, Jimmy Carter Library; Letter, Edmund Muskie and William D. Hathaway to Jimmy Carter, February 22, 1977, "Water Project Briefing, 3/10/77 [O/A 6748]" Folder, Box 50, Office of Congressional Liaison Moore, Jimmy Carter Library.

14. Memorandum, Dan Tate to Frank Moore, February 23, 1977, "Water Projects, 2/18/77–10/6/78 [CF, O/A 625]" Folder, Box 50, Office of Congressional Liaison Moore, Jimmy Carter Library.

15. *Congressional Record*, 95th Congress, 1st Session, 1977, Volume 123, part 5:5742.
16. Memorandum, Stu Eizenstat to Secretary of Defense, et al., February 28, 1977, "Water Project Briefing, 3/10/77 [O/A 6748]" Folder, Box 50, Office of Congressional Liaison Moore, Jimmy Carter Library.
17. Letter, Jimmy Carter to Wayne Sanstead, March 1, 1977, "Water Projects, 2/18/77–10/6/78 [CF, O/A 625]" Folder, Box 50, Office of Congressional Liaison Moore, Jimmy Carter Library.
18. Letter, [B.] Kevin Molloy to Jim Purks, March 28, 1977, "Water Projects, 1/77–4/77 [1]" Folder, Box 29, Eleanor Weaver's Subject Files, White House Press Office Media Liaison Office, Jimmy Carter Library; Letter, Jim Purks to Kevin Molloy, March 28, 1977, "Water Projects, 1/77–4/77 [1]" Folder, Box 29, Eleanor Weaver's Subject Files, White House Press Office Media Liaison Office, Jimmy Carter Library; Letter, Gerald L. Pond to Jimmy Carter, April 2, 1977, "Water Projects, 1/77–4/77 [1]" Folder, Box 29, Eleanor Weaver's Subject Files, White House Press Office Media Liaison Office, Jimmy Carter Library; Letter, Jim Purks to Gerald L. Pond, April 11, 1977, "Water Projects, 1/77–4/77 [1]" Folder, Box 29, Eleanor Weaver's Subject Files, White House Press Office Media Liaison Office, Jimmy Carter Library.
19. Letter, B. Kevin Molloy to Jason Friedman, March 11, 2017. Email Correspondence.
20. The following senators met with Eizenstat and Moore: James Abourezk (D-SD), Dewey F. Bartlett (R-OK), Quentin N. Burdick (D-ND), Robert C. Byrd (D-WV), Alan Cranston (D-CA), John C. Danforth (R-MO), Dennis DeConcini (D-AZ), Pete V. Domenici (R-NM), Wendell H. Ford (D-KY), Jake Garn (R-UT), Barry Goldwater (R-AZ), Mike Gravel (D-AK), Clifford P. Hansen (R-WY), Gary Hart (D-CO), Orrin G. Hatch (R-UT), William D. Hathaway (D-Maine), Sam Hayakawa (R-CA), Ernest F. Hollings (D-SC), Walter Huddleston (D-KY), J. Bennett Johnston (D-LA), Russell B. Long (D-LA), George McGovern (D-SD), Sam Nunn (D-GA), Harrison Schmitt (R-NM), John C. Stennis (D-MS), Strom Thurmond (R-SC), Malcolm Wallop (R-WY), and Milton R. Young (R-ND). Similarly, the following members of Congress were at the meeting, too: James Abdnor (R-SD), Bill Alexander (D-AR), John B. Anderson (R-IL), Mark Andrews (R-ND), D. Douglas Barnard (D-GA), John B. Breaux (D-LA), William S. Cohen (R-ME), Butler Derrick (D-SC), Frank E. Evans (D-CO), Richard H. Ichord (D-MO), Edgar L. Jenkins (D-GA), Harold T. "Bizz" Johnson (D-CA), James P. Johnson (R-CO), Martha Keys (D-KS), John J. McFall (R-CA), K. Gunn McKay (D-UT), David D. "Dan" Marriott (R-UT), John E. Moss (D-CA), Carl D. Perkins (D-KY), Larry Pressler (R-SD), John J. Rhodes (R-AZ), Teno Roncalio (D-WY), Eldon D. Rudd (R-AZ), Arlan Stangeland (R-MN), Bob Stump (D-AZ), Morris K. Udall (D-AZ), and Wesley W. Watkins (D-OK). See White House Projects Meeting, March 10, 1977, "Water Projects, 3/77" Folder, Box 42, Plains File, Subject File, Transition: State and Defense Options, Jimmy Carter Library; Meeting with members of Congress on Water Resource Projects, March 10, 1977, "Water Projects, 3/77" Folder, Box 42, Plains File, Subject File, Transition: State and Defense Options, Jimmy Carter Library; Memorandum, Rick Hutcheson to Frank Moore, March 7, 1977, "Water Project Briefing, 3/10/77 [O/A 6748]" Folder, Box 50, Office of Congressional Liaison Moore, Jimmy Carter Library; Memorandum, Frank Moore to Jimmy Carter, March 4, 1977, "Water Project Briefing, 3/10/77 [O/A 6748]" Folder, Box 50, Office of Congressional Liaison Moore, Jimmy Carter Library.
21. Meeting, Stu Eizenstat and Frank Moore with Members of Congress, March 9, 1977, "Water Project Briefing, 3/10/77 [O/A 6748]" Folder, Box 50, Office of Congressional Liaison Moore, Jimmy Carter Library.
22. Remarks, Bert Lance to Members of Congress, March 10, 1977, "Water Projects, 1/77–4/77 [1]" Folder, Box 29, Eleanor Weaver's Subject Files, White House Press Office Media Liaison Office, Jimmy Carter Library.
23. *Congressional Record*, 95th Con-

Chapter Notes—4

gress, 1st Session, 1977, Volume 123, part 6:7503–5.

24. Letter, Ann Dye to Frank Moore, March 14, 1977, "Water Projects, 2/18/77–10/6/78 [CF, O/A 625]" Folder, Box 50, Office of Congressional Liaison Moore, Jimmy Carter Library; Michael Baron,e "The beginning of the end for Nancy Pelosi?" *New York Post* (November 28, 2014). Available online at http://nypost.com/2014/11/28/the-beginning-of-the-end-for-nancy-pelosi/; Burton I. Kaufman and Scott Kaufman, *The Presidency of James Earl Carter, Jr.* (Lawrence: University of Kansas Press, 2006), 23; Norman Ornstein, "Can Clinton Still Emerge a Winner; Here's What to Do," *Roll Call* (May 27, 1993). Available online through Lexis-Nexis Academic. (Accessed September 19, 2006.)

25. Memorandum, Kathy Fletcher to Stu Eizenstat, March 15, 1977, "Water Project Review—Basic Documents 1977 [C/F, O/A 169] [1]" Folder, Box 50, Domestic Policy Staff, Kathy Fletcher's Subject Files, Jimmy Carter Library.

26. Letter, Jimmy Carter to Members of Congress, March 16, 1977, "Water Projects, 1/77–4/77 [1]" Folder, Box 29, Eleanor Weaver's Subject Files, White House Press Office Media Liaison Office, Jimmy Carter Library; Letter, Jimmy Carter to Members of Congress, March 16, 1977, "Water Projects, 2/18/77–10/6/78 [CF, O/A 625]" Folder, Box 50, Office of Congressional Liaison Moore, Jimmy Carter Library.

27. Michelle Norris, "Sifting Through the Friday News Dump," *NPR: All Things Considered* (June 30, 2005). Available online at http://www.npr.org/templates/story/story.php?storyId=4725120. An excellent explanation of this practice comes from Aaron Sorkin (via dialogue delivered by Bradley Whitford in *The West Wing*, Season 1, Episode 13, which aired January 26, 2000). The episode title was "Take Out the Trash Day," a euphemism for the Friday news dump.

28. Memorandum, Stu Eizenstat to Jimmy Carter, March 18, 1977, "Water Projects (2/77–3/77) and (Undated) [CF, O/A 46] [1]" Folder, Box 315, Eizenstat, Staff Offices Domestic Policy Staff, Jimmy Carter Library; Memorandum, Bert Lance to Jimmy Carter, March 16 or 17, 1977, "Water Projects (2/77–3/77) and (Undated) [CF, O/A 46] [1]" Folder, Box 315, Eizenstat, Staff Offices Domestic Policy Staff, Jimmy Carter Library; *Congressional Record*, 95th Congress, 1st Session, 1977, Volume 123, part 7:8306–18; *Congressional Record*, 95th Congress, 1st Session, 1977, Volume 123, part 8: 9116–9, 9122, 9473–5, 9480–2. For other examples of senators and representatives speaking out about their local projects, see *Congressional Record*, 95th Congress, 1st Session, 1977, Volume 123, part 6:7505–6, 7595–6; *Congressional Record*, 95th Congress, 1st Session, 1977, Volume 123, part 7:7891, 8782–4, 8885–7; *Congressional Record*, 95th Congress, 1st Session, 1977, Volume 123, part 8:9130, 9511–2, 9542, 9708–10, 9732–4; *Congressional Record*, 95th Congress, 1st Session, 1977, Volume 123, part 8:10011; *Congressional Record*, 95th Congress, 1st Session, 1977, Volume 123, part 9:10587–9.

29. Memorandum, Kitty Schirmer and Kathy Fletcher to Stu Eizenstat, March 18, 1977, "Water Projects (2/77–3/77) and (Undated) [CF, O/A 46] [1]" Folder, Box 315, Eizenstat, Staff Offices Domestic Policy Staff, Jimmy Carter Library; Memorandum, Kitty Schirmer and Kathy Fletcher to Stu Eizenstat, March 11, 1977, "Water Projects (2/77–3/77) and (Undated) [CF, O/A 46] [1]" Folder, Box 315, Eizenstat, Staff Offices Domestic Policy Staff, Jimmy Carter Library; Memorandum, Jim Purks to Rick Hutcheson, March 25, 1977, "Water Projects, 1/77–4/77 [1]" Folder, Box 29, Eleanor Weaver's Subject Files, White House Press Office Media Liaison Office, Jimmy Carter Library. Fletcher had just been exonerated from a he said/she said potential leak scandal. Allegedly, Fletcher leaked a larger list of water projects and stated that 90% to 95% of them "would be recommended for termination." Fletcher countered that the leak was in fact the bungling of the Bureau of Reclamation. Carter defended Fletcher, corroborating her story with the stories of the other administration representatives who had access to the sensitive material at the meeting in question. Carter rejected

Chapter Notes—4

a recommendation by Hutcheson to insulate Fletcher—that is segregate her—from participation in future water project meetings to eliminate the possibility that she would continue to be pegged as the leak. See Note, Rick Hutcheson to Stu Eizenstat, March 22, 1977, "Water Projects (2/77–3/77) and (Undated) [CF, O/A 46] [1]" Folder, Box 315, Eizenstat, Staff Offices Domestic Policy Staff, Jimmy Carter Library; Memorandum, Stu Eizenstat to Jimmy Carter, March 15, 1977, "Water Projects (2/77–3/77) and (Undated) [CF, O/A 46] [1]" Folder, Box 315, Eizenstat, Staff Offices Domestic Policy Staff, Jimmy Carter Library; Memorandum, Stu Eizenstat to Jimmy Carter, March 22, 1977, "Water Projects (2/77–3/77) and (Undated) [CF, O/A 46] [1]" Folder, Box 315, Eizenstat, Staff Offices Domestic Policy Staff, Jimmy Carter Library; Note, Joanne [?] to Stu [Eizenstat], March 8, 1977, "Water Projects (2/77–3/77) and (Undated) [CF, O/A 46] [1]" Folder, Box 315, Eizenstat, Staff Offices Domestic Policy Staff, Jimmy Carter Library.

30. Letter, Ivan Swift to Frank Moore, March 28, 1977, "Water Projects, 2/18/77–10/6/78 [CF, O/A 625]" Folder, Box 50, Office of Congressional Liaison Moore, Jimmy Carter Library; Don Walker, "Ban on Paintsville Dam Lifted along with Other Projects," *Lexington Herald* (March 24, 1977), A1, A20.

31. Draft Memorandum, Frank Moore to Jimmy Carter, March 31, 1977, "Water Project Review—Basic Documents 1977 [C/F, O/A 169] [1]" Folder, Box 50, Domestic Policy Staff, Kathy Fletcher's Subject Files, Jimmy Carter Library.

32. Memorandum, Frank Moore to [Jimmy Carter], April, 5, 1977, "Water Projects, 2/18/77–10/6/78 [CF, O/A 625]" Folder, Box 50, Office of Congressional Liaison Moore, Jimmy Carter Library.

33. Kaufman and Kaufman, 35.

34. Note, Craig [Raupe] to Frank [Moore], April 6, 1977, "Water Projects, 2/15/77–4/16/77 [O/A 6473]" Folder, Box 50, Office of Congressional Liaison Moore, Jimmy Carter Library.

35. Memorandum, Stu Eizenstat to Frank Moore, et al., April 16, 1977, "Water Projects, 2/15/77–4/16/77 [O/A 6473]" Folder, Box 50, Office of Congressional Liaison Moore, Jimmy Carter Library; Memorandum, Stu Eizenstat to Jimmy Carter, et al., April 16, 1977, "Water Projects, 2/15/77–4/16/77 [O/A 6473]" Folder, Box 50, Office of Congressional Liaison Moore, Jimmy Carter Library; Memorandum, Dan Tate to Frank Moore, April 16, 1977, "Water Projects, 2/18/77–10/6/78 [CF, O/A 625]" Folder, Box 50, Office of Congressional Liaison Moore, Jimmy Carter Library.

36. Memorandum, Stu Eizenstat to Cecil Andrus, April 16, 1977, "Water Projects (4/77–5/77) [CF, O/A 46] [2]" Folder, Box 315, Staff Offices, Domestic Policy Staff, Eizenstat, Jimmy Carter Library; Memorandum, Stu Eizenstat to the President, April 16, 1977, "Water Projects (4/77–5/77) [CF, O/A 46] [2]" Folder, Box 315, Staff Offices, Domestic Policy Staff, Eizenstat, Jimmy Carter Library.

37. Note, Jimmy Carter to Stu Eizenstat, April 15. 1977, "Water Projects (4/77–5/77) [CF, O/A 46] [2]" Folder, Box 315, Staff Offices, Domestic Policy Staff, Eizenstat, Jimmy Carter Library.

38. Statement on Water Projects, April 18, 1977, "Water Projects, 1/77–4/77 [1]" Folder, Box 29, Eleanor Weaver's Subject Files, White House Press Office Media Liaison Office, Jimmy Carter Library.

39. Letter, Richard D. Lamm to Jimmy Carter, April 20, 1977, "Water Projects (4/77–5/77) [CF, O/A 46] [1]" Folder, Box 315, Staff Offices, Domestic Policy Staff, Eizenstat, Jimmy Carter Library; Letter, Stu Eizenstat to Richard D. Lamm, April 20, 1977, "Water Projects (4/77–5/77) [CF, O/A 46] [1]" Folder, Box 315, Staff Offices, Domestic Policy Staff, Eizenstat, Jimmy Carter Library.

40. Draft Letter, [Jimmy Carter] to Members of the House Appropriations Committee, May 1977, "Water Projects, 2/18/77–10/6/78 [CF, O/A 625]" Folder, Box 50, Office of Congressional Liaison Moore, Jimmy Carter Library; Meeting, Jim Wright, Bizz Johnson, Tom Bevill, Gunn McKay, Jamie Whitten, and Jimmy Carter, May 2, 1977, "Water Projects (4/77–5/77) [CF, O/A 46] [1]" Folder, Box 315, Staff Offices, Domestic Policy Staff, Eizenstat, Jimmy Carter Library.

Chapter Notes—4

41. *Congressional Record*, 95th Congress, 1st Session, 1977, Volume 123, part 17:21028–9.

42. Memorandum, Water Mondale, Stu Eizenstat, and Frank Moore to Jimmy Carter, May 4, 1977, "Water Projects (4/77–5/77) [CF, O/A 46] [2]" Folder, Box 315, Staff Offices, Domestic Policy Staff, Eizenstat, Jimmy Carter Library.

43. *Congressional Record*, 95th Congress, 1st Session, 1977, Volume 123, part 12:13790–3. For other arguments similar to McKay's, see, for example, *Congressional Record*, 95th Congress, 1st Session, 1977, Volume 123, part 10:12524–6; *Congressional Record*, 95th Congress, 1st Session, 1977, Volume 123, part 11:12755–9; *Congressional Record*, 95th Congress, 1st Session, 1977, Volume 123, part 13:15260–1; *Congressional Record*, 95th Congress, 1st Session, 1977, Volume 123, part 14:17056–7; *Congressional Record*, 95th Congress, 1st Session, 1977, Volume 123, part 16:19606–7; *Congressional Record*, 95th Congress, 1st Session, 1977, Volume 123, part 17:21058–9.

44. *Congressional Record*, 95th Congress, 1st Session, 1977, Volume 123, part 14:17260.

45. Memorandum, Stu Eizenstat and Frank Moore to Jimmy Carter, June 6, 1977, "Water Projects (4/77–5/77) [CF, O/A 46] [2]" Folder, Box 315, Staff Offices, Domestic Policy Staff, Eizenstat, Jimmy Carter Library; Memorandum, Kathy Fletcher to Stu Eizenstat, June 6, 1977, "Water Projects (4/77–5/77) [CF, O/A 46] [2]" Folder, Box 315, Staff Offices, Domestic Policy Staff, Eizenstat, Jimmy Carter Library; Memorandum, Frank Moore to Jimmy Carter, June 6, 1977, "Water Projects (4/77–5/77) [CF, O/A 46] [2]" Folder, Box 315, Staff Offices, Domestic Policy Staff, Eizenstat, Jimmy Carter Library.

46. Note, Rick Hutcheson to Frank Moore, et al., June 23, 1977, "Water Projects, 2/18/77–10/6/78 [CF, O/A 625]" Folder, Box 50, Office of Congressional Liaison Moore, Jimmy Carter Library; Memorandum, Stu Eizenstat to [Jimmy Carter], June 20, 1977, "Water Projects, 2/18/77–10/6/78 [CF, O/A 625]" Folder, Box 50, Office of Congressional Liaison Moore, Jimmy Carter Library.

47. Memorandum, Rick Merrill to Frank Moore, June 27, 1977, "Water Projects, 2/18/77–10/6/78 [CF, O/A 625]" Folder, Box 50, Office of Congressional Liaison Moore, Jimmy Carter Library; Memorandum, Stu Eizenstat to [Jimmy Carter], June 20, 1977, "Water Projects, 2/18/77–10/6/78 [CF, O/A 625]" Folder, Box 50, Office of Congressional Liaison Moore, Jimmy Carter Library. For a description of Rick Merrill's job at this time, see, for example, Jim Free's exit interview. Available online at https://www.jimmycarterlibrary.gov/assets/documents/oral_histories/exit_interviews/Free.pdf. (Accessed May 22, 2017.)

48. *Congressional Record*, 95th Congress, 1st Session, 1977, Volume 123, part 17:21806–10.

49. *Congressional Record*, 95th Congress, 1st Session, 1977, Volume 123, part 17:21805, 21821.

50. *Congressional Record*, 95th Congress, 1st Session, 1977, Volume 123, part 17:21830–7.

51. *Congressional Record*, 95th Congress, 1st Session, 1977, Volume 123, part 17:21837.

52. *Congressional Record*, 95th Congress, 1st Session, 1977, Volume 123, part 17:21838, 21844, 21853; *Congressional Record*, 95th Congress, 1st Session, 1977, Volume 123, part 22:28156, 27676. For other statements, see, for example, *Congressional Record*, 95th Congress, 1st Session, 1977, Volume 123, part 20:24892–3, 25410; *Congressional Record*, 95th Congress, 1st Session, 1977, Volume 123, part 22:28600.

53. *Congressional Record*, 95th Congress, 1st Session, 1977, Volume 123, part 19:24331–2, 24493; John B. Oakes, "The Pork Barrel Challenge," *The New York Times* (July 21, 1975), 23.

54. Jimmy Carter, "Public Works Appropriations Bill Statement on Signing H.R. 7553 Into Law," August 8, 1977. Available online by Gerhard Peters and John T. Woolley, *The American Presidency Project*. Available online at https://www.presidency.ucsb.edu/documents/public-works-appropriations-bill-statement-signing-hr-7553-into-law.

55. *Ibid.*

56. Jimmy Carter: "The President's News Conference," July 12, 1977. Online by Gerhard Peters and John T. Woolley, *The American Presidency Project*. Available online at http://www.presidency.ucsb.edu/documents/the-presidents-news-conference-109.

Chapter 5

1. *Congressional Record*, 96th Congress, 2nd Session, 1980, Volume 126, part 7:8580–1.

2. "Recommendations For The Treatment of Civilian and Military Offenders of the Vietnam Era," no date, "Pardon, etc. Vietnam War, 01/1977–10/1978" Folder, Box 41, White House Counsel's Office Files, Jimmy Carter Library.

3. Specifically, on March 29, 1975, President Ford signed Proclamation 4360, Terminating Registration Procedures Under Military Selective Service Act, eliminating the registration requirement for all 18–25-year-old male citizens. See Gerald R. Ford, Proclamation, "Proclamation 4360—Terminating Registration Procedures Under the Military Selective Service Act, As Amended. March 29 1975," *Weekly Compilation of Presidential Documents* Volume 11, Number 14 (April 7, 1975), 318–19.

4. Bernard Rostker, *I Want You! The Evolution of the All-Volunteer Force* (Santa Monica: RAND Corporation, 2006). Rostker's book provides and exhaustively informative account of the modern All-Volunteer Force but his chapter on the renewal of the registration under Carter focuses more on the role—his role—as Director of the Selective Service than it does on Carter's actions. He even admits in a footnote that the narrative slips into the first person surrounding some events. For Ford's decision to let draft registration lapse, see pages 418–23. For Carter's position in 1979, see pages 417–418. For Eizenstat's statement, see pages 428–29.

5. Détente is generally defined as a general cooling in otherwise strained relations. The success of Carter's détente policy and his foreign policy in general is something of significant contention amongst historians. See, for example, Donald S. Spencer, *The Carter Implosion: Jimmy Carter and the Amateur Style of Diplomacy* (New York: Praeger, 1988); John Dumbrell, *The Carter Presidency: A Re-Evaluation* (Manchester, New York: Manchester University Press, 1993); Burton I. Kaufman and Scott Kaufman, *The Presidency of James Earl Carter, Jr.* (Lawrence: University of Kansas Press, 2006).

6. Rostker, 431, 424, 436; "House Vote on Draft Bill," *The New York Times* (August 13, 1941).

7. Jimmy Carter, "State of the Union Address 1980" (January 23, 1980). Available online at http://www.jimmycarterlibrary.org/documents/speeches/su80jec.phtml. (Accessed May 3, 2010.)

8. The proclamation said, "The Congress of the United States has made available the funds (H.J. Res. 521, approved by me on June 27, 1980), which are needed to initiate this registration, beginning with those born on or after January 1, 1960." See Jimmy Carter, Proclamation, "Registration Under the Military Selective Service Act: Proclamation 4771. July 2, 1980," *Weekly Compilation of Presidential Documents* Volume 16, Number 27 (July 7, 1980), 1275–1276; Congress, House, Committee on Armed Services, *Presidential Recommendations for Selective Service Reform*, 96th Congress 2nd Session, Report. Rostker 439–441; Beth Bailey, *America's Army: Making the All-Volunteer Force* (Cambridge: Belknap Press, 2009), 130–131.

9. *Congressional Record*, 96th Congress, 2nd Session, 1980, Volume 126, part 1:858; *Congressional Record*, 96th Congress, 2nd Session, 1980, Volume 126, part 11:13604. For similar remarks from Byrd, see also *Congressional Record*, 96th Congress, 2nd Session, 1980, Volume 126, part 11:14624–14625. See also, for example, *Congressional Record*, 96th Congress, 2nd Session, 1980, Volume 126, part 1:340, 560–561. For a discussion of Byrd's statesmanship, see David R. Tarr and Ann O'Connor, eds., *Congress A to Z*, 3rd ed. (Washington, D.C.: Congressional Quarterly, Inc., 1999), 45–46.

10. *Congressional Record*, 96th Congress, 2nd Session, 1980, Volume 126, part 5:5529; *Congressional Record*, 96th

Chapter Notes—5

Congress, 2nd Session, 1980, Volume 126, part 7:8331, 8577–8, 8593, 8597, 8637; *Congressional Record*, 96th Congress, 2nd Session, 1980, Volume 126, part 11:14295–301; Richard Halloran, "President's Draft Registration Plan Arouses Skepticism at Senate Hearing," *The New York Times* (March 12, 1980), A12. See also, for similar exchanges, *Congressional Record*, 96th Congress, 2nd Session, 1980, Volume 126, part 5:5642–5643, 5773–5774. For a discussion of Kemp's politics in the 1970s, see Jack Kemp, *An American Renaissance: A Strategy for the 1980's* (New York: Harper and Row, 1978), chapters one and two. For positions similar to Kemp's, see, for example, *Congressional Record*, 96th Congress, 2nd Session, 1980, Volume 126, part 6:7141–7142.

11. For these conversations and other examples like them, see *Congressional Record*, 96th Congress, 2nd Session, 1980, Volume 126, part 7:8581, 8591, 8613; *Congressional Record*, 96th Congress, 2nd Session, 1980, Volume 126, part 4:4829; *Congressional Record*, 96th Congress, 2nd Session, 1980, Volume 126, part 11:14278–9.

12. *Congressional Record*, 96th Congress, 2nd Session, 1980, Volume 126, part 7:8597. There were many other members quoting similar and the same polls at various points through these debates. See, for example, *Congressional Record*, 96th Congress, 2nd Session, 1980, Volume 126, part 4:4486; *Congressional Record*, 96th Congress, 2nd Session, 1980, Volume 126, part 5:6197; *Congressional Record*, 96th Congress, 2nd Session, 1980, Volume 126, part 7:8320–8321, 8604; *Congressional Record*, 96th Congress, 2nd Session, 1980, Volume 126, part 10:13263–13264.

13. *Congressional Record*, 96th Congress, 2nd Session, 1980, Volume 126, part 7:9120–9121; *Congressional Record*, 96th Congress, 2nd Session, 1980, Volume 126, part 10:12602–12603; *Congressional Record*, 96th Congress, 2nd Session, 1980, Volume 126, part 11:13576; "The 'Draft Debate' is Over," *The Washington Post* (June 6, 1980), A16.

14. "Carter: Register Women for Draft: Congressional Leaders Say Proposal Is Doomed," *The Post* (West Palm Beach, Florida) (February 9, 1980), A1, A10.

15. *Congressional Record*, 96th Congress, 2nd Session, 1980, Volume 126, part 2:1508; *Congressional Record*, 96th Congress, 2nd Session, 1980, Volume 126, part 7:8622. Seiberling was campaigning to serve Kent, Ohio (and the rest of the Ohio fourteenth district), when the Kent State massacre occurred. He represented that district for the next sixteen years, from 1971 until 1987.

16. *Congressional Record*, 96th Congress, 2nd Session, 1980, Volume 126, part 11:13599–13604, 14282–7, 14304–14305. The text of King's speech has been printed in many places. See, for example, Martin Luther King, Jr., "Declaration of Independence from the War in Vietnam," *Ramparts* (May 1967), 33–37.

17. For similar statements, see, for example, *Congressional Record*, 96th Congress, 2nd Session, 1980, Volume 126, part 3:4137. Many more dismissed all pretense of a self-fulfilling prophecy and spent their time on the floor denouncing registration as if it was a call for a draft. Many took the opportunity to voice the argument made a decade earlier that conscription is tantamount to involuntary servitude. See, for example, *Congressional Record*, 96th Congress, 2nd Session, 1980, Volume 126, part 2:1510–1512; *Congressional Record*, 96th Congress, 2nd Session, 1980, Volume 126, part 4:5018–5019; *Congressional Record*, 96th Congress, 2nd Session, 1980, Volume 126, part 7:8578, 8593. Others, like Representative Ron Paul (R-TX), lambasted the draft as a system of weakness. "The draft is symbolic of totalitarianism. It is not in the American tradition to endorse the draft. Volunteerism is the nature of a free society, a voluntary army is the only alternative." See *Congressional Record*, 96th Congress, 2nd Session, 1980, Volume 126, part 7:8592. For another example of this sort of rhetoric, see *Congressional Record*, 96th Congress, 2nd Session, 1980, Volume 126, part 3:4152. For Boland's comment, see *Congressional Record*, 96th Congress, 2nd Session, 1980, Volume 126, part 7:8603.

18. Jimmy Carter, Statement, "Selective Service Revitalization: Statement on the Registration of Americans for the Draft. February 8, 1980," *Weekly Compilation of*

Presidential Documents Volume 16, Number 6 (February 11, 1980), 289–91; Jimmy Carter, Remarks, "Registration Under the Military Selective Service Act: Remarks on Signing Proclamation 4771. July 2, 1980," *Weekly Compilation of Presidential Documents* Volume 16, Number 27 (July 7, 1980), 1274–275; Rostker, 438; Registration Proposed in 1980: Men, Women, in Carter Draft Plan," *Lodi News-Sentinel* (February 9, 1980), 1. The same story ran as "Draft Approval Cautious," *Daytona Beach Morning Journal* (Florida) (February 9, 1980), 5A.

19. "Women in Draft Plan," *Gadsden Times* (Gadsden, Alabama) (February 8, 1980), 1, 8; "Reaction to Plan Critical," *Lodi News-Sentinel* (February 9, 1980), 1; *Congressional Record*, 96th Congress, 2nd Session, 1980, Volume 126, part 1:906–907; *Congressional Record*, 96th Congress, 2nd Session, 1980, Volume 126, part 2:1918; *Congressional Record*, 96th Congress, 2nd Session, 1980, Volume 126, part 4:4804–4805. For similar arguments, see also *Congressional Record*, 96th Congress, 2nd Session, 1980, Volume 126, part 2:2130–2131.

20. Bailey, 132.

21. *Rostker v. Goldberg* 453 U.S. 57 (1981); Rostker, 443–46; Linda K. Kerber, "'A Constitutional Right to be Treated Like … Ladies': Women, Civic Obligation and Military Service." *The University of Chicago Law School Roundtable* 95 (1993); Rostker, 443–46.

22. Eric Bradner, "U.S. military opens combat positions to women." *CNN* (December 3, 2015). Available online at http://www.cnn.com/2015/12/03/politics/u-s-military-women-combat-positions/index.html. (Accessed on March 8, 2016.)

23. *Congressional Record*, 96th Congress, 2nd Session, 1980, Volume 126, part 7:8594; *Congressional Record*, 96th Congress, 2nd Session, 1980, Volume 126, part 10:13277; *Congressional Record*, 96th Congress, 2nd Session, 1980, Volume 126, part 11:14272

24. *Congressional Record*, 96th Congress, 2nd Session, 1980, Volume 126, part 19:24715; "Reagan Retains Draft Registration," *Park City Daily News* (Bowling Green, Kentucky) (January 8, 1982), 16; "Draft Sign-Up Continued By Reagan Order," *Times Daily* (Florence, Alabama) (January 6, 1982), 1; Military Manpower Task Force, "A Report to the President on Selective Service Registration," December 15, 1981.

25. *Congressional Record*, 96th Congress, 2nd Session, 1980, Volume 126, part 12:15988–15989; *Congressional Record*, 96th Congress, 2nd Session, 1980, Volume 126, part 14:18926; George C. Wilson, "Navy Chief Breaks with Carter, Urges Return to Military Draft," *The Washington Post* (June 20, 1980), A1.

26. *Congressional Record*, 96th Congress, 2nd Session, 1980, Volume 126, part 7:8625; *Congressional Record*, 96th Congress, 2nd Session, 1980, Volume 126, part 12:148370–14838.

27. Jimmy Carter, Remarks, "Remarks at the Democratic Congressional Campaign Committee Victory Luncheon. August 14, 1980," *Weekly Compilation of Presidential Documents* Volume 16, Number 33 (August 18, 1980), 1529–531.

28. Jimmy Carter, Remarks, "Remarks and a Question-and-Answer Session at a Townhall Meeting. September 15, 1980," *Weekly Compilation of Presidential Documents* Volume 16, Number 33 (August 18, 1980), 1725–738. Carter made similar remarks at other question-and-answer stops on the campaign trail. See for example, Jimmy Carter, Remarks, "Remarks and a Question-and-Answer Session at a Town Meeting. September 22, 1980," *Weekly Compilation of Presidential Documents* Volume 16, Number 33 (August 18, 1980), 1869–883.

29. *Congressional Record*, 96th Congress, 2nd Session, 1980, Volume 126, part 19:24715; Doug Bandow, "Draft Registration: The Politics of Institutional Immortality," *Cato Policy Analysis* No. 214 (August 15, 1994). Available online at https://www.cato.org/publications/policy-analysis/draft-registration-politics-institutional-immortality. (Accessed May 3, 2010.)

Chapter 6

1. Statement, "Jimmy Carter on Senate Bill 1" "Pre-Convention Issues Statements"

Chapter Notes—6

Folder, Box 91, Records of the 1976 Campaign Committee to Elect Jimmy Carter, 1976, Jimmy Carter Library; "Address by Jimmy Carter Announcing his Candidacy for the 1976 Democratic Presidential Nomination to the National Press Club," (December 12, 1974). Available online at http://www.4president.org/speeches/carter1976announcement.htm. (Accessed December 11, 2009.)

2. "The Watergate Window," *The New York Times* (June 12, 1978), A18; Andrew Rudalevige, *The New Imperial Presidency: Renewing Presidential Power after Watergate* (Ann Arbor: University of Michigan Press, 2005), 112–13, 210.

3. Memorandum, American Civil Liberties Union to the Members of the United States Senate, August 26, 1976, "Wiretapping" Folder, Box 35, Records of Domestic Policy Staff, Jimmy Carter Library.

4. Congress, House, Subcommittee on Courts, Civil Liberties, and the Administration of Justice of the Committee on the Judiciary, *Foreign Intelligence Surveillance Act* (Washington, D.C.: Government Printing Office, 1976), 1; Letter, Bruce A. Lehman to Anita Gutierez [sic], March 30, 1977, "Wiretapping" Folder, Box 35, Records of Domestic Policy Staff, Jimmy Carter Library. The reference back to Franklin Delano Roosevelt and the long duree of lax wiretap standards is ubiquitous in the literature. See also David Atkins, "Wiretap Legislation: Past and Present," *First Principles* 3:1 (September 1977), 2. A copy of this article was in the "Wiretapping" Folder, Box 35, Records of Domestic Policy Staff, Jimmy Carter Library; Letter, Bruce A. Lehman to Anita Gutierez [sic], March 30, 1977, "Wiretapping" Folder, Box 35, Records of Domestic Policy Staff, Jimmy Carter Library; *Congressional Record*, 95th Congress, 1st Session, Volume 123, part 8:9274. David Atkins, a student at Columbia University and an intern with the Project on National Security & Civil Liberties, published a thorough analysis of the Carter bill grounded in a through history of wiretapping legislation. Atkins notes: "There are two themes which characterize the forty year history of wiretap law and practice: congressional inaction and executive branch arrogance. Every administration since Franklin Roosevelt's has claimed that a vague notion called 'inherent Presidential power' confers the right to conduct 'national security' surveillance without needing a court order to make it legal."

5. *Congressional Record*, 95th Congress, 1st Session, Volume 123, part 8:9274–9275.

6. *Olmstead v. United States* 277 U.S. 438 (1928); *Katz v. United States* 389 U.S. 347 (1967); *Berger v. New York* 388 U.S. 41 (1967).

7. *United States v. United States District Court for the Eastern District of Michigan* 407 U.S. 297 (1972).

8. John M. Goshko, "White House to Ask Legal Curb on Taps in Security Probes," *The Washington Post* (April 7, 1977), A12. A copy of the article was found in the "Wiretapping" Folder, Box 35, Records of Domestic Policy Staff, Jimmy Carter Library.

9. Memorandum, American Civil Liberties Union to the Members of the United States Senate, August 26, 1976, "Wiretapping" Folder, Box 35, Records of Domestic Policy Staff, Jimmy Carter Library; Congress, Senate, Committee on the Judiciary, Subcommittee on Criminal Laws and Procedures, *Foreign Intelligence Surveillance Act of 1977*, 95th Congress, 1st Session, Hearing, pages 74–85.

10. Congress, Senate, Select Committee to Study Governmental Operations With Respect to Intelligence Activities, *Final report of the Select Committee to Study Governmental Operations with Respect to Intelligence Activities, United States Senate* (Washington, D.C.: Government Printing Office, 1976). Parts are reprinted in Donald Musch, ed., *Civil Liberties and the Foreign Intelligence Surveillance Act* (Dobbs Ferry: Oceana Publications, Inc., 2003). Church's committee would be established on a permanent basis in 1976 as the Select Committee on Intelligence. For the Carter camps' take on the Church committee, see, for example, Memorandum, Burt Wides to Sam Bleicher, 1976, "Wiretapping—Domestic Surveillance Privacy 1" Folder, Box 37, Sam Bleicher's Subject Files, 1976, Jimmy Carter Library. For other discussion of the Church Committee and its infamous

report, see, for example, "Investigations: Nobody Asked: Is it Moral?" *Time* (May 10, 1976), 32–34; Gary Hart, "Liberty and Security," *U.S. National Security, Intelligence and Democracy: From the Church Committee to the War on Terror*, Russell A. Miller, ed. (London: Routledge, 2008).

11. Gerald R. Ford, "United States Foreign Intelligence Activities, Executive Order 11905. February 18, 1976." *Weekly Compilation of Presidential Documents* Volume 12, Number 8 (February 23, 1976), 234–43; Gerald R. Ford, Executive Order, "United States Foreign Intelligence Activities," February 18, 1976, "Wiretapping—Domestic Surveillance Privacy 2" Folder, Box 37, Sam Bleicher's Subject Files, 1976, Jimmy Carter Library; Center for National Security Issues—Washington, D.C., "President Ford's Intelligence Proposals: A Charter for Abuse," *Intelligence Report* 1:2 (March 1976). A copy of the entire pamphlet is in Sam Bleicher's papers and the records of the Domestic Policy Staff. See "Wiretapping—Domestic Surveillance Privacy 1" Folder, Box 37, Sam Bleicher's Subject Files, 1976, Jimmy Carter Library; "Wiretapping" Folder, Box 35, Records of Domestic Policy Staff, Jimmy Carter Library.

12. Memorandum, Michael Mullen [to Sam Bleicher], [1976], "Wiretapping—Domestic Surveillance Privacy 1" Folder, Box 37, Sam Bleicher's Subject Files, 1976, Jimmy Carter Library. Mullen also criticized the "Criminal Law Standard" and the role of judges, but those arguments were not as well developed.

13. Project SHAMROCK allowed the NSA to intercept and examine all international telegrams and mine them for intelligence. As part of the CHAOS program, the CIA collected intelligence and developed files on New Left activists. MERRIMAC applied the same surveillance to antiwar activists.

14. Memorandum, Burt Wides to Sam Bleicher, [1976], "Wiretapping—Domestic Surveillance Privacy 1" Folder, Box 37, Sam Bleicher's Subject Files, 1976, Jimmy Carter Library. For explanations of the various nefarious programs and operations, see especially *Final report of the Select Committee to Study Governmental Operations with Respect to Intelligence Activities, United States Senate*, op cit.

15. More specifically, the letter said, "S 3197 prohibits the court from forcing the government agent to demonstrate that the target is truly a threat to national security and that the wiretap will in fact produce evidence of the target's clandestine activities. This leaves the bill as little more than a sham, giving only the appearance of meaningful safeguards against unwarranted invasions of privacy." See Memorandum, American Civil Liberties Union to the Members of the United States Senate, August 26, 1976, "Wiretapping" Folder, Box 35, Records of Domestic Policy Staff, Jimmy Carter Library. This memo is a shortened version of a larger article. See "Electronic Eavesdropping: Watergate Comes Full Circle," *Congressional Quarterly* XXXI:34 (August 25, 1973), 2321–324.

16. *Ibid.*

17. Jimmy Carter, "Intelligence Oversight Board. May 4, 1977," *Weekly Compilation of Presidential Documents* Volume 13, Number 19 (May 9, 1977), 658–59; Jimmy Carter, "President's Foreign Intelligence Advisory Board. Executive Order 11984. May 4, 1977." *Weekly Compilation of Presidential Documents* Volume 13, Number 19 (May 9, 1977), 659; Jimmy Carter, Executive Order, 11985 "United States Foreign Intelligence Activities. May 13, 1977," *Weekly Compilation of Presidential Documents* Volume 13, Number 20 (May 16, 1977), 719–20. *Washington Post* reporter John M. Goshko explained, "Following the arrival of the Carter administration, [Attorney General Edward Levi's] successor, [Griffin Bell], decided that, instead of attempting to revive the old bill, an attempt should be made to draft new legislation with a better change of passage. The aim is to substitute a judicial warrant requirement for the controversial present system that assumes the President's right under his 'inherent constitutional powers' to authorize electronic eavesdropping in foreign intelligence cases." See John M. Goshko, "White House to Ask Legal Curb on Taps in Security Probes," *The Washington Post* (April 7, 1977), A12. A copy of the article was found in the "Wiretapping"

Chapter Notes—6

Folder, Box 35, Records of Domestic Policy Staff, Jimmy Carter Library.

18. Letter, Robert W. Kastenmeier to Griffin B. Bell, March 2, 1977, "Wiretapping Legislation" Folder, Box 36, Records of Domestic Policy Staff, Jimmy Carter Library; Letter, Bruce A. Lehman to Anita Gutierez [sic], March 30, 1977, "Wiretapping" Folder, Box 35, Records of Domestic Policy Staff, Jimmy Carter Library; *Congressional Record*, 95th Congress, 1st Session, Volume 123, part 8:9274–9275. Elsewhere in Lehman's letter he cited the Kastenmeier quote of Chief Justice Earl Warren from *United States v. Robel* 389 U.S. 258, 264 (1967): "This concept of 'national defense' cannot be deemed an end in itself. Justifying an exercise of... power designed to promote such a goal. Implicit in the term 'national defense' is the notion of defending those values and ideals which set the Nation apart.... It would indeed be ironic if in the name of national defense, we would sanction the subversion of one of those liberties... which make the defense of the Nation worthwhile." For other examples of West Wing support, see, for example, Memorandum, Annie [Gutierrez] to Stu [Eisenstat], April 21, 1977, "Wiretapping" Folder, Box 35, Records of Domestic Policy Staff, Jimmy Carter Library; Letter, Frederick D. Baron to Annie Gutierrez, May 6, 1977, "Wiretapping" Folder, Box 35, Records of Domestic Policy Staff, Jimmy Carter Library; Letter, Frederick D. Baron to Annie Gutierrez, May 16, 1977, "Wiretapping" Folder, Box 35, Records of Domestic Policy Staff, Jimmy Carter Library; Memorandum, Annie Gutierrez to Stu Eizenstat, May 9, 1977, "Wiretapping" Folder, Box 35, Records of Domestic Policy Staff, Jimmy Carter Library.

19. Transcript, "Remarks of the President Upon Announcement of Amendments to Foreign Intelligence Surveillance Act of 1977," May 18, 1877, "Wiretapping" Folder, Box 35, Records of Domestic Policy Staff, Jimmy Carter Library; "The President's Appointments Today," *The Washington Post* (May 18, 1977), A5.

20. Letter, Griffin Bell to the Speaker [of the] House of Representatives, May 18, 1977, "Wiretapping" Folder, Box 35, Records of Domestic Policy Staff, Jimmy Carter Library.

21. Bill McAllister and Christopher Dickey, "U.S. in Conflict on Wiretap Evidence," *The New York Times* (March 10, 1978), A2. A copy of the article is in the "Wiretapping Legislation" Folder, Box 36, Records of Domestic Policy Staff, Jimmy Carter Library. For other descriptions of the case, see, for example, Tom Wicker, "Inherent Power Again," *The New York Times* (February 14, 1978), A32; Tom Wicker, "The Need for S 1566," *The New York Times* (April 21, 1978), A27. Copies of the editorials are in the "Wiretapping Legislation" Folder, Box 36, Records of Domestic Policy Staff, Jimmy Carter Library.

22. "National Security Surveillance," *The Washington Post* (April 14, 1978), A16. A copy of the article is in the "Wiretapping Legislation" Folder, Box 36, Records of Domestic Policy Staff, Jimmy Carter Library.

23. Statement, Department of Justice, February 10, 1978, "Wiretapping Legislation" Folder, Box 36, Records of Domestic Policy Staff, Jimmy Carter Library.

24. The *Time* magazine article went on to say, "The U.S. Government pursued its prosecution with immense care and zeal, for more was at stake than the fates of a pair of inept spies. The trial... set the stage for the testing of a crucial constitutional question: whether a U.S. President can order wiretaps without a judicial warrant in cases involving national security. Much of the evidence used in the case against Truong and Humphrey, accused of passing classified documents to Communist Viet Nam, was developed after bugging devices and a hidden camera revealed the conspiracy. Even though Congress is now considering a bill to ban warrantless surveillance, the Justice Department wanted to pursue its case in the courts. If Truong and Humphrey could be convicted and their conviction sustained on appeal, U.S. Presidents could continue to order the surveillance of suspected foreign espionage agents without prior court approval." See "Nation: The Odd Couple," *Time* (May 29, 1978), 26–27. Regarding Kennedy's position, see Nicholas M. Horrock, "Senate Passes Bill to Bar

Chapter Notes—6

Bugging in U.S. Without Court Order," *The New York Times* (April 21, 1978), A1. A copy of the article was found in the "Wiretapping Legislation" Folder, Box 36, Records of Domestic Policy Staff, Jimmy Carter Library. Horrock is quoting Kennedy's statements made on the House floor. See *Congressional Record* 95th Congress, 2nd Session, Volume 124, part 9:108867.

25. Christopher Dickey and Jane Seaberry, "U.S. to Defend Warrantless Taps," *The New York Times* (March 11, 1978), D8; "Judges and 'foreign intelligence,'" *The Washington Star* (April 22, 1978), A10. A copy of both articles are in the "Wiretapping Legislation" Folder, Box 36, Records of Domestic Policy Staff, Jimmy Carter Library.

26. *Congressional Record*, 95th Congress, 1st Session, Volume 123, part 13:15222–32. For other examples of the bipartisan support for this bill—and members of Congress like Kennedy and Bayh saying as such—see, for example, *Congressional Record*, 95th Congress, 2nd Session, Volume 124, part 9:10887–10890.

27. *Congressional Record*, 95th Congress, 1st Session, Volume 123, part 13:15207, 15456, 15624; *Congressional Record*, 95th Congress, 1st Session, Volume 123, part 29: 37070–1, 37655, 37815. Kennedy blamed S 3197's failure on time running out and that S 1566 was a continuation "[picking] up where last year's left off." For the quote and another example of Kennedy emphasizing the continuity between the 1976 and 1977 bills, see Congress, Senate, Committee on the Judiciary, Subcommittee on Criminal Laws and Procedures, *Foreign Intelligence Surveillance Act of 1977*, 95th Congress, 1st Session, Hearing, page 1.

28. Congress, Senate, Committee on the Judiciary, Subcommittee on Criminal Laws and Procedures, *Foreign Intelligence Surveillance Act of 1977*, 95th Congress, 1st Session, Hearing, page 1.

29. Congress, Senate, Committee on the Judiciary, Subcommittee on Criminal Laws and Procedures, *Foreign Intelligence Surveillance Act of 1977*, 95th Congress, 1st Session, Hearing, page 26.

30. When Baron referred to "last year's bill," he was also referring to the previous (Ford) administration and the previous attorney general (Levi). See Congress, Senate, Committee on the Judiciary, Subcommittee on Criminal Laws and Procedures, *Foreign Intelligence Surveillance Act of 1977*, 95th Congress, 1st Session, Hearing, pages 45–46.

31. *Congressional Record*, 95th Congress, 2nd Session, Volume 124, part 9:10897. Senators Gaylord Nelson (D-WI) and Charles Mathias (R-MD) made similar comments. See pages 10903 and 10905.

32. Senator William Scott (R-VA)—who would later retire at the end of this session—was the lone "nay" vote. On occasion of the bill's passage, Senator Birch Bayh (D-IN) said the act "will bring an end to the practice of electronic surveillance by the executive branch without a court order in the United States." See "Senate Votes to Ban Warrantless Spying," *The Washington Post* (April 21, 1978), A3; Congress, Senate, Committee on the Judiciary, *Foreign Intelligence Surveillance Act of 1977* (Washington, D.C.: Government Printing Office, 1977), Report; *Congressional Record*, 95th Congress, 2nd Session, Volume 124, part 6:6800; *Congressional Record*, 95th Congress, 2nd Session, Volume 124, part 9:10886–10911, 11100; *Congressional Record*, 95th Congress, 2nd Session, Volume 124, part 13:16812. The Carter administration worked with members of Congress to help the bill through the legislative process. See, for example, Memo, Orin Kramer to Annie Gutierrez, September 10, 1977, "Wiretapping Legislation" Folder, Box 36, Records of Domestic Policy Staff, Jimmy Carter Library; Letter, Herman Schwartz to Orin S. Kramer, August 17, 1977, "Wiretapping Legislation" Folder, Box 36, Records of Domestic Policy Staff, Jimmy Carter Library; Letter, Annie M. Gutierrez to Herman Schwartz, October 6, 1977, "Wiretapping Legislation" Folder, Box 36, Records of Domestic Policy Staff, Jimmy Carter Library; Daniel Gilmore, "Electronic Surveillance," *United Press International* (February 27, 1978), no page. A copy of the article is in the "Wiretapping Legislation" Folder, Box 36, Records of Domestic Policy Staff, Jimmy Carter Library. For examples of congressional debate, see *Congressional Record*,

95th Congress, 2nd Session, Volume 124, part 21:28128, 28133–28136, 28144; *Congressional Record,* 95th Congress, 2nd Session, Volume 124, part 21:28427, 28895–28900; *Congressional Record,* 95th Congress, 2nd Session, Volume 124, part 23:31531, 31614, 31623; *Congressional Record,* 95th Congress, 2nd Session, Volume 124, part 25:33778–33789; *Congressional Record,* 95th Congress, 2nd Session, Volume 124, part 26:34844–34846; *Congressional Record,* 95th Congress, 2nd Session, Volume 124, part 27:36409–36418; *Congressional Record,* 95th Congress, 2nd Session, Volume 124, part 28:37650, 38771, 38084, 38086.

33. George Lardner, Jr., "Carter Signs Bill Limiting Foreign Intelligence Surveillance," *The Washington Post* (October 26, 1978), A2.

34. Address, Griffin B. Bell to Yale Law Journal Banquet, April 20, 1978, "Wiretapping Legislation" Folder, Box 36, Records of Domestic Policy Staff, Jimmy Carter Library.

35. *Congressional Record,* 95th Congress, 2nd Session, Volume 124, part 21:28399.

36. For a description of the immediate impact of the 1978 Foreign Intelligence Surveillance Act, see, for example, Whitfield Diffie and Susan Landau, *Privacy on the Line: The Politics of Wiretapping and Encryption* (Cambridge: The MIT Press, 1998, 2007), 140, 202–03.

37. For Reagan's actions, see, for example, Stanley I. Kutler, *The Wars of Watergate: The Last Crisis of Richard Nixon* (New York: A. A. Knopf, 1990), 588.

38. Ronald Kessler, *The Bureau: The Secret History of the FBI* (New York: St. Martin's Press, 2002), 438–43; Terry D. Turchie and Kathleen M. Puckett, *Homeland Insecurity: How Washington Politicians Have Made America Less Safe* (Palisades: History Publishing Company, 2008).

39. Diffie and Landau, 280; Lawrence Wright, *The Looming Tower: Al-Qaeda and the Road to 9/11* (New York: A. A. Knopf, 2006), 354.

40. Andrew Rudalevige, *The New Imperial Presidency: Renewing Presidential Power after Watergate* (Ann Arbor: University of Michigan Press, 2005), 243–48.

41. For the quote, see Diffie and Landau, 280–85. This conclusion is corroborated elsewhere. See Bruce Fein, "Presidential Authority to Gather Foreign Intelligence," *Presidential Studies Quarterly* 37:1 (March 2007), 23–36; Timothy Scahill, "The Domestic Security Enhancement Act of 2003: A Glimpse into a Post–PATRIOT Act Approach to Combating Domestic Terrorism," *CR: The New Centennial Review* 6.1 (Spring 2006) 69–94; Donald Musch, ed., *Civil Liberties and the Foreign Intelligence Surveillance Act* (Dobbs Ferry: Oceana Publications, Inc., 2003).

Chapter 7

1. For a discussion of Hoover and Roosevelt, see Justice White's dissent in *Immigration and Naturalization Service v. Chadha, et al.* 462 U.S. 919 (1983). For further discussion of the origins of the legislative veto, see Barbara Hinkson Craig, *The Legislative Veto: Congressional Control of Regulation* (Boulder: Westview Press, 1983), chapter 2; Martha Liebler Gibson, *Weapons of Influence: The Legislative Veto, American Foreign Policy, and the Irony of Reform* (Boulder: Westview Press, 1992), chapter 2; Jessica Korn, *The Power of Separation: American Constitutionalism and the Myth of the Legislative Veto* (Princeton: Princeton University Press, 1996); Walter J. Oleszek, *Congressional Procedures and the Policy Process,* 3rd ed. (Washington, D.C.: Congressional Quarterly Press, 1989), 266–68.

2. Joseph Cooper and Patricia A. Hurley, "The Legislative Veto: A Policy Analysis," *Congress & the Presidency* 10:1 (Spring 1983), 1. Fifteen legislative vetoes were passed during Franklin Delano Roosevelt's administration, followed by eighteen during the Harry Truman administration, thirty-one during the Dwight Eisenhower administration, twenty-two during the John F. Kennedy administration, and thirty-six during the Lyndon Johnson administration. However, during the Richard Nixon administration—including the Gerald R. Ford interregnum—that number jumped to 115. See Article,

Chapter Notes—7

"Legislative Veto and the Constitution—A Reexamination," March 1978, "Legislative Veto—Articles & Testimony" Folder, Box 43, Records of the Domestic Policy Staff (Carter Administration), 1976–1981, Jimmy Carter Library; Bernard Schwartz, "Legislative Veto and the Constitution—A Reexamination," *George Washington Law Review* 46:3 (March 1978), 351–2; Arthur John Keefe, "The Legislative Veto: Now You See it, Now You Don't (I)," *American Bar Association Journal* 63 (September 1977), 1296–1300. For Keefe's quote, see page 1296. For a discussion of the 96th Congress' nickname, see Oleszek, 275–6.

3. Evidence of Levitas' nickname is ubiquitous in the literature and in the papers of Carter's staff. See, for example, Barbara Hinkson Craig, *Chadha: The Story of an Epic Constitutional Struggle* (New York: Oxford University Press, 1988), ix. For the term "Watergate class" and Levitas crusade for the device, see chapter 2. For a discussion of voting participation, see Richard L. Hall, *Participation in Congress* (New Haven: Yale University Press, 1996). For the term "legislative participation," see page 1. For a discussion of the added difficulty for freshmen representatives to distinguish themselves, see pages 102–03.

4. Carter began as cordial as possible but that eventually developed into balance—how to be fair but firm with Congress on legislative vetoes as well as on other issues. See, for example, "Carter Fires a Salvo," *Time* (August 28, 1978), 10–11.

5. The Supreme Court case, *Immigration and Naturalization Service v. Chadha, et al.* 462 U.S. 919 (1983), will be discussed in more detail at the end of this chapter.

6. Memorandum, Robert B. Barnett to Carter-Mondale Transition Team, December 4, 1976, "Legislative Veto (12/76–6/80), 12/1976–06/1980" Folder, Box 42, Records of the Domestic Policy Staff (Carter Administration), 1976–1981, Jimmy Carter Library.

7. United States Constitution, Article 1, Section 7, Clause 2: "Every Bill which shall have passed the House of Representatives and the Senate, shall, before it become a Law, be presented to the President of the United States; If he approve he shall sign it, but if not he shall return it, with his Objections to that House in which it shall have originated, who shall enter the Objections at large on their Journal, and proceed to reconsider it. If after such Reconsideration two thirds of that House shall agree to pass the Bill, it shall be sent, together with the Objections, to the other House, by which it shall likewise be reconsidered, and if approved by two thirds of that House, it shall become a Law. But in all such Cases the Votes of both Houses shall be determined by Yeas and Nays, and the Names of the Persons voting for and against the Bill shall be entered on the Journal of each House respectively. If any Bill shall not be returned by the President within ten Days (Sundays excepted) after it shall have been presented to him, the Same shall be a Law, in like Manner as if he had signed it, unless the Congress by their Adjournment prevent its Return, in which Case it shall not be a Law."

8. United States Constitution, Article 1, Section 7, Clause 3: "Every Order, Resolution, or Vote to which the Concurrence of the Senate and House of Representatives may be necessary (except on a question of Adjournment) shall be presented to the President of the United States; and before the Same shall take Effect, shall be approved by him, or being disapproved by him, shall be repassed by two thirds of the Senate and House of Representatives, according to the Rules and Limitations prescribed in the Case of a Bill."

9. Memorandum, Robert B. Barnett to Carter-Mondale Transition Team, December 4, 1976, "Legislative Veto (12/76–6/80), 12/1976–06/1980" Folder, Box 42, Records of the Domestic Policy Staff (Carter Administration), 1976–1981, Jimmy Carter Library.

10. Senate Government Operations Report, *Study on Federal Regulation* Volume II, February 1977, "Legislative Veto Paper (9/29/79–1/8/80), 09/29/1979–01/08/1980" Folder, Box 44, Records of the Domestic Policy Staff (Carter Administration), 1976–1981, Jimmy Carter Library; Congress, Senate, Committee on Government Operations, *Study on Federal Regulation*, 95th Congress, 1st Session, Study. For the quote, see pages 116–17.

Chapter Notes—7

11. *Ibid.*, 117, 122.

12. *Congressional Record*, 95th Congress, 1st Session, 1977, Volume 123, part 1:347; *Congressional Record*, 95th Congress, 1st Session, 1977, Volume 123, part 16:19871; *Congressional Record*, 95th Congress, 1st Session, 1977, Volume 123, part 18:22470–2, 22772, 22998, 23063; *Congressional Record*, 95th Congress, 1st Session, 1977, Volume 123, part 19:23481. For the quote, see page 22471.

13. Signing Statement, Jimmy Carter, July 28, 1977, "Legislative Veto—Bills with Veto Provisions (1978)" Folder, Box 43, Records of the Domestic Policy Staff (Carter Administration), 1976–1981, Jimmy Carter Library; *Congressional Record*, 95th Congress, 1st Session, 1977, Volume 123, part 21:26185.

14. Specifically, HR 11112 called for "A bill to amend section 553 of title 5, United States Code, to require submission to Congress of rules promulgated thereunder, and to provide for disapproval of such rules by enactment of a joint resolution of disapproval," in essence every rule would be subject to legislative veto. Memorandum, John M. Harmon to Robert J. Lipshutz and Stuart E. Eizenstat, March 23, 1978, "Legislative Veto (12/76–6/80), 12/1976–06/1980" Folder, Box 42, Records of the Domestic Policy Staff (Carter Administration), 1976–1981, Jimmy Carter Library. For the commentary on Levitas, see Craig, *Chadha*, chapter two. For the quotes, see page 38.

15. Memorandum, Si Lazarus to Bo Cutter and Harrison Wellford, April 13, 1978, "Legislative Veto (12/76–6/80), 12/1976–06/1980" Folder, Box 42, Records of the Domestic Policy Staff (Carter Administration), 1976–1981, Jimmy Carter Library; Memorandum, Dale McOmber to Bo Cutter, April 26, 1978, "Legislative Veto (12/76–6/80), 12/1976–06/1980" Folder, Box 42, Records of the Domestic Policy Staff (Carter Administration), 1976–1981, Jimmy Carter Library.

16. *Congressional Record*, 95th Congress, 2nd Session, 1978, Volume 124, part 1:531–2.

17. McIntyre had just assumed the position at OMB because of the Bert Lance affair, his previous boss and the man who last held his job left amidst scandal and disgrace of alleged nefarious business practices. Though McIntyre had worked in the OMB and under Lance, there was initial skepticism as to whether he had the intestinal fortitude for the job. See "Soft Touch at the OMB," *Time* (June 5, 1978), 74. Quick to prove naysayers wrong, McIntyre laid out the rules for the FTC bill. "The House-passed version of H.R. 3816 contains an amendment providing for Congressional review and possible veto of FTC rules. This amendment states that the FTC must submit a copy of each rule to the Congress at the time it is promulgated and that no such rule could become effective (1) if both Houses adopt a concurrent resolution disapproving it within 90 calendar days of continuous session after promulgation, or (2) if, within 60 days after promulgation, one House adopts a "concurrent" disapproval resolution and transmits it to the other House, and the other House does not disapprove the resolution within 30 calendar days of continuous session." See Letter, Griffin B. Bell to Warren Magnuson, January 27, 1978, "Legislative Veto—FTC (1/30/78–2/28/78), 01/30/1978–02/28/1978" Folder, Box 43, Records of the Domestic Policy Staff (Carter Administration), 1976–1981, Jimmy Carter Library; Memorandum, Rick Neustadt to Stu Eizenstat, et al., January 28, 1978, "Legislative Veto—FTC (1/30/78–2/28/78), 01/30/1978–02/28/1978" Folder, Box 43, Records of the Domestic Policy Staff (Carter Administration), 1976–1981, Jimmy Carter Library; Letter, James T. McIntyre to Harley O. Staggers, January 31, 1978, "Legislative Veto—FTC (1/30/78–2/28/78), 01/30/1978–02/28/1978" Folder, Box 43, Records of the Domestic Policy Staff (Carter Administration), 1976–1981, Jimmy Carter Library.

18. Neustadt followed up the next week with a barrage of thank-you notes for their efforts on HR 3816 to the following people: Edward Merlis, Staff Director, Senate Committee on Commerce, Science, and Transportation; Peter Kinzler, Counsel, House Subcommittee on Consumer Protection and Finance; Martha Maloney, Senate Subcommittee on Consumer. Si Lazarus sent a similar pat-on-the-back

letter to Neustadt commending his work. See Memorandum, Rick Neustadt to Stu Eizenstat, et al., February 9, 1978, "Legislative Veto—FTC (1/30/78–2/28/78), 01/30/1978–02/28/1978" Folder, Box 43, Records of the Domestic Policy Staff (Carter Administration), 1976–1981, Jimmy Carter Library; Letter, Richard M. Neustadt to Edward Merlis, February 20, 1978, "Legislative Veto—FTC (1/30/78–2/28/78), 01/30/1978–02/28/1978" Folder, Box 43, Records of the Domestic Policy Staff (Carter Administration), 1976–1981, Jimmy Carter Library; Letter, Richard M. Neustadt to Peter Kinzler, February 20, 1978, "Legislative Veto—FTC (1/30/78–2/28/78), 01/30/1978–02/28/1978" Folder, Box 43, Records of the Domestic Policy Staff (Carter Administration), 1976–1981, Jimmy Carter Library; Letter, Richard M. Neustadt to Martha Maloney, February 20, 1978, "Legislative Veto—FTC (1/30/78–2/28/78), 01/30/1978–02/28/1978" Folder, Box 43, Records of the Domestic Policy Staff (Carter Administration), 1976–1981, Jimmy Carter Library; Memorandum, Si Lazarus to Rick Neustadt, February 20, 1978, "Legislative Veto—FTC (1/30/78–2/28/78), 01/30/1978–02/28/1978" Folder, Box 43, Records of the Domestic Policy Staff (Carter Administration), 1976–1981, Jimmy Carter Library.

19. Memorandum, Rick Neustadt to Jim Free, February 22, 1978, "Legislative Veto—FTC (1/30/78–2/28/78), 01/30/1978–02/28/1978" Folder, Box 43, Records of the Domestic Policy Staff (Carter Administration), 1976–1981, Jimmy Carter Library; Fact Sheet, FTC Amendments of 1978 (HR 3816); Fact Sheet, no date, "Legislative Veto—FTC (3/4/78–11/12/79), 03/04/1978–11/12/1979" Folder, Box 43, Records of the Domestic Policy Staff (Carter Administration), 1976–1981, Jimmy Carter Library; Article, "'Congressional Veto' Stalls FTC Bill," March 18, 1978, "Legislative Veto—FTC (3/4/78–11/12/79), 03/04/1978–11/12/1979" Folder, Box 43, Records of the Domestic Policy Staff (Carter Administration), 1976–1981, Jimmy Carter Library; Irwin B. Arieff, "Congressional Veto Stalls FTC Bill," *Congressional Quarterly* (March 18, 1978), 701.

20. Memorandum, Si Lazarus to Rick Neustadt, March 6, 1978, "Legislative Veto—FTC (3/4/78–11/12/79), 03/04/1978–11/12/1979" Folder, Box 43, Records of the Domestic Policy Staff (Carter Administration), 1976–1981, Jimmy Carter Library; Article, "House Defeats Compromise on FTC Bill," March 4, 1978, "Legislative Veto—FTC (3/4/78–11/12/79), 03/04/1978–11/12/1979" Folder, Box 43, Records of the Domestic Policy Staff (Carter Administration), 1976–1981, Jimmy Carter Library.

21. Memorandum for the File, Rick Neustadt, March 22, 1978, "Legislative Veto—Chron, 3/22/78–2/5/80, 03/22/1978–02/05/1980" Folder, Box 43, Records of the Domestic Policy Staff (Carter Administration), 1976–1981, Jimmy Carter Library; Memorandum, Mike Sohn to Rick Neustadt, March 27, 1978, "Legislative Veto—Chron, 3/22/78–2/5/80, 03/22/1978–02/05/1980" Folder, Box 43, Records of the Domestic Policy Staff (Carter Administration), 1976–1981, Jimmy Carter Library.

22. Memorandum, Rick Neustadt to David Rubenstein and Si Lazarus, March 28, 1978, "Legislative Veto—Chron, 3/22/78–2/5/80, 03/22/1978–02/05/1980" Folder, Box 43, Records of the Domestic Policy Staff (Carter Administration), 1976–1981, Jimmy Carter Library.

23. Memorandum, Rick Neustadt to Stu Eizenstat, August 23, 1978, "Legislative Veto—FTC (3/4/78–11/12/79), 03/04/1978–11/12/1979" Folder, Box 43, Records of the Domestic Policy Staff (Carter Administration), 1976–1981, Jimmy Carter Library; Memorandum, Stu Eizenstat and Rick Neustadt to Frank Moore and Les Francis, September 1, 1978, "Legislative Veto—FTC (3/4/78–11/12/79), 03/04/1978–11/12/1979" Folder, Box 43, Records of the Domestic Policy Staff (Carter Administration), 1976–1981, Jimmy Carter Library; Memorandum, Rick Neustadt to Les Francis, et al., August 25, 1978, "Legislative Veto—FTC (3/4/78–11/12/79), 03/04/1978–11/12/1979" Folder, Box 43, Records of the Domestic Policy Staff (Carter Administration), 1976–1981, Jimmy Carter Library.

24. As this domestic policy battle waged in Washington, D.C., Jimmy Carter

Chapter Notes—7

had already begun his marathon twelve-day foreign policy negotiating session with Egyptian President Anwar Sadat and Israeli Prime Minister Menachem Begin at Camp David. On September 17, 1978, Carter emerged from seclusion with the two world leaders and announced the eponymous Camp David Accords. See Memorandum, Rick Neustadt to Stu Eizenstat, September 6, 1978, "Legislative Veto—FTC (3/4/78–11/12/79), 03/04/1978–11/12/1979" Folder, Box 43, Records of the Domestic Policy Staff (Carter Administration), 1976–1981, Jimmy Carter Library.

25. *Congressional Record,* 95th Congress, 2nd Session, 1978, Volume 124, part 21:28528–35, 28682; *Congressional Record,* 95th Congress, 2nd Session, 1978, Volume 124, part 24:32323–35.

26. *Congressional Record,* 95th Congress, 2nd Session, 1978, Volume 124, part 24:32330.

27. *Congressional Record,* 95th Congress, 2nd Session, 1978, Volume 124, part 24:32332, 32335.

28. Memorandum of Meeting, Legislative Veto Meeting, April 12, 1978, "Legislative Veto—Presidential Statement, 6/28/78 (4/12/78–6/1/78), 04/12/1978–06/1/1978" Folder, Box 44, Records of the Domestic Policy Staff (Carter Administration), 1976–1981, Jimmy Carter Library; Memorandum, Rick Neustadt to Bill Cable, April 15, 1978, "Legislative Veto—Presidential Statement, 6/28/78 (4/12/78–6/1/78), 04/12/1978–06/1/1978" Folder, Box 44, Records of the Domestic Policy Staff (Carter Administration), 1976–1981, Jimmy Carter Library; Memorandum, Rick Neustadt, to Si Lazarus and Larry Simms, May 22, 1978, "Legislative Veto—Presidential Statement, 6/28/78 (4/12/78–6/1/78), 04/12/1978–06/1/1978" Folder, Box 44, Records of the Domestic Policy Staff (Carter Administration), 1976–1981, Jimmy Carter Library.

29. Memorandum, Larry L. Simms to Robert J. Lipshutz and Stuart E. Eizenstat, April 21, 1978, "Legislative Veto—Presidential Statement, 6/28/78 (4/12/78–6/1/78), 04/12/1978–06/1/1978" Folder, Box 44, Records of the Domestic Policy Staff (Carter Administration), 1976–1981, Jimmy Carter Library; Draft Memorandum for the President, "Administration Policy Regarding Legislative Vetoes," April 21, 1978, Larry L. Simms to Robert J. Lipshutz and Stuart E. Eizenstat, April 21, 1978, "Legislative Veto—Presidential Statement, 6/28/78 (4/12/78–6/1/78), 04/12/1978–06/1/1978" Folder, Box 44, Records of the Domestic Policy Staff (Carter Administration), 1976–1981, Jimmy Carter Library.

30. Memorandum, John M. Harmon to Robert J. Lipshutz and Stuart E. Eizenstat, June 6, 1978, "Legislative Veto—Presidential Statement, 6/28/78 (6/6/78–6/29/78), 06/06/1978–06/29/1978" Folder, Box 44, Records of the Domestic Policy Staff (Carter Administration), 1976–1981, Jimmy Carter Library.

31. Letter, Griffin [Bell] to Rick [Neustadt], no date, "Legislative Veto—Presidential Statement, 6/28/78 (6/6/78–6/29/78), 06/06/1978–06/29/1978" Folder, Box 44, Records of the Domestic Policy Staff (Carter Administration), 1976–1981, Jimmy Carter Library.

32. Memorandum, Rick Neustadt to Stu Eizenstat, June 16, 1978, "Legislative Veto—Presidential Statement, 6/28/78 (6/6/78–6/29/78), 06/06/1978–06/29/1978" Folder, Box 44, Records of the Domestic Policy Staff (Carter Administration), 1976–1981, Jimmy Carter Library; Memorandum, Stu Eizenstat and Rick Neustadt to the President, June 19, 1978, "Legislative Veto—Presidential Statement, 6/28/78 (6/6/78–6/29/78), 06/06/1978–06/29/1978" Folder, Box 44, Records of the Domestic Policy Staff (Carter Administration), 1976–1981, Jimmy Carter Library. For a discussion of Muskie's politics, see Theo Lippman, Jr., and Donald C. Hansen, *Muskie* (New York: W. W. Norton and Company, 1971). For his relationship with Carter, see Carter, *Keeping Faith,* 37, 61, 67, 519–21, 536–38, 558.

33. As part of Carter's style, he often met with members of Congress or brought them to the White House—especially if they disagreed with him on an issue. Part skillful wooing, part comity and deference, Carter wanted to make sure all voices were heard and all positions defended on any given issue. See "Just Call Him Mister," *Time* (February 21, 1977), 11–12. For discussion

of the circumstances of this meeting, see Letter, Stu Eizenstat to the President, June 20, 1978, "Legislative Veto—Presidential Statement, 6/28/78 (6/6/78–6/29/78), 06/06/1978–06/29/1978" Folder, Box 44, Records of the Domestic Policy Staff (Carter Administration), 1976–1981, Jimmy Carter Library; Letter, Rick Hutcheson to Stu Eizenstat, June 21, 1978, "Legislative Veto—Presidential Statement, 6/28/78 (6/6/78–6/29/78), 06/06/1978–06/29/1978" Folder, Box 44, Records of the Domestic Policy Staff (Carter Administration), 1976–1981, Jimmy Carter Library.

34. Press Release, Jimmy Carter to Congress of the United States, June 21, 1978, "Legislative Veto, 6/21/78–5/7/79" Folder, Box 107, Records of the Office of Congressional Liaison (Carter Administration), 1976–1981, Jimmy Carter Library; Jimmy Carter, Message, "Legislative Vetoes: Message to Congress, June 21, 1978," *Weekly Compilation of Presidential Documents* Volume 14, Number 25 (June 26, 1978), 1146–49.

35. Ibid.

36. Memorandum, Rick Neustadt to Stu Eizenstat, June 22, 1978, "Legislative Veto—Presidential Statement, 6/28/78 (6/6/78–6/29/78), 06/06/1978–06/29/1978" Folder, Box 44, Records of the Domestic Policy Staff (Carter Administration), 1976–1981, Jimmy Carter Library.

37. Article, "O'Neill Backs President in Row Over Veto Rights," June 23, 1978, "Legislative Veto—Presidential Statement, 6/28/78 (6/6/78–6/29/78), 06/06/1978–06/29/1978" Folder, Box 44, Records of the Domestic Policy Staff (Carter Administration), 1976–1981, Jimmy Carter Library; "O'Neill Backs President in Row Over Veto Rights," *The New York Times* (June 23,1978), A8.

38. Craig, *The Legislative Veto*, chapter four; Korn, chapter five.

39. Shirley Hufstedler was new to her post but her name had been kicked around as a possible appointee to the Carter administration since 1976. See "Jimmy's Talent File," *Time* (December 20, 1976), 12–14.

40. Memorandum, Benjamin R. Civiletti to Shirley M. Hufstedler, June 5, 1980, "Legislative Veto Issue (2), 04/28/1980–12/12/1980" Folder, Box 5, Shirley M. Hufstedler Collection, Jimmy Carter Library. For discussion of Hufstedler's promotion, see Carter, *Keeping Faith*, 60, 76.

41. Memorandum, Shirley M. Hufstedler to F. James Rutherford, et al., June 6, 1980, "Legislative Veto Issue (2), 04/28/1980–12/12/1980" Folder, Box 5, Shirley M. Hufstedler Collection, Jimmy Carter Library; Memorandum, Benjamin R. Civiletti to Shirley M. Hufstedler, June 5, 1980, "Legislative Veto Issue (2), 04/28/1980–12/12/1980" Folder, Box 5, Shirley M. Hufstedler Collection, Jimmy Carter Library; Article, "Turf Wars: Ed Strikes Back," Jule 1980, "Legislative Veto" Folder, Box 16, Records of the Domestic Policy Staff (Carter Administration), 1976–1981, Jimmy Carter Library; "Turf Wars: Ed Strikes Back," *Federal Focus* 5:7 (July 1980), 1–8.

42. Memorandum, Shirley M. Hufstedler to the President, July 21, 1980, "Legislative Veto" Folder, Box 16, Records of the Domestic Policy Staff (Carter Administration), 1976–1981, Jimmy Carter Library.

43. Congress, House, Committee on Education and Labor, Subcommittee on Elementary, Secondary, and Vocational Education, Oversight Hearing on Congressional Disapproval of Education Regulations, 96th Congress, 2nd Session, September 18, 1980, Hearing, pages 1–2.

44. Ibid., 3–23. For Goodling's question, see page 23.

45. Ibid., 23–25.

46. Ibid., 26, 41.

47. Ibid., 27–37.

48. Ibid., 64–79, 82. For her interrogation, see pages 79–91. For the quote, see page 82.

49. Note, Betsy Levin to Shirley M. Hufstedler, November 12, 1980, "Legislative Veto Issue (2), 04/28/1980–12/12/1980" Folder, Box 5, Shirley M. Hufstedler Collection, Jimmy Carter Library; Note, Lloyd N. Cutler to Shirley M. Hufstedler, October 16, 1980, "Legislative Veto Issue (2), 04/28/1980–12/12/1980" Folder, Box 5, Shirley M. Hufstedler Collection, Jimmy Carter Library; Letter, Shirley M. Hufstedler to Carl D. Perkins, December 16, 1980, "Legislative Veto Issue (2), 04/28/1980–12/12/1980" Folder, Box 5,

Shirley M. Hufstedler Collection, Jimmy Carter Library; Letter, Carl D. Perkins to Shirley M. Hufstedler, November 20, 1980, "Legislative Veto Issue (2), 04/28/1980–12/12/1980" Folder, Box 5, Shirley M. Hufstedler Collection, Jimmy Carter Library.

50. Statement, Ken Kramer, December 12, 1980, "Legislative Veto Issue (2), 04/28/1980–12/12/1980" Folder, Box 5, Shirley M. Hufstedler Collection, Jimmy Carter Library. Kramer's coplaintiffs were Representatives Trent Lott (R-MS), Larry Hopkins (R-KY), John Ashbrook (R-OH), Robert Lagomarsino (R-CA), Tennyson Guyer (R-OH), L. A. "Skip" Bafalis (R-FL), Thomas Petri (R-WI), Jon Hinson (R-MS), John Erlenborn (R-IL), Edward J. Derwinski (R-IL), Willis Gradison (R-OH), Maneal Lujan (R-NM), Robert Walker (R-PA), Larry McDonald (D-GA), Daniel Crane (R-IL), W. Henson Moore (R-LA), James M. Collins (R-TX), and Senators William Armstrong (R-CO), Carl Levin (D-MI), Pete Domenici (R-NM), and Barry Goldwater (R-AZ); Craig, *The Legislative Veto*, 90–91.

51. *Immigration and Naturalization Service v. Chadha, et al.* 462 U.S. 919 (1983). See also, Craig, *Chadha*, chapter 1; Gibson, chapter 3; *Congressional Record*, 94th Congress, 1st Session, 1975, Volume 121, part 3:40247, 40800.

52. Craig, *Chadha*, chapter 7 and epilogue; Barbara Hinkson Craig, *The Legislative Veto*, epilogue.

Conclusion

1. Team Fix, "The CBS News Republican debate transcript, annotated," *The Washington Post* (February 13, 2016). Available online at https://www.washingtonpost.com/news/the-fix/wp/2016/02/13/the-cbs-republican-debate-transcript-annotated/. (Accessed February 19, 2016.)

2. George E. Reedy, *The Twilight of the Presidency* (New York: New American Library, 1970), 168, 179.

3. Carter's farming roots and populist style was embodied in the title of his aircraft. While Ford flew around the nation campaigning in Air Force One, Carter campaigned in a jet named Peanut One.

See M. B. Darwin, "Of Peanuts and Politicians," *American Speech* 53:2 (Summer 1978), 166; Yanek Mieczkowski, *Gerald Ford and the Challenges of the 1970s* (Lexington: University Press of Kentucky, 2005), 321.

4. Arthur M. Schlesinger, Jr., *The Imperial Presidency* (Boston: Houghton Mifflin, 1973, 1989), xxviii, 417.

Postscript

1. Technically, Trump is not the first to use the phrase, despite his claim that he invented it. Most notably, Ronald Reagan used it in his campaign in 1980. See, for example, Matt Taibbi, "Donald Trump Claims Authorship of Legendary Reagan Slogan; Has Never Heard of Google," *Rolling Stone* (March 25, 2015). Available at https://www.rollingstone.com/politics/politics-news/donald-trump-claims-authorship-of-legendary-reagan-slogan-has-never-heard-of-google-193834/. (Accessed April 15, 2019.)

2. Nate Silver, "Will Donald Trump Be Impeached?" *FiveThirtyEight* (May 22, 2017). Available at https://fivethirtyeight.com/features/chance-donald-trump-impeached/. (Accessed October 6, 2017); David R. Mayhew, *Congress: the Electoral Connection* (New Haven: Yale University Press, 1974).

3. Silver's Ford quote comes from the *Congressional Record*. "The only honest answer is that an impeachable offense is whatever a majority of the House of Representatives considers [it] to be at a given moment in history; conviction results from whatever offense or offenses two-thirds of the other body considers to be sufficiently serious to require removal of the accused from office." See, *Congressional Record*, 91st Congress, 2nd Session, Volume 116, part 9:11913; "Tracking Congress In The Age Of Trump." Available online at https://projects.fivethirtyeight.com/congress-trump-score/. (Accessed October 6, 2017); Julia Azari, Perry Bacon, Jr., and Harry Enten, "Even The Biggest Scandals Can't Kill Party Loyalty," *FiveThirtyEight* (May 16, 2017). Available online at https://fivethirtyeight.com/features/even-the-

biggest-scandals-cant-kill-party-loyalty/. (Accessed October 6, 2017.)

4. Susan J. Douglas, "Trump's Anti-Mandate," *In These Times* (January 2017), 18.

5. Julia Azari, "Every president claims to have a mandate. Does Trump actually have one?" *Vox* (November 17, 2016). Available online at https://www.vox.com/the-big-idea/2016/11/17/13658374/trump-mandate-history-presidential-politics. (Accessed October 28, 2017); Julia Azari, "Trump Came In As A Weak President, And He's Made Himself Weaker," *FiveThirtyEight* (August 1, 2017). Available online at https://fivethirtyeight.com/features/trump-weak-president/?ex_cid=538twitter. (Accessed October 6, 2017); Richard E. Neustadt, *Presidential Power: The Politics of Leadership* (New York: John Wiley & Sons, 1960). For an updated version of Neustadt's argument, see Richard E. Neustadt, *Presidential Power and the Modern Presidents: The Politics of Leadership From Roosevelt to Reagan* (New York: The Free Press, 1991). On the subject of apotheosis, Reedy later elaborated, "The trend is clear. Over the passage of the years, what was little more than managerial authority has become power over the life of the nation itself. The right to check this power still rests in Congress and the courts. But the ability to check assumes the capacity to offer alternatives, to explain them to the public, and to manage a structure that carries them out. In the modern age, when action with little time for reflection becomes increasingly urgent, these capabilities are lessened with each passing day for every arm of the government except the presidency." George E. Reedy, *The Twilight of the Presidency* (New York: New American Library, 1970), 39–46. (For the quote, see page 46.) As an extension of the Neustadt logic, I have always appreciated Norman Ornstein's description. He framed the power to persuade as a balance between Gunther Gebel-Williams and Gulliver. "A president's power is defined by his relations with Congress. A president must exercise power in many arenas, persuading many audiences at home and abroad. But the key test for a president's clout or success is how he is judged in dealing with Congress: Does he master them, or do they master him?.... The successful president... comes across like animal tamer Gunther Gebel-Williams: He gets into the ring with the Congressional lions and tigers, cracks the whip, and, although they growl and roar, they still get up on their tiny little stools and perform. But if a president looks like Gulliver, a pitiful, helpless giant dominated by Congressional Lilliputians, then watch out." See Norman Ornstein, "Can Clinton Still Emerge a Winner; Here's What to Do," *Roll Call* (May 27, 1993). Available online through Lexis-Nexis Academic. (Accessed September 19, 2006.)

6. Julia Azari, "The Fight Over The State of The Union Was About The Future of Democracy," *FiveThirtyEight* (January 29, 2019). Available online at https://fivethirtyeight.com/features/the-fight-over-the-state-of-the-union-was-about-the-future-of-democracy/. (Accessed March 30, 2019); Julia Azari, "Forget Norms. Our Democracy Depends On Values," *FiveThirtyEight* (May 24, 2018). Available online at https://fivethirtyeight.com/features/forget-norms-our-democracy-depends-on-values/. (Accessed March 30, 2019.)

7. Peter Baker, "For Trump, the Reality Show Has Never Ended," *The New York Times* (October 10, 2017). Available at https://www.nytimes.com/2017/10/10/us/politics/trump-corker-feud-tweet-liddle-bob.html. (Accessed October 11, 2017.)

8. Adam Serwer, "Trump the Toddler," *The Atlantic* (January 10, 2019). Available online at https://www.theatlantic.com/ideas/archive/2019/01/trump-the-toddler-wants-a-wall/580021/. (Accessed March 30, 2019.)

9. James Fallows, "From Donald Trump, a New Low," *The Atlantic* (September 30, 2017). Available online at https://www.theatlantic.com/notes/2017/09/from-donald-trump-a-new-low/541647/?utm_source=eb. (Accessed October 6, 2017); Donald Trump, Twitter Post, September 30, 2017. Available online at https://twitter.com/realDonaldTrump/status/914089003745468417; Donald Trump, Twitter Post, September 30, 2017. Available online at https://twitter.com/realDonaldTrump/status/914089888596754434.

10. David J. Cook, "Toiling in Trump's Vineyard of Alternative Facts Lining Its Random Walk," *DePaul Journal for Social Justice* 10:2 (Summer 2017), 1–9.

11. Jeffrey Crouch, Mark J. Rozell, and Mitchel A. Sollenberger, "The Law: The Unitary Executive Theory and President Donald J. Trump," *Presidential Studies Quarterly* 47:3 (September 2017), 561–73; Jeffrey Crouch, Mark J. Rozell, and Mitchel A. Sollenberger, "President Obama's Signing Statements and the Expansion of Executive Power," *Presidential Studies Quarterly* 43:4 (December 2013), 883–89; Stephen Skowronek, "The Conservative Insurgency and Presidential Power: A Developmental Perspective on the Unitary Executive," *Harvard Law Review* 122:8 (October 2009), 2070–103 (for the quote, see pages 2074 and 2075); Ezra Klein, "4 political scientists are tracking whether Trump is damaging American democracy," *Vox* (October 5, 2017). Available online at https://www.vox.com/policy-and-politics/2017/10/5/16414338/trump-democracy-authoritarianism. (Accessed October 21, 2017.)

12. Julia Azari, "Trump's presidency signals the end of the Reagan era," *Vox* (December 1, 2016). Available online at https://www.vox.com/mischiefs-of-faction/2016/12/1/13794680/trump-presidency-reagan-era-end; Stephen Skowronek, *The Politics Presidents Make: Leadership from John Adams to George Bush* (Cambridge: Belknap Press, 1993); Richard Kreitner, "What Time Is It? Here's What the 2016 Election Tells Us About Obama, Trump, and What Comes Next," *The Nation* (November 22, 2016). Available at https://www.thenation.com/article/what-time-is-it-heres-what-the-2016-election-tells-us-about-obama-trump-and-what-comes-next/. (Accessed October 6, 2017); Peter Beinart, "Why Trump Supporters Believe He Is Not Corrupt," *The Atlantic* (August 22, 2018). Available online at https://www.theatlantic.com/ideas/archive/2018/08/what-trumps-supporters-think-of-corruption/568147/?utm_content=edit-promo&utm_source=facebook&utm_medium=social&utm_term=2018-12-21T16%3A30%3A17&utm_campaign=the-atlantic. (Accessed March 30, 2019.)

13. Dylan Matthews, "Trump is wasting his congressional majority—like Jimmy Carter did," *Vox* (August 4, 2017). Available online at https://www.vox.com/policy-and-politics/2017/8/4/16075196/trump-legislative-failure-carter. (Accessed October 6, 2017.)

14. See for example, Kevin Liptak, "Trump: 'Nobody knew health care could be so complicated,'" *CNN* (February 28, 2017). Available online at http://www.cnn.com/2017/02/27/politics/trump-healthcare-complicated/index.html. (Accessed October 6, 2017.)

15. A running total of Trump's golf habits can be found at https://factba.se/topic/calendar. Many articles have been written about the politics of Trump golfing. See for example, Chris Cillizza, "Donald Trump's huge golf hypocrisy," *CNN* (January 3, 2018). Available online at https://www.cnn.com/2018/01/03/politics/donald-trump-golf-analysis/index.html. (Accessed April 1, 2019.)

Bibliography

Primary Sources

"Air Force One: Facts and History of 707 as Air Force One." Available online at http://www.707sim.com/air-force-one.html. (Accessed March 27, 2007.)

Ali, Safia Samee. "What Is the Emoluments Clause and What Does It Mean for the President?" *NBC News* (June 12, 2017). Available at https://www.nbcnews.com/news/us-news/what-emoluments-clause-what-does-it-mean-president-n771081. (Accessed October 11, 2017.)

Arieff, Irwin B. "Congressional Veto Stalls FTC Bill." *Congressional Quarterly* (March 18, 1978), 701.

Bandow, Doug. "Draft Registration: The Politics of Institutional Immortality." *Cato Policy Analysis* No. 214 (August 15, 1994). Available online at https://www.cato.org/publications/policy-analysis/draft-registration-politics-institutional-immortality. (Accessed May 3, 2010.)

Carter, Jimmy. "Inaugural Address." (January 20, 1977.) Online by Gerhard Peters and John T. Woolley, *The American Presidency Project*. Available online at http://www.presidency.ucsb.edu/documents/inaugural-address-0.

―――. *Keeping Faith: Memoirs of a President*. Toronto: Bantam Books, 1982.

―――. *The Public Papers of Jimmy Carter 1977*, 2 Books. Washington, D.C.: Government Printing Office, 1977.

―――. "State of the Union Address 1980" (January 23, 1980). Available online at http://www.jimmycarterlibrary.org/documents/speeches/su80jec.phtml. (Accessed May 3, 2010.)

"Carter: Register Women for Draft: Congressional Leaders Say Proposal Is Doomed." *The Post* (West Palm Beach, Florida) (February 9, 1980), A1, A10.

CNBC News. 2017.

Congress. House. Committee on Armed Services. *Presidential Recommendations for Selective Service Reform*. 96th Congress, 2nd Session. Report.

―――. ―――. Committee on Appropriations. Subcommittee on the Treasury, Postal Service, and General Government Appropriations. *Federal Expenditures at San Clemente and Key Biscayne*. 93rd Congress, 1st Session, 1973. Hearing.

―――. ―――. Committee on Education and Labor. Subcommittee on Elementary, Secondary, and Vocational Education. *Oversight Hearing on Congressional Disapproval of Education Regulations*. 96th Congress, 2nd Session. September 18, 1980, Hearing.

―――. ―――. Committee on International Relations. *Vietnam Humanitarian Assistance and Evacuation Act of 1975*. 94th Congress, 1st Session. Report.

―――. ―――. Committee on the Judiciary. Subcommittee on Administrative Practice and Procedure. *Clemency Program Practices and Procedures*. 93rd Congress, 2nd Session, Hearing.

Bibliography

_____. _____. Committee on the Judiciary. Subcommittee on Courts, Civil Liberties, and the Administration of Justice. *Foreign Intelligence Surveillance Act.* 1976. Publication.

_____. Senate. Committee on Government Operations. *Study on Federal Regulation.* 95th Congress, 1st Session. Study.

_____. _____. Subcommittee on Criminal Laws and Procedures. *Foreign Intelligence Surveillance Act of 1977.* 95th Congress, 1st Session. Hearing.

Congressional Quarterly Weekly Report, 37:40 (October 6, 1979), 2199.

Congressional Record, 1972–1981.

Cornwell, Susan. "Trump health secretary to repay cost of private jet travel." *Reuters* (September 28, 2017). Available at https://www.reuters.com/article/us-usa-trump-expenses/trump-health-secretary-to-repay-cost-of-private-jet-travel-idUSKCN1C32WH. (Accessed October 6, 2017.)

Diamond, Dan, and Rachana Pradhan. "Price's private-jet travel breaks precedent." *Politico* (September 19, 2017). Available at http://www.politico.com/story/2017/09/19/tom-price-chartered-planes-flights-242908?cmpid=sf. (Accessed October 7, 2017.)

Douglas, Susan J. "Trump's Anti-Mandate." *In These Times* (January 2017), 18.

"Draft Approval Cautious." *Daytona Beach Morning Journal* (Florida) (February 9, 1980), 5A.

"Draft Sign-Up Continued By Reagan Order." *Times Daily* (Florence, Alabama) (January 6, 1982), 1.

"Electronic Eavesdropping: Watergate Comes Full Circle." *Congressional Quarterly* XXXI:34 (August 25, 1973), 2321–2324.

Fahrenthold, David A., and Jonathan O'Connell. "What is the 'Emoluments Clause'? Does it apply to President Trump?" *Washington Post* (January 23, 2017). Available at https://www.washingtonpost.com/politics/what-is-the-emoluments-clause-does-it-apply-to-president-trump/2017/01/23/12aa7808-e185-11e6-a547-5fb9411d332c_story.html?utm_term=.309aa2576fe2. (Accessed October 7, 2017.)

Fallows, James. "From Donald Trump, a New Low." *The Atlantic* (September 30, 2017). Available at https://www.theatlantic.com/notes/2017/09/from-donald-trump-a-new-low/541647/?utm_source=eb. (Accessed October 6, 2017.)

_____. "The Passionless Presidency." *The Atlantic* 243:5 (May 1979), 33–48.

Farrar, Susan. "Yacht Carter banished is coming back." *Atlanta Constitution* (August 25, 1983), 12-A.

Federal Register. 1974–1981.

FiveThirtyEight. 2017–2019.

Ford, Gerald R. *A Time to Heal: The Autobiography of Gerald R. Ford.* New York: Harper and Row, 1979.

The Gallup Poll Cumulative Index: Public Opinion, 1935–1997. Lanham: Rowman & Littlefield, 1999, 331–336, 349–351, 354–358.

Gallup Polls, 1974–2017.

Gerald Ford Library. Charles E. Goodell Papers.

_____. Gerald R. Ford Congressional Papers.

_____. John O. Marsh Files.

_____. Melvin R. Laird Papers.

_____. Paul Theis and Robert Orben Files.

_____. Philip W. Buchen Files (White House Counsel's Office).

_____. President Ford Committee Campaign Records.

_____. Presidential Handwriting File.

_____. Robert J. Horn Files.

_____. White House Central Files Subject File.

Graham, David A. "Trump: When the President Says It, That Means It's True." *The Atlantic* (March 23, 2017). Available at https://www.theatlantic.com/politics/archive/2017/03/trump-time-interview-ex-post-facto/520551/. (Accessed October 6, 2017.)

Bibliography

Harrington, Rebecca. "A loophole in the 25th Amendment lets 14 people remove a sitting President from office." *Business Insider* (October 12, 2017). Available at http://www.independent.co.uk/news/world/americas/donald-trump-impeachment-25th-amendment-remove-sitting-president-mike-pence-white-house-a7996681.html. (Accessed October 21, 2017.)
Jimmy Carter Library. Hugh Carter Files.
_____. Margaret McKenna Files.
_____. Records of the Domestic Policy Staff (Carter Administration), 1976–1981.
_____. Records of the 1976 Campaign Committee to Elect Jimmy Carter, 1976.
_____. Records of the Office of Congressional Liaison (Carter Administration), 1976–1981.
_____. Records of the Speechwriters Office, 1977–1981.
_____. Shirley M. Hufstedler Collection.
_____. White House Central Files.
_____. White House Counsel's Office Files.
_____. White House Press Office Files.
_____. White House Vertical File.
King, Martin Luther, Jr. "Declaration of Independence from the War in Vietnam." *Ramparts* (May 1967), 33–37.
Kreitner, Richard. "What Time Is It? Here's What the 2016 Election Tells Us About Obama, Trump, and What Comes Next." *The Nation* (November 22, 2016). Available at https://www.thenation.com/article/what-time-is-it-heres-what-the-2016-election-tells-us-about-obama-trump-and-what-comes-next/. (Accessed October 6, 2017.)
Liptak, Kevin. "Trump: 'Nobody knew health care could be so complicated.'" *CNN* (February 28, 2017.) Available at http://www.cnn.com/2017/02/27/politics/trump-health-care-complicated/index.html. (Accessed October 6, 2017.)
Lodi News-Sentinel. 1980.
Los Angeles Times. 2017.
Meyer, Josh. "NSA warned White House against using personal email." *Politico* (September 29, 2017). Available at http://www.politico.com/story/2017/09/29/white-house-private-email-nsa-warning-243324?cmpid=sf. (Accessed on October 6, 2017.)
Military Manpower Task Force. "A Report to the President on Selective Service Registration." December 15, 1981.
The New York Times. 1972–2017.
Podhoretz, John. "Democrats' best hope for 2020: Oprah." *New York Post* (September 27, 2017). Available at http://nypost.com/2017/09/27/democrats-best-hope-for-2020-oprah/. (Accessed October 6, 2017.)
Presidential Studies Quarterly, 2013–2017.
"Reagan Retains Draft Registration," *Park City Daily News* (Bowling Green, Kentucky) (January 8, 1982), 16.
Sequoia. Available at http://www.sequoiayacht.com/aboutus.htm. (Accessed February 9, 2009.)
Sklar, Rachel. "Ford Coverage: Nixon, Chevy Chase And Football, But Something's Missing." *Huffington Post* (December 27, 2006). Available online at https://www.huffingtonpost.com/entry/ford-coverage-nixon-chevy_b_37218?guccounter=1&guce_referrer=aHR0cHM6Ly93d3d3d3d3d3d3d3d3d3dcuZ29vZ2xlLmNvbS8&guce_referrer_sig=AQAAAGO0-QUj8_fdy-0FQ6Zmk8nRN5g4mlWIA2VQF79JRPh0JMfCojJrQ7xZgeUckCEZCjcDDxgRfP2-Oocg5Y-d7sbkQ16BD_fWC2uR7iI-VPKgUr2PcA3YIWN6fFrDAPMIBGSXxk1Gu_LrvV51bZMP9LiTVqUVr40eni_0QergBGES. (Accessed January 17, 2009.)
Team Fix. "The CBS News Republican debate transcript, annotated." *Washington Post* (February 13, 2016). Available online at https://www.washingtonpost.com/news/the-fix/wp/2016/02/13/the-cbs-republican-debate-transcript-annotated/. (Accessed February 19, 2016.)
Time. 1970–2017.

Bibliography

"Turf Wars: Ed Strikes Back." *Federal Focus* 5:7 (July 1980), 1–8.
Twitter, 2017.
USS *Pueblo*. Available at http://www.usspueblo.org/. (Accessed February 9, 2009.)
"VC-137B/C Stratoliner." Available online at http://www.globalsecurity.org/military/systems/aircraft/vc-137.htm. (Accessed March 27, 2007.)
Vox. 2016–2019.
The Washington Post. 1974–2017.
The Washington Star. 1981.
Weekly Compilation of Presidential Documents. 1974–1981.
Winsor, Morgan. "Richard Nixon, Bill Clinton both faced impeachment over obstruction of justice." *ABC News* (May 17, 2017). Available at http://abcnews.go.com/US/richard-nixon-bill-clinton-faced-impeachment-obstruction-justice/story?id=47460022. (Accessed October 11, 2017.)
"Women in Draft Plan." *Gadsden Times* (Gadsden, Alabama) (February 8, 1980), 1, 8.

Secondary Sources

Adler, David Gray, and Larry N. George, eds. *The Constitution and the Conduct of American Foreign Policy*. Lawrence: University of Kansas Press, 1996.
Azari, Julia R. *Delivering the People's Message: The Changing Politics of the Presidential Mandate*. Ithaca: Cornell University Press, 2014.
Bailey, Beth. *America's Army: Making the All-Volunteer Force*. Cambridge: Belknap Press, 2009.
Bailey, Beth, and David Farber, eds. *America in the 70s*. Lawrence: University Press of Kansas, 2004.
Baskir, Lawrence M., and William A. Strauss. *Chance and Circumstance: The Draft, The War and The Vietnam Generation*. New York: Alfred A. Knopf, Inc., 1978.
Bennett, G. H. *The American Presidency 1945–2000: Illusions of Grandeur*. Thrupp: Sutton Publishing, 2000.
Bernstein, Carl, and Bob Woodward. *All the President's Men*. New York: Simon & Schuster, 1974.
Black, Charles L., Jr. "The Presidency and Congress." *Washington and Lee Law Review*, 32:4 (Fall 1975), 841–854.
Black, Earl, and Merle Black. *The Rise of Southern Republicans*. Cambridge: Harvard University Press, 2002.
Cavan, Sherri. *20th Century Gothic: America's Nixon*. San Francisco: Wigan Pier Press, 1979.
Cook, David J. "Toiling in Trump's Vineyard of Alternative Facts Lining Its Random Walk." *DePaul Journal for Social Justice* 10:2 (Summer 2017), 1–9.
Cooper, Joseph, and Patricia A. Hurley. "The Legislative Veto: A Policy Analysis." *Congress & the Presidency* 10:1 (Spring 1983), 1–24.
Craig, Barbara Hinkson. *Chadha: The Story of an Epic Constitutional Struggle*. New York: Oxford University Press, 1988.
_____. *The Legislative Veto: Congressional Control of Regulation*. Boulder: Westview Press, 1983.
Darwin, M. B. "Of Peanuts and Politicians." *American Speech* 53:2 (Summer 1978), 166.
Diffie, Whitfield, and Susan Landau. *Privacy on the Line: The Politics of Wiretapping and Encryption*. Cambridge: The MIT Press, 1998, 2007.
Dumbrell, John. *The Carter Presidency: A Re-Evaluation*. Manchester, New York: Manchester University Press, 1993.
Fein, Bruce. "Presidential Authority to Gather Foreign Intelligence." *Presidential Studies Quarterly* 37:1 (March 2007), 23–36.

Bibliography

Genovese, Michael A. *The Power of the American Presidency: 1789–2000*. New York: Oxford University Press, 2001.

Gergen, David. *Eyewitness to Power: The Essence of Leadership Nixon to Clinton*. New York: Simon & Schuster, 2000.

Gibson, Martha Liebler. *Weapons of Influence: The Legislative Veto, American Foreign Policy, and the Irony of Reform*. Boulder: Westview Press, 1992.

Gillon, Steve M. *"That's Not What We Meant to Do": Reform And Its Unintended Consequences in Twentieth-Century America*. New York: W. W. Norton & Company, 2000.

Greene, John Robert. *The Presidency of Gerald R. Ford*. Lawrence: University of Kansas Press, 1995.

Greenstein, Fred I. *The Presidential Difference: Leadership Style From FDR to Clinton*. New York: The Free Press, 2000.

Haas, Garland A. *Jimmy Carter and the Politics of Frustration*. Jefferson: McFarland & Company, Inc., 1992.

Hall, Richard L. *Participation in Congress*. New Haven: Yale University Press, 1996.

Hargrove, Edwin C. *Jimmy Carter as President: Leadership and the Politics of the Public Good*. Baton Rouge: Louisiana State University Press, 1988.

Hébert, F. Edward, with John McMillan. *"Last of the Titans": The Life and Times of Congressman F. Edward Hébert of Louisiana*. Lafayette: Center for Louisiana Studies, 1976.

Jones, Charles O. *The Trusteeship Presidency: Jimmy Carter and the United States Congress*. Baton Rouge: Louisiana State University Press, 1988.

Jones, Joseph, and Lori Olafson, eds. *War Resistersin Retrospect: Papers from the 2007 Our Way Home Peace Event and Reunion*. Ottawa: National Research Council of Canada Press, 2009.

Kaufman, Burton I., and Scott Kaufman. *The Presidency of James Earl Carter, Jr.* Lawrence: University of Kansas Press, 2006.

Kaufman, Scott, ed. *A Companion to Gerald R. Ford and Jimmy Carter*. Malden: John Wiley & Sons, 2016.

Keefe, Arthur John. "The Legislative Veto: Now You See it, Now You Don't (I)." *American Bar Association Journal* 63 (September 1977), 1296–1300.

Kemp, Jack. *An American Renaissance: A Strategy for the 1980's*. New York: Harper and Row, 1978.

Kerber, Linda K. "'A Constitutional Right to be Treated Like ... Ladies': Women, Civic Obligation and Military Service." *The University of Chicago Law School Roundtable* 95 (1993).

Kessler, Ronald. *The Bureau: The Secret History of the FBI*. New York: St. Martin's Press, 2002.

Koch, Edward I., and William Rauch. *Politics*. New York: Simon & Schuster, 1985.

Koch, Edward I., with Daniel Paisner, *Citizen Koch: An Autobiography*. New York: St. Martin's Press, 1992.

Koenig, Louis W. *The Chief Executive*. New York, Texas: Harcourt, Brace & World, 1960.

Korn, Jessica. *The Power of Separation: American Constitutionalism and the Myth of the Legislative Veto*. Princeton: Princeton University Press, 1996.

Kriner, Douglas L. "Taming the Imperial Presidency: Congress, Presidents and the Conduct of Military Action," PhD Dissertation, Harvard University, 2006.

Kutler, Stanley I. *The Wars of Watergate: The Last Crisis of Richard Nixon*. New York: A. A. Knopf, 1990.

Levine, Suzanne Braun, and Mary Thom. *Bella Abzug: How One Tough Broad from the Bronx Fought Jim Crow and Joe McCarthy, Pissed Off Jimmy Carter, Battled for the Rights of Women and Workers, Rallied Against War and for the Planet, and Shook Up Politics Along the Way*. New York: Farrar, Straus and Giroux, 2007.

Lippman, Theo, Jr., and Donald C. Hansen. *Muskie*. New York: W. W. Norton and Company, 1971.

Bibliography

Mayhew, David R. *Congress: The Electoral Connection*. New Haven: Yale University Press, 1974.

Melanson, Philip H. *The Secret Service: The Hidden Story of an Enigmatic Agency*. New York: Carroll & Graf Publishers, 2002.

Mieczkowski, Yanek. *Gerald Ford and the Challenges of the 1970s*. Lexington: University Press of Kentucky, 2005.

Miller, Russell A., ed. *U.S. National Security, Intelligence and Democracy: From the Church Committee to the War on Terror*. London: Routledge, 2008.

Mollenhoff, Clark R. *The President Who Failed: Carter Out of Control*. New York: The Free Press, 1980.

Musch, Donald, ed. *Civil Liberties and the Foreign Intelligence Surveillance Act*. Dobbs Ferry: Oceana Publications, Inc., 2003.

Neustadt, Richard E. *Presidential Power and the Modern Presidents: The Politics of Leadership From Roosevelt to Reagan*. New York: The Free Press, 1991.

_____. *Presidential Power: The Politics of Leadership*. New York: John Wiley & Sons, 1960.

O'Brien, Michael. *Philip Hart: The Conscience of the Senate*. East Lansing: Michigan State University Press, 1995.

O'Connor, John F. "The Emoluments Clause: An Anti-Federalist Intruder in a Federalist Constitution." *Hofstra Law Review* 24:1 (1995), 91–178.

Oleszek, Walter J. *Congressional Procedures and the Policy Process*. 3rd ed. Washington, D.C.: Congressional Quarterly Press, 1989.

Paulsen, Michael Stokes. "Is Lloyd Bentsen Unconstitutional?" *Stanford Law Review* 46:4 (April 1994), 907–918.

Plaxton, Sharon Rudy. "To Reconcile A Nation: Gerald Ford, Jimmy Carter, and the Question of Amnesty 1974–1980." Doctoral Thesis, Queen's University, December 1995.

Reedy, George E. *The Twilight of the Presidency*. New York: New American Library, 1970.

Reveley III, W. Taylor. *War Powers of the President and Congress: Who Holds the Arrows and Olive Branch?* Charlottesville: University of Virginia Press, 1981.

Rostker, Bernard. *I Want You! The Evolution of the All-Volunteer Force*. Santa Monica: RAND Corporation, 2006.

Rudalevige, Andrew. *The New Imperial Presidency: Renewing Presidential Power after Watergate*. Ann Arbor: University of Michigan Press, 2005.

Scahill, Timothy. "The Domestic Security Enhancement Act of 2003: A Glimpse into a Post–PATRIOT Act Approach to Combating Domestic Terrorism." *CR: The New Centennial Review* 6:1 (Spring 2006), 69–94.

Schlesinger, Arthur M., Jr. *The Imperial Presidency*. Boston: Houghton Mifflin, 1973, 1989.

Skowronek, Stephen. "The Conservative Insurgency and Presidential Power: A Developmental Perspective on the Unitary Executive." *Harvard Law Review* 122:8 (October 2009), 2070–103.

_____. *The Politics Presidents Make: Leadership from John Adams to George Bush*. Cambridge: Belknap Press, 1993.

Spencer, Donald S. *The Carter Implosion: Jimmy Carter and the Amateur Style of Diplomacy*. New York: Praeger, 1988.

Tarr, David R., and Ann O'Connor, eds. *Congress A to Z*. 3rd ed. Washington, D.C.: Congressional Quarterly, Inc., 1999.

Thomas, Ann Van Wynen, and A. J. Thomas, Jr. *The War-Making Powers of the President: Constitutional and International Law Aspects*. Dallas: Southern Methodist University Press, 1982.

Thompson, Kenneth W., ed. *The Carter Presidency: Fourteen Intimate Perspectives of Jimmy Carter*. Lanham: University Press of America, 1990.

Tillman, Seth Barrett. "Business Transactions and President Trump's 'Emoluments' Problem." *Harvard Journal of Law & Public Policy* 40:3 (March 2017) 759–771.

Bibliography

Tower, John G. *Consequences: A Personal and Political Memoir.* Boston: Little, Brown and Company, 1991.
Treen, David C., ed. *Can You Afford this House?* Edison: Caroline House Press, 1978.
Uslaner, Eric M. "Comity in Context: Confrontation in Historical Perspective." *British Journal of Political Science* 21:1 (January 1991), 45–77.
_____. *The Decline of Comity in Congress.* Ann Arbor: University of Michigan Press, 1993.
Wilson, Joan Hoff. *Herbert Hoover: Forgotten Progressive.* Boston: Little, Brown and Company, 1975.

Index

Abourezk, James: on water policy 83; on wiretapping 123–24
Abzug, Bella: on draft dodgers 35; on Gerald Ford's draft dodger clemency program 40–41
accountability: Gerald Ford on 113; Jack Watson on 23–24; Jimmy Carter on 16, 20, 69–70, 110, 119
Adams, Brock 87
Addabbo, Joseph: on draft registration of women 105–6
Affordable Care Act (2010) 164; *see also* Obamacare
Afghanistan: Soviet invasion of (1979) 98–99, 108
Air Force One 63
Alexander, Clifford, Jr. 74, 81, 87
All the President's Men (film) 28
American Bar Association: Jimmy Carter's speech to (1976) 19–20
American Civil Liberties Union (ACLU): on wiretapping 111, 112–13, 117
Anderson, John: on draft registration 107
Anderson, Patrick 21; on campaign strategy (1976) 17
Andrus, Cecil 74, 81, 87; on water policy 89
Arendsee, Richard W.: on *Sequoia* 63
Arieff, Irwin B. 138
Atchafalaya channelization project 71–72, 78
attorney general: Jimmy Carter on politics and 19; *see also specific attorneys general*
Auburn Dam 75, 92
AuCoin, Les: on draft registration of women 105
austerity: Jerry Brown on 14, 26; Jimmy Carter's policy toward 14, 18–19, 21, 22, 24, 26, 50–51, 52, 55, 58, 68–69, 70;

John F. Kennedy on 52; Joseph Kraft on 54; *Sequoia* sale and 56, 61–62

Baker, Howard: on draft registration 103
Baker, Peter 162
Barnett, Robert B.: on legislative vetoes 130–35
Baron, Frederick D.: on wiretapping 123
Bayh, Birch: on wiretapping 121, 124
Begin, Menachem 63
Bell, Griffin 44, 118, 119; on legislative vetoes 142–43, 145; on wiretapping 122–23, 124–25
Berger v. New York (1967) 112
Bevill, Tom 90
Biaggi, Mario 135
Blumenthal, Mike 66
Boland, Edward: on draft registration 103, 105
Boner, William: on draft registration 103
Bongardt, Steve 126
Brown, Harold 56; on draft registration 101; *Sequoia* sale and 59
Brown, Jerry: austerity policy of 14, 26
Brown v. Walker (1896) 34–35
Bureau of Reclamation 85
Burger, Warren 153
Burke, Edward 99
Burke-Wadsworth Act (1940) 99
Burton, Phillip 57, 81
Bush, George W.: presidential power expansion under 163; wiretapping policy of 126–27
Byrd, Harry: on draft registration 100–101
Byrd, Robert C.: on draft registration 103; on water policy 85

Cache Valley water project 72
Caddell, Patrick H.: "Internal Working

Index

Paper on Political Strategy" (1976) authored by 25–27
Califano, Joseph A., Jr.: on draft registration 100–101
Camp David 63–64, 139
Carter, Hugh 53; on presidential auto use 66; on *Sequoia* sale 55–56
Carter, Lillian: on Jimmy Carter's presidential candidacy 15
Carter, Rosalynn 28, *50*; in presidential election (1976) 15
Central Arizona Project (CAP) 75–76, 76, 83
Central Intelligence Agency (CIA): "Operation CHAOS" of 114–15, 117
Central Utah Project: Bonneville Unit of 74, 90
Chadha, Jagdish 152–53
Christian faith: of Jimmy Carter 33, 43
Church, Frank 113
Church Committee 113, 121; on presidential power 114, 116, 117
Civiletti, Benjamin: on legislative vetoes 146–47, 148, 149
Claytor, W. Graham, Jr. 59
Cleland, Max 45
clemency: defined 33; Gerald Ford's draft dodger 31–32, 33, 35, 37, 38–42, 44, 47–48
Clemency Review Board 39
Clinton, Bill: on draft registration 109; impeachment of 160
USS *Cole*: bombing of (2001) 126
comity: Donald Trump and 159, 161–63; Gerald Ford and 39–40; Griffith Bell and 122; Jimmy Carter and 13, 16, 25, 26, 34, 46, 47, 73, 82, 85, 86, 87, 109, 118, 119, 129, 136, 139, 143–44, 150, 152, 154 157–58; Richard Nixon and 49; *see also* decency; dignity
Communications Act (1934) 111–12
communications policy: of Jimmy Carter 29–30
confidence in government: Jimmy Carter on 20–21; *see also* trust
Corker, Bob: on Donald Trump 161–62, 163
Cornelison, Joseph: on *Sequoia* sale 60–61
corruption: of Donald Trump 160–61; Jimmy Carter on 20; of Ronald Reagan 158
Council on Environmental Quality 74, 77
Crane, Philip: on draft dodgers 36

Cranston, Alan: on water policy 85
credibility gap: Jimmy Carter's understanding of 21
Cuomo, Mario: on governing versus campaigning 24
Cutler, Lloyd: on draft registration 99; on legislative vetoes 148, 151
Cutter, Bo: on legislative vetoes 137

Dayton Floodwall 84
decency: Jimmy Carter and 16; *see also* comity; dignity
DeConcini, Dennis: on water policy 83
Democratic Party primary (1976) 15–18
Department of Education (DOE): legislative veto of regulations of 146–52
Department of Veterans' Affairs: draft dodgers and 45
Derwinski, Edward J.: on draft dodgers 36
Des Moines, Iowa: Jefferson-Jackson Day Dinner in (1977) 66; Jimmy Carter's speech in (1976), 22
Dickerson, John 155
Dickey, Christopher: on wiretapping 119
Dickey-Lincoln School Lakes Project 77–78
dignity: of Donald Trump 159–65; Jimmy Carter and 29, 66, 143, 145; *see also* comity; decency
Dole, Bob: on Myers Amendment 46; on wiretapping 116
draft dodgers *32*; Gerald Ford on 31–32, 33, 37, 38–42; Jimmy Carter's amnesty for 31–48, 97–98; Patrick Caddell on 26; Richard Nixon on 31, 34, 37
draft registration: Jimmy Carter on 99–100, 108–9; reinstatement of 97–109
Duck River Dam 79
Dukakis, Michael: austerity policy of 26
Dye, Ann: on water policy 81–82
Dylan, Bob 26

Eastland, James: on wiretapping 121
Eckhardt, Robert: on draft registration 101; on legislative vetoes 138, 139–40
Edwards, Don: on draft dodgers 35; on legislative vetoes 140
Ehrlichman, John 115
Eilberg, Joshua 153
Eizenstat, Stuart ("Stu") 24, 82, 84, 86, 87, 136, 137, 138, 139, 143, 145; on Congressional relations 73; on draft registration 98; on legislative vetoes

210

Index

142, 144; on Myers Amendment 46; on openness and responsiveness 13–14, 15; on presidential chauffeurs 64; on water policy 77, 78, 80, 83, 89, 90–91
Equal Rights Amendment (ERA) 105
Erdahl, Arlen 149
ethics, code of: of Jimmy Carter 15–18, 19–21, 24–25
Executive Order 11803 (1974) 38
Executive Protection Service: uniforms of 49

failure: Jimmy Carter as 155
Federal Bureau of Investigation (FBI) 126; COINTELPRO program of 115; Jimmy Carter's wiretapping use of 119; Richard Nixon's abuse of 18
Fletcher, Kathy: on water policy 82, 83–84, 91
Flynt, Larry, Jr. 57, 60
Ford, Gerald 13, 28, *38*, *43*; on draft dodgers 31–32, 33, 37, 38–42, 42–43, 47–48; on draft registration 98, 107; on "Hail to the Chief" 52; on impeachment 160; national healing carried out by 25–26; political stock of 156; presidential credibility of 50; in presidential election (1976) 16–17; Richard Nixon pardoned by 29, 31, 39, 40, 41, 47, 50, 116, 129, 156; on wiretapping 113–14, 116, 118, 119
Ford, William: on legislative vetoes 149–50
foreign intelligence surveillance *see* wiretapping
Foreign Intelligence Surveillance Act (1978) 110, 114, 118–26, 157
Free, Jim: on water policy 91

Gallagher, Jack 60
Garn, Jake: on wiretapping 121
Garrison Diversion water project 79
Garvey, Robert R.: on *Sequoia* sale 61
General Education Provisions Act (1974): Section 431 debated 148–51
Goldberg, Robert 106
Goldwater, Barry: on draft dodgers 36; on draft registration of women 105; on Gerald Ford's draft dodger clemency program 40; on water policy 76, 83, 93–94
González, Henry: on Ronald Reagan seeking a new presidential yacht 62
Goodling, William 149

Goshko, John M. 112
government spending *see* spending
Graves, Ernest 73
Green, Bill: on draft registration 102
Gulf of Tonkin Resolution (1964) 47
Gully, W.L. ("Bill") 58

"Hail to the Chief": Gerald Ford on playing of 52; Jimmy Carter on playing of 26, 51, 165
Hall, Sam: on draft dodgers 36
Halloran, Richard 101
Harmon, John M: on legislative vetoes 136, 142, 149, 150
Hart, Gary: on Jimmy Carter's austerity 69
Hart, Philip A.: on draft dodgers 35
Haskell, Floyd: on water policy 92–93
Hatfield, Mark: on draft registration 100, 101, 104, 107, 108; on Myers Amendment 45–46
Hathaway, William 77
Hayes, Rutherford B. 54, 56
Hayward, Thomas B.: on draft registration 108
Hébert, F. Edward: on Gerald Ford's draft dodger clemency program 39–40
Heinz, John: on draft registration 101–2
helicopters: Jimmy Carter's sale of 19, 67–68
Hollings Ernest ("Fritz"): on Myers Amendment 46
Holt, Marjorie: on draft registration of women 106
Hoover, Herbert: legislative vetoes and 128, 152, 153, 154
Horton, Frank: on draft dodgers 35
Huddleston, Walter: on wiretapping 121
Hufstedler, Shirley 146; on legislative vetoes 147–48, 150–51
Humphrey, Hubert H.: on water policy 85
Humphrey, Ronald Louis: warrantless wiretapping of 119–20
Hurricane Maria (2017) 162
Hyde, Henry: on wiretapping 125

Immigration and Naturalization Service v. Chadha (1983) 130, 152–54
impeachment 159–60; as Congressional power 132; threat to Richard Nixon 31, 156
imperial presidency: defined 49–50, 124, 156–57; under Donald Trump 165; Foreign Intelligence Surveillance Act

211

Index

(1978) passed in reaction to 110; Gary Hart on 69; Henry Hyde on 125; Jack Watson on 23; Jimmy Carter on 51–52, 55, 124, 161; of Richard Nixon 49–50, 68, 128–29; Stu Eizenstat on 14; Walter Mondale on 115; Watergate class of legislators elected to counter 113
Impoundment Control Act (1974) 73, 83
Inouye, Daniel: on wiretapping 121
Internal Revenue Service (IRS) 16; "Special Services Staff" of 115

Jackson, Henry ("Scoop") 18; on draft registration of women 105
Jenrette, John W., Jr.: on *Sequoia* sale 57–58
Johnson, Andrew: impeachment of 160
Johnson, Harold T. ("Bizz") 88, 91
Johnson, Lyndon Baines: comity and, 40; Congressional relations of 153; legislative vetoes and 128, 129; wiretapping and 111–12
Johnston, J. Bennett: on Atchafalaya channelization project 71–72; on water policy 93
Jordan, Hamilton 23, 65; on presidential accountability 24

Kastenmeier, Robert: on wiretapping 111, 118
Katz v. United States (1967) 112
Keith, Damon: on wiretapping 112
Kemp, Jack F.: on draft registration 102
Kennedy, Edward ("Ted"): on draft registration 107; on Gerald Ford's draft dodger clemency program 39; on Jimmy Carter's draft dodger pardon 44; on wiretapping 120–21, 121, 123, 124
Kennedy, John F. 66; austerity policy of 52
Kester, John G.: on *Sequoia* sale 61
King, Martin Luther, Jr.: civil disobedience of 36; on Vietnam War 104; wiretapping of 115
King, Martin Luther, Sr. 26
Knievel, Evel 57
Knight, H.S.: on presidential auto use 66
Koch, Edward I.: on draft dodgers 35
Kraft, Joseph: on Jimmy Carter's sincerity 54
Kramer, Ken: on legislative vetoes 151–52
Kucera, Danny 108
KUED radio (Salt Lake City) 74

Lamm, Richard: on water policy 88
Lance, Bert: on water policy 81, 83
Larsen, Leonard: on water policy 77
Lazarus, Simon 137, 138
leadership style: of Jimmy Carter 21–22, 24–25, 109
legacy: of Jimmy Carter 155, 158; of Richard Nixon 15, 16, 19, 28
legislative style: of Jimmy Carter 157
legislative vetoes 128–54; Jimmy Carter on 129–30, 136, 144–45, 153
Levin, Betsy: on legislative vetoes 151
Levin, Carl 152
Levitas, Elliott: legislative vetoes and 129, 134–35, 136, 137, 138–39, 140, 144, 149, 150, 153
limousines: Jerry Brown on 14; Jimmy Carter on politicians' use of 22, 52, 54; Jimmy Carter's sale of 19, 51, 64–67, 68, 165; Patrick Caddell on 26
Lincoln, Abraham: presidential yachting of 54
Lipshutz, Robert J. 136; on legislative vetoes 142; on Myers Amendment 46; on *Sequoia* sale 61
Long, Russell B. 77–78; on water policy 85
Los Angeles, California: Jimmy Carter's speech in (1976), 21

MacNeil, Robert: on Jimmy Carter's austerity policy 69
Malloy, Thomas Aquinas 59, 60
Maloney, Jim 66–67
Mansfield, Mike: on Gerald Ford's draft dodger clemency program 40
Martin, Judith: on *Sequoia* sale 56–57, 59, 59–60, 61–62
Martinez, Tony 109
Mathias, Charles: on wiretapping 120, 121
Mazzoli, Romano L. 72; on water policy 94
McAllister, Bill: on wiretapping 119
McClellan, John: on wiretapping 121
McDonald, Larry 152
McGovern, George: on draft registration 104–5; on water policy 75, 76, 83
McIntyre, Jim 137, 138
McIntyre, Thomas 71; on water policy 93–94
McKay, Gunn: on water policy 90
McKenna, Margaret 46; on *Sequoia* sale 60, 61

Index

McKinney, Stewart: on draft registration 102
McOmber, Dale 137
Merrill, Rick: on water policy 91–92
Michel, Robert: on draft registration 97
Michigan State University: fight song of played, 52
Mihdhar, Khalid al- 126
Mitchell, Parren: on draft registration 102
Molloy, B. Kevin 79; on Jimmy Carter 79–80
Mondale, Walter *20*; on presidential role 27–28; vice-presidential role of 27; water policy and 85, 89; on wiretapping 114–16
Montgomery, Sonny: on draft registration 108
Moore, Frank 57, 77, 78, 137, 138, 143, 145; on austerity 52; water policy and 80, 83, 85, 89, 90–91
Moore, Henson: on legislative vetoes 140
Moore, John L., Jr.: on transparency and comity 25
Mudd, Roger 53
Mullen, Michael 114; on wiretapping 116–17
Murphy, John: on legislative vetoes 135–36
Muskie, Edward 77, 78, 143
Myers, John T.: on Jimmy Carter's draft dodger pardon 45–46
Myers Amendment (1977) 45–47

National Organization for Women (NOW): on draft registration of women 105
National Park Service: as prospective *Sequoia* owner 57
National Security Agency (NSA): SHAMROCK program of 117; wiretapping role of 116, 121, 127
Navy Historical Museum: as prospective *Sequoia* owner 55
Neal, Stephen: on draft registration of women 106
Nelson, Gaylord: on wiretapping 120, 121
Nessen, Ron 52
Neustadt, Richard: legislative veto policy and 137–38, 139, 141, 142, 143, 145–46; on presidential power 161
"A New Beginning" statement (1976) 19
Nixon, Richard: comity and 40; Congressional relations of 153; on draft dodgers 31, 34, 37; imperial presidency of 49–50, 68, 128–29; legacy of 15, 16, 19, 28; legislative vetoes and 129; military procurement policy of 97; pardon of 29, 31, 39, 40, 41, 47, 50, 116, 129, 156; on presidential yacht sales 60; resignation of 156, 160; on wiretapping 115, 118, 119, 124
Nunn, Sam: on draft registration 101

Oahe Irrigation project 75, 76, 83
Oakes, John B.: on Atchafalaya channelization project 72; on pork-barrel spending 94–95, 95
Obama, Barack: golfing of criticized 165; presidential legacy of 159; presidential power expansion under 163
Obamacare 159; *see also* Affordable Care Act (2010)
Office of Management and Budget (OMB) 23, 74
Olmstead v. United States (1928) 111, 112
Omnibus Crime Control and Safe Streets Act (1968) 112, 113, 125
O'Neill, Tip 141; on legislative vetoes 145–46
openness: Griffin Bell on 123; Jimmy Carter on 16, 18–19, 22, 110, 124; Joseph Kraft on 54; Stu Eizenstat on 14; Walter Mondale on 28; *see also* secrecy; transparency

Paintsville Dam 84
Panetta, Leon: on draft registration 104
pardon: as presidential power 33; of Richard Nixon 29, 31, 39, 40, 41, 47, 50, 116, 129, 156
Pelosi, Nancy 161
Pennsylvania Avenue (Washington, D.C.): Jimmy Carter's walk down, during presidential inauguration (1977) *50*, 51, 53, 54
Perkins, Carl D. 151; on water policy 84
Pertschuk, Michael 139
Philadelphia, Pennsylvania: presidential debate in (1976) *43*, 43–44
Pond, Gerald L. 79
pork-barrel legislation: John B. Oakes on 72, 94–95; water projects as 71, 74, 75, 78, 85, 86–87, 92–93, 95, 96
Powell, Jody 61; on austerity 53
Powell, Lewis F., Jr.: on wiretapping 112–13
presidential election (1976) 16–22; Phil-

Index

adelphia debate during, 43–44; Watergate as issue in 15, 16–17, 17–18, 19, 20, 25, 44, 51, 69, 110, 114; wiretapping as issue in 114–18
presidential election (1980) 165; draft registration as an issue in 107–9
presidential transition (1976–1977) 13, 23–30
Presidential Yacht Trust: as *Sequoia* owner 63
Proclamation 4771 (1980) 100
Proxmire, William: on presidential automobile use 65; on water policy 78
Public Works for Water and Power Development and Energy Research Appropriation bill (1977) 90–96; Jimmy Carter on 95
Purks, Jim 79

Rapid City, South Dakota: Jimmy Carter's campaign speech (1976) in 18–19
Rather, Dan 31
Raupe, Craig: on water policy 85–86
Reagan, Ronald 165; Donald Trump compared to 163–64; on draft registration 107–8, 109; in presidential election (1976) 17, 18, 21–22; presidential memory of 155; presidential yachts and 62–63; scandals of 158, 160; on wiretapping 125–26
Reedy, George: on presidential power 155–56, 161
Rehnquist, William: on draft registration of women 106
Rhodes, John 81
Ribicoff, Abraham: on legislative vetoes 135
Richard Russell Dam 72
Ringle, Ken: on *Sequoia* sale 63–64
Roche, Francis B. 59
Rodino, Peter: on wiretapping 118–19, 121
Roncalio, Teno: on water policy 76–77
Roosevelt, Franklin Delano: draft registration policy of 99; Hundred Days of, as model for Jimmy Carter's presidency 28, 76; on legislative vetoes 128, 153; presidential power enhanced under 69; wiretapping and 111, 120, 123, 124
Rostker, Bernard: on draft registration 98, 99, 109
Rostker v. Goldberg (1981) 106
Rubenstein, David 24
Rubio, Marco: on Ronald Reagan 155

Sadat, Anwar 63
Sanstead, Wayne 79
Sargent, John D. 34
Saturday Night Massacre (1973) 16, 116
Scherther, Leon: on *Sequoia* sale 60
Schirmer, Kitty: on water policy 84
Schlafly, Phyllis: on draft registration of women 105
Schlesinger, Arthur M.: imperial presidency concept of 49, 124, 156–57
Schmitt, Harrison H.: on draft registration 101
Schroeder, Patricia: on draft registration 101
scrutiny of government: Jimmy Carter on 16, 20, 95
secrecy: Jimmy Carter on 17–18, 29; *see also* openness; transparency
Seiberling, John: on draft registration 104
Selective Training and Service Act (1940) *see* Burke-Wadsworth Act (1940)
Sequoia: sale of 24, 53–64, 67, 157, 165
Shanahan, Joe 37
Simms, Larry: on legislative vetoes 142
Sisk, Bernice: on water policy 75
Sohn, Michael 139
Soviet Union: Afghanistan invasion of (1979) 98–99, 108
Speakes, Larry 63
Special Discharge Review Program 32–33, 44–45
spending: Jimmy Carter on 19, 22, 73–74, 87, 89–90, 95; *see also* austerity; pork-barrel legislation
Staggers, Harley: on legislative vetoes 140
Stennis, John C. 91, 101; on draft registration 108
Stump, Bob: on Jimmy Carter's transparency 76
Summer Olympics (1980): U.S. boycott of 99, 108
symbolic gestures: Jimmy Carter's use of 58, 99, 157; Richard Nixon's use of 49

Talmadge, Herman 115
Tate, Dan: on water policy 77–78
Tennessee-Tombigbee Waterway project 79, 92
Thurmond, Strom 124; on draft dodgers 37; on Gerald Ford's draft dodger clemency program 40; *Sequoia* sale and 57–58; on wiretapping 121, 122
transparency: Jimmy Carter on, 13, 14–

214

Index

15, 16, 18–19, 22, 29, 73, 76, 83–84, 110; *Sequoia* sale and 62; *see also* openness; secrecy
Tropp, Richard: on Gerald Ford's draft dodger clemency program 41
Truman, Harry: wiretapping and 111
Trump, Donald *160*; comity and 159; Jimmy Carter compared to 164–65; presidential dignity of 159–65; on presidential power 163; presidential style of 161–63; Ronald Reagan compared to 163–64
Truong Dinh Hung: warrantless wiretapping of 119–20
trust: Jimmy Carter on 29, 69–70; Patrick Caddell on 26; *see also* confidence in government
Tucker, Jim 72; on water policy 94

Ulman, Leon: on Myers Amendment 46
Union of Soviet Socialist Republics (U.S.S.R) *see* Soviet Union
U.S. Army Corps of Engineers 78, 85
U.S. Congress: amnesty powers of 34, 45–47; draft dodger reconciliation debated in 34–38; Jimmy Carter's relationship with 22, 27, 72, 73, 74–75, 77–78, 80–81, 83, 86, 95–96, 122–24; "Watergate class" of 113; *see also* legislative vetoes
U.S. Constitution: Donald Trump and 163; legislative vetoes and 130–33, 136, 144–45, 147–48, 149–50; presidential pardon power in 33, 34, 36, 46; presidential wiretapping justified by 111, 112, 115, 117, 120, 122, 124, 125
U.S. Navy: Gerald Ford in 33; Jimmy Carter in 33; pay in 102; presidential yachts and 55, 56–57, 59, 61; *see also* Navy Historical Museum
United States v. United States District Court for the Eastern District of Michigan (1972) 112–13, 123, 124
University of Michigan: fight song of 52
Upton, Herb 58

USA PATRIOT Act (2001) 126–27
Utley, Robert M.: on *Sequoia* sale 59

Vance, Cyrus 143
Vietnam War 31, 47, 49, 69; as issue in presidential election (1976) 17–18, 19, 22, 25, 51–52; Jimmy Carter on 18, 19, 43–44, 51–52, 99; legacies of 33, 41, 43–44, 51–52, 129, 156, 157; Martin Luther King, Jr. on 104; *see also* draft dodgers

Wadsworth, James 99
Walker, Don: on Paintsville Dam 84
Warren, Charles 81
water projects 71–96, 158, 164
Watergate scandal 28, 122; as issue in presidential election (1976) 15, 16–17, 17–18, 19, 20, 25, 44, 51, 69, 110, 114; Jimmy Carter on 18, 19, 20, 22, 51–52, 110; legacies of 13, 16, 51–52, 113, 116, 124–25, 129, 153, 156, 157; wiretapping in 113, 121
Watson, Jack 14, 19, 23; on presidential accountability 23–24
Waxman, Henry 140
Weinberger, Caspar: on draft registration 107–8
Wellford, Harrison 137
White, Lawrence: on Foreign Intelligence Surveillance Act (1978) 126
Wides, Burt: on wiretapping 117
Wilson, Bob: on draft dodger amnesty 36
Wilson, George 108
wiretapping 110–27, 157; Jimmy Carter on 114, 118–25
women: draft registration of debated 105–6
Wright, Jim 81, 88, 91

yachts: used by U.S. presidents 54; *see also Sequoia*
Yatesville Dam 84
Young, Milton: on water policy 93

215

www.ingramcontent.com/pod-product-compliance
Ingram Content Group UK Ltd.
Pitfield, Milton Keynes, MK11 3LW, UK
UKHW041956140426
5217IPUK00015B/832